The Book of Handicrafts

for all the family

with instructions and patterns for new and traditional crafts

Edited by
EVE HARLOW

LONGMEADOW
PRESS

Contents

Authors and Contributors

Audrey Hersch
Valerie Janitch
Bruce Angrave
Irena Clanfield
Alison Richards
Diana Biggs
Anne Hulbert

Katie Dyson
Patricia Philpott
Pam Hartland
Joyce Thyer
Lynette Syme
Shirley Lane
Jill Newton

David Constable
Anne Croot
Maxine Fitter
Frances Diplock
Ruth Francis
Len Cacutt

Mary Konior
Frances Rhodes
Jane Simpson
Lydia Cole-Powney
Mary Rhodes
Margaret Beautement

First published in the USA by
Longmeadow Press, PO Box 16, Rowayton Station,
Norwalk, Connecticut 06353

ⓒ 1975 Hennerwood Publications Limited

ISBN 0 904230 04 X

Produced by Mandarin Publishers Limited
Hong Kong

Printed in England by Jarrold & Sons Limited

Introduction

It is not necessary to be an artist to be good at handicrafts – many beautiful pieces of folk-art were created by untrained hands – and what ordinary people create today may well be treasured by collectors of handicrafts tomorrow!

All the things in this book were created by imaginative people, many of them professional craftsmen and women. This does not mean that a beginner cannot make something similarly attractive – once he has the knowhow.

You can learn about a new craft by tackling an easy project and then later, progress to something a little more ambitious. The projects are planned in sequence to lead you naturally from the basic techniques to those more complex and you will find that the instructions do not assume a prior knowledge – everything is made as simple as possible to understand. And once you have become skillful at one craft you will want to try others, perhaps combining two or three to produce something really original. Readers who, perhaps, already enjoy a particular craft, will discover new ideas and designs to stimulate them and go on to explore less familiar techniques and combinations.

Many of the projects in this book are for making furnishings – quilts, rugs, wall hangings, lampshades and pictures – as well as for dozens of small decorative accessories for every room. With the help of this book you can learn how to make useful and attractive things for your home for a fraction of the price they would cost to buy. Other chapters show how to make personal handicraft accessories – jewelry, bags and belts – and have new designs for knitted, crocheted or embroidered clothes. Throughout there are patterns for things to make as gifts of all different kinds. A wide variety of materials are included and information is given at the end as to their availability.

You will learn something of the origins of handicrafts too – the mythology and pagan-worship behind corn-dollies, the ancient story of macramé – and the comparatively humble beginnings of patchwork and appliqué.

Handicrafts are an absorbing – and profitable – pastime for all the family and among the exciting ideas in these pages there is something for everyone.

Feltcraft

Felt is a satisfying medium for craft work. It is
easy to cut out, does not fray and pieces can be
joined with the simplest seams or glued
together. It is an ideal fabric to decorate with
embroidery or appliqué and above all, it is
fairly inexpensive and comes in a wide range
of colours.

Ring o' Rosie

Rosie is an attractive display stand for jewelry and will hold rings, necklaces, bracelets on her outstretched arms. She stands 8in (20cm) high.

Materials required:

Two pieces of ⅜in (9mm) wooden dowel, A: 8in (20cm) long; B: 6in (15cm) long
3in (7.5cm) diameter circle ½in (1cm) plywood, thick
9in (23cm) felt squares, mustard, and green
12in (30cm) felt square, bright pink
Scraps of beige, white and green felt
Length of thick white wool yarn
Kapok or other suitable filling
Approx. ½oz (14.2g) medium size gold beads
Wood adhesive.
Clear drying adhesive

To make the Rosie

Drill a recess in the centre of circular piece of plywood to fit the end of dowel A. Use a knife to taper the dowel if necessary. Cover the circular piece above and below with red felt. To fit the two pieces of dowel together as shown in Fig 1, pare away some of the wood from the middle of dowel B and again on dowel A, 2½in (6cm) from the square end. Glue and then tie B across A as shown.

Hands and arms Cut two pieces of beige felt each 1½in x 1in (3.5cm x 2.5cm). Oversew short ends together on each piece to make a ring. Run a gathering thread round one edge and draw up, to fit onto the end of dowel B for hands. Use a touch of adhesive to hold hands in place. Cover the arms with white yarn, winding it round closely and covering the edge of the felt. Cut a strip of red felt. Glue where felt hands join the wool arms.

Head Cut a piece of beige felt 2½in x 5½in (6cm x 14cm) for the head. Join short ends to make a ring. Run gathering threads around one edge and draw up tightly. Stuff firmly, run gathering threads around other edge, push onto end of dowel A as far as it will go and draw up to fit the dowel neck. Cut a strip of beige felt 1in x 6in (2.5cm x 15cm) for the neck and roll around the dowel under the head. Glue to secure and stitch the head to the neck. (Fig 2).

Bodice For the bodice, cut a piece of mustard felt 2½in x 5½in (6cm x 14cm). Approximately 1½in (3.5cm) in from the shorter ends, cut two ¾in (2cm) vertical slits, ½in (1cm) down from the top edge. Slip these slits over the arms and join the shorter edges up the centre back. Gather and stuff as for the head, sew bodice to neck. (Fig 3).

Skirt The skirt is a piece of pink felt 5in x 9in (12.5cm x 23cm). Join short edges. Gather one long edge and slip the skirt onto the dowel below the bodice. Stuff and finish as for the head. (See Fig 4).

There should now be about ½in (1cm) of dowel projecting from the lower gathered edges of the skirt. Glue this firmly into the centre of the wooden base.

Skirt decoration Make eight pink and eight green felt beads. For one bead, cut a strip of felt 9in x 1in (23cm x 2.5cm) wide. Taper each long side so that one end is pointed. Fold in wide end ½in (1cm). Hold, fold down and dab adhesive lightly along centre of strip to narrow end. Roll strip lightly from wide to narrow end. Sew felt beads, in alternating colours, around lower edge of skirt, with a small gold bead in the centre of each. Cut a strip of mustard felt ½in x 11in (1cm x 28cm) and pink the edges. Glue around the skirt above felt beads and finally sew gold beads along centre of strip.

To finish bodice, head and apron

Glue a few loops of white yarn at the top of the bodice to suggest a portion of blouse, and glue a narrow strip of green felt to edge it. Stitch gold beads around the green strip. Roll two narrow strips of green for buttons and stick to the bodice with a gold bead sewn in the centre of each. Attach threads to the centre of the doll's forehead and string three or four lengths of gold beads to either side of the head for hair. Cut a triangle of pink felt measuring 7½in (19cm) along one long edge and 5in (12.5cm) along each of the other two edges. Glue lightly to cover the head. Catch ends together under the chin. Cut two small circles of green felt for eyes and one in pink for mouth. Glue and stitch to face. (Fig 5).

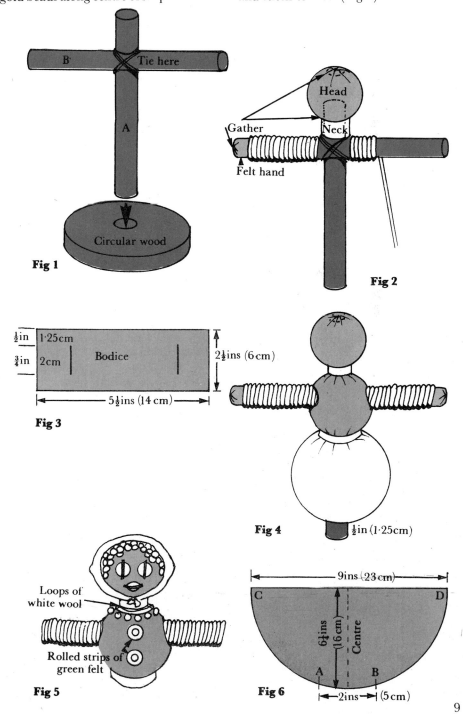

Fig 1 Tie here B A Circular wood

Fig 2 Head Neck Gather Felt hand

Fig 3 ½in 1·25cm ¾in 2cm Bodice 2½ins (6cm) 5½ins (14 cm)

Fig 4 ½in (1·25cm)

Fig 5 Loops of white wool Rolled strips of green felt

Fig 6 9ins (23 cm) C D 6¼ins (16cm) Centre A B 2ins (5 cm)

Apron Cut apron from mustard felt. (Fig 6). Cut pocket measuring 5in x 1⅝in *(12.5cm x 4cm)*. Gather up one long edge and oversew to apron at A-B. Pin corners of pocket to outside edges of apron and cut to round off lower corners. Baste in place. Cut a white felt apron, slightly larger on the curved edge than Fig 6 and pink the edge. Put under mustard felt. Work running stitches through all the layers of felt on dotted line. Gather up straight edges of both layers together. Draw up to 2in *(5cm)*. Stitch around doll's waist. Cut a narrow strip of white for a waistband. Glue and stitch.

Embroidered Tree

A charming piece of decoration to make for a Christmas table in felt with a few glittering beads and some sequins.

Materials required for two trees:
8in *(20cm)* square pink felt
Scraps of white and mustard felt
Sequins
Beads
Sewing thread
Embroidery threads
Gold threads

To make a tree

Cut circle of pink felt 8in *(20.5cm)* in diameter. Cut circle in half. One circle will make two trees. Embroider the semi-circles, either by sewing machine or by hand. Suitable stitches are chain stitch, stem stitch, cross stitch and French knots. Add small beads and sequins as required. Seam the straight edges together. Cut out a white felt star. The trunk of the tree illustrated is made using a 6in *(15cm)* length of sturdy wire, covered in white felt. Make a base from non-bake clay available in craft shops and push the wire or a short length of thin wooden dowel into it. If the dowel is still loose when the clay has dried, glue it into the base. Cover the trunk with felt. Paint the base. (See page 8).

Sewing Kit to Wear

Here is an idea for a complete sewing kit, attached to the ends of a tape measure. While working wear the tape measure around your neck so that everything you need is conveniently at hand. Try to find a tape measure that has a hole at each end or, if necessary, make the holes and finish them off with an eyelet.

Materials required:
Coloured felt squares
Trimmings
Buckram or thin cardboard
Small amount of Kapok or other suitable filling
Thin cord
Small snap fastener
Fabric adhesive
Tape measure
Scissors
Thimble
Skein of assorted thread
Needles and pins

To make the sewing kit

Pin cushion Cut two 3in *(7.5cm)* squares of contrasting felt for the pin cushion. Oversew together on three sides, stuff firmly and oversew the fourth side to close.

Thimble case Cut two circles 2in *(5cm)* in diameter from contrasting colour felt. Oversew around two-thirds of the circle. Stitch a snap fastener inside the opening to close.

Thread holder Cut two 2in *(5cm)* squares of contrasting colour felt for the thread holder. Overcast two opposite sides.

Scissors case Trace the pattern for the scissors case from the outline given (Fig 7), adjusting the dimensions and shape as necessary. Cut the shape out of felt twice for the back and cut the front, lower section out once. Cut out the back shape again in buckram or thin cardboard, slightly smaller than the pattern. Glue the stiffening material between the two back pieces and baste the front section into position. Oversew all around the edge with contrasting colour thread and then oversew back again in the opposite direction, crossing the first row of stitches.

To finish

To assemble the sewing kit, knot one end of the cord and stitch the knot to one corner of the pin cushion. Cut the cord off about 3in *(7.5cm)* long, thread

through the hole in the tape measure and knot the other end. Stitch the knot to the thimble case. Repeat with the scissors case and thread holder. Trim each item as illustrated.

Pixie Ring

Five little pixies make a charming nursery mobile for a baby or toddler.

Materials required:

5 table tennis balls
Brightly coloured felt squares
Flesh-coloured poster paint
Black poster paint
Pipe cleaners
4yds *(3.66m)* brown double knitting yarn
Large and small coloured beads
9in *(23cm)* diameter lampshade ring or 29in *(72.5cm)* flexible wire curved into a ring and twisted at the ends to secure
1 small brass curtain ring
32in *(81cm)* braid trimming
Black sewing thread
Black buttonhole twist
Fabric adhesive
Clear drying adhesive
Tracing paper

To make the pixies

Trace off and cut out separate paper patterns for one hand, the jerkin and the trousers, following the broken lines for the hand and trousers. Cut a 3in *(7.5cm)* diameter half-circle for the hat (Fig 8). Cut the hand shape out twice in flesh-coloured felt, and the jerkin and trousers twice each in a brightly coloured felt. Cut out the hat shape once in a felt to match either the jerkin or the trousers. Stitch two small coloured beads down the centre of one jerkin piece for front buttons. Place the back jerkin piece flat and glue a hand at each end of the sleeve using fabric adhesive as shown in the Fig 8. Glue one trouser piece to the jerkin back applying adhesive on the upper part only and positioning as shown. Cut a piece of pipe cleaner 4in *(10cm)* long and bend it into the shape of the coloured line in the diagram. Glue into position.

Glue the second trouser piece over the first and finally the front of the jerkin. Spread fabric adhesive all over sleeves and across top and down each side. To make the head, pierce a small hole in a table tennis ball with a knitting needle and then paint the ball with flesh-colour paint. When the paint is dry, push the ball down over the protruding pipe cleaner. To make the hair, cut a piece of cardboard about 4in *(10cm)*

Fig 7

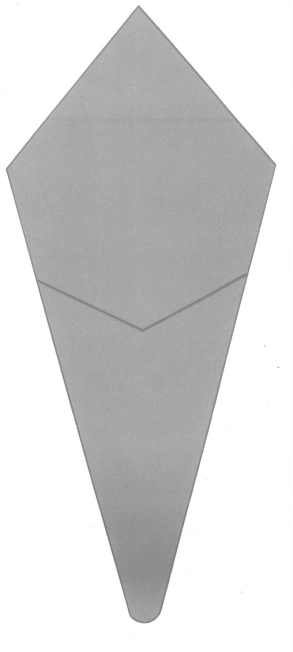

Materials required:
15in *(38cm)* of 36in *(90cm)* wide hessian [burlap]
27in *(68cm)* thick white cord
Stiff buckram
Coloured felt squares: flesh, black, brown, medium blue, dark blue, yellow and white.
Scrap of striped ribbon or fabric
36in *(91cm)* ric-rac braid
Fabric adhesive

To make the bag

Turn and press a 4in *(10cm)* hem onto the right side along each selvedge (see Fig 9). Stitch each end of the turning, taking ½in *(1cm)* seam, as indicated by dotted line. Fold the fabric in half along the line indicated on the diagram, right sides facing and join the side seams as far as the lower edge of the selvedge edge. Finish off very securely. Trim seams and turn bag and hems to right side. Cut two pieces of buckram each measuring 12in x 3½in *(30cm x 9cm)*, and fit one inside each top hem. Fix the buckram to the facing with glue or catch selvedge neatly to the inside of the bag. Cut the cord in half, binding each end securely, and stitch to the front and back with ends 6in *(18cm)* apart, to form handles.

Collage design

Enlarge a pattern for the figure from Fig 10. To do this, trace off the design and mark the tracing into squares. Draw a similar squared grid 7in *(17.5cm)* deep and transfer the traced design to the grid, reproducing it line for line.

Head Cut out the whole head in flesh colour felt, extending the neck as indicated by the coloured line. Embroider the mouth in stem stitch and cut the eyes in black felt. Glue them into position. Cut the hair in brown felt and glue over the top of the head. Cut a circle of deep yellow felt for the hat, and stick this behind the head.

Suit Cut the suit top in medium-blue

deep and wind the brown yarn around it about 15 times. Slide the loops off the cardboard and tie tightly in the middle. Cut the ends and spread the yarn out into a circle. Glue the yarn to the ball with clear drying adhesive, the tied centre at the crown and trim the ends neatly. Paint in the eyes. Form the hat into a cone and glue the straight edges together. Stick the hat onto the hair. Make four more pixies in the same way.

To assemble the mobile

Knot the end of a piece of black thread and catch it firmly to the top of a hat. Slide a large bead to rest on top of the hat and then tie the other end of the thread to the lampshade or wire ring, about 6in *(15cm)* above the figure.
Attach the remaining pixies equally around the circle in the same way.
Cut four 15in *(38cm)* lengths of black buttonhole twist. Loop each one through the curtain ring and knot about 1½in *(3.5cm)* above the cut ends of each pair. Then tie each doubled thread at quarterly intervals round the ring.

Sailor-boy Tidy Bag

Hang a felt-collage tidy bag in a boy's room and it is more likely that pyjamas will be tidied away neatly inside each morning!

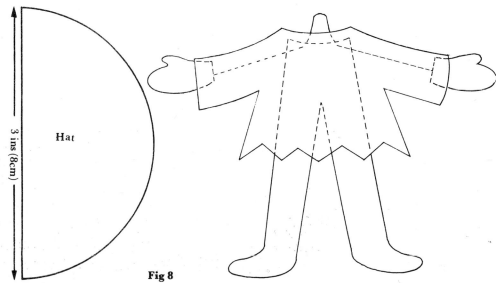

3 ins *(8cm)*

Hat

Fig 8

felt, cutting the centre front opening even with the inside edges of the collar. Cut a rectangle of striped ribbon or fabric as indicated and glue this behind the suit top, as illustrated. Cut the two collar pieces in white felt and glue into position. Cut the hands in flesh felt and glue the wrists behind cuffs. Now glue this body over lower edge of neck, as pattern.

Trousers Cut the trousers in dark blue felt, extending the top edge and the legs as shown by the coloured lines. Glue trousers behind the lower edge of the suit top. Cut the boots in black felt, and glue over the lower edges of the trousers. Glue the whole figure to centre front of the bag. Encircle the figure with a 9in *(23cm)* diameter circle of ric-rac braid or other decorative trimming.

Pencil Flowers

Felt flower heads fit on to the ends of pencils for a bright bazaar item or for a gift for a child.

Materials required:
Felt scraps in assorted colours
Matching sewing threads
Small beads
Pencils

To make the flowers
Two types of flower heads are illustrated, a daisy and a five-petalled flower. The stem is the same for both flowers. The centres are circles of felt cut out with pinking shears or with the edges snipped into a fringe.

Petalled flower Trace off the petal shape and the stem from Fig. 11. Draw the outline onto thin cardboard and cut out the shapes to make templates. Use the templates to cut out five petals and one stem. Cut circles for the centre and pink or fringe the edges. Stitch five petals

together at the points. Make a knot on the end of thread and bring the needle through the centre of the flower so that the knot is underneath. Slip first the larger circle and then the smaller onto the needle and push them down onto the flower. Stitch one or more small beads to the flower centre and fasten the thread off on the wrong side. To make up the stem, seam the two straight edges and fit the stem to the pencil end. Stitch the flower head to the stem.

Daisies Cut out the daisy flower shape, two centres and one stem. Make up the daisy flower in the same way as for the five-petalled flower.

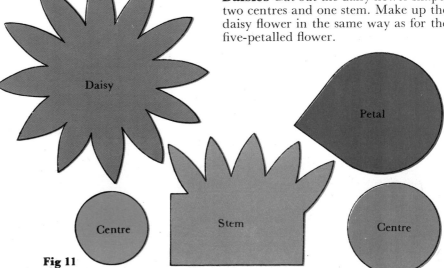

Fig 9

Fig 10

Fig 11

Daisy

Petal

Centre

Stem

Centre

4ins (10cm)

fold
Selvedge

Right side of fabric

28ins (71cm)

Selvedge
fold

15ins (38cm)

Papercraft

Paper Sculpture

Paper sculpture is thought to have originated in Poland during the First World War. It is related to the Japanese art of paper folding 'Origami'.
Paper sculpture was in vogue during and after the Second World War in Britain, when it was effectively used in the decoration of commercial and government exhibitions.

Paper, when used for sculpture, imposes its own limitations. The shapes which form the basis of all paper sculpture are simple – cones, cylinders and box forms. All the subtleties of sculptural form must be suggested by these fundamental shapes. This limitation demands an extremely creative standard of invention. Paper sculpture is not necessarily as transient an art as the medium suggests. Correctly made and protected – as in a deep glazed frame, it is as permanent as a water-colour, which after all is painted on paper.

TOOLS AND MATERIALS

Cutting tools The tools required are a pair of sharp scissors and a utility knife with a renewable pointed blade. These knives can be bought from artists' supply shops, craft stores and model maker's shops. Next, a suitable surface should be found to cut on when the knife is used. A sheet of glass ensures a clean cut and does not blunt the knife, but heavy hardboard or linoleum can be used for a cutting board if preferred.

Paper The basic ingredient of this form of sculpture is, of course, paper, and it is important to obtain sheets of the best quality you can afford, in various thicknesses, strong enough to stand up well and sufficiently pliable to bend easily. Poor quality paper should not be used as it will not 'roll' without cracking. Coloured paper is effective in paper sculpture. If only white is available and a coloured effect is desired, paint the paper before starting. Remember that 'white' paper comes in different shades of white and unless a contrast of tones and textures is intended, only one kind of paper should be used in a given piece of work.

Adhesives Glue is needed for fixing the paper. A clear impact adhesive is recommended for most jobs. A small stapler is useful for sculpture work.

Other equipment Lay aside a pencil and eraser, tracing paper for sketching out and designing the shapes, a straight edge or metal edged ruler and some pieces of wooden dowel, of various thicknesses from $\frac{1}{8}$ in *(3mm)* to $\frac{3}{8}$ in *(9mm)* diameter. These are to roll the paper around when coiled and curved shapes are required.

WORKING WITH PAPER

Before cutting the paper, mark the lines to be cut in pencil. Cut lines with a utility knife against a ruler edge, cutting evenly and firmly. It may be necessary to cut along a line two or three times until the paper is cut through. Use scissors for curved edges and complicated shapes although with practice, most lines can be cut with a pointed blade.

Scoring Scoring paper means cutting halfway through the paper and is a technique which enables paper to be folded with a clean sharp edge, without the surface breaking or wrinkling. Interesting light and shade effects can be obtained by scoring.

Curling Paper is given a curved 'bias' by drawing the strip between a straight edge, such as a ruler or scissors blade, and the thumb.

Curling gives soft, light and shade effects.

SIMPLE FOLDS AND CUTS

Before starting a more complex project, try cutting and folding paper, to get the feeling of the medium, as shown in the illustration overleaf and in Fig 1. Make some boxes, cones, hexagons, etc; pleat paper by scoring; curve some strips by the method described. Make cuts in a sheet of stiff paper and observe the shadows cast by the cut edges.

Score lines to be made on the surface of the paper are shown as solid lines. Those to be made on the reverse are shown as broken lines.

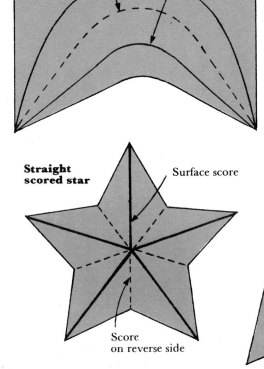

Fig 1   **Curved score exercise**

Score on reverse side

Surface score

Straight scored star

Surface score

Score on reverse side

Curved score exercise

Surface score

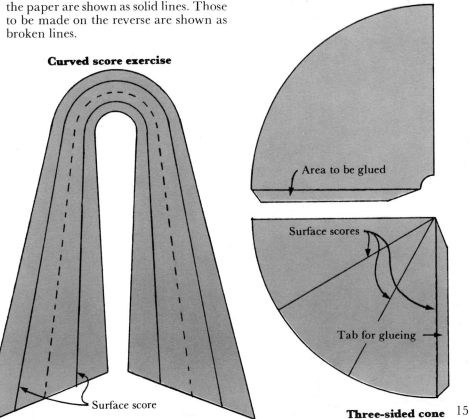

Cone

Area to be glued

Surface scores

Tab for glueing

Three-sided cone   15

Bouquet of Roses

Make a posy of roses as an introduction to paper sculpture.

Materials required:
White water-colour paper
Length of dowel
Steel garden wire
Scissors
Ruler
Utility knife

To make the bouquet

The wrapper of the bouquet is a round-shaped piece of paper coiled into a cone shape and then stapled, except that the shape of the paper is specially designed to form the spiral edges of the wrapper. The leaves are cut out of stiff paper, using scissors or a knife. The leaves are then rolled around a piece of dowel to give them a convex bias and then scored on the wrong side, up the centre line, pressing lightly with the knife and a ruler. The sides of the leaf are then bent forward along the score line. The flowers are the most interesting part of the sculpture and are formed from the spiral shape in the diagram (Fig 2). Cut out along the lines and give the paper a curved 'bias' by drawing the strip of the spiral between the edge of a ruler and the thumb. The spiral is then rolled by hand around a thin dowel, starting from the outer end so that the innermost part of the spiral design forms the outermost petal of the rose. The dowel is then withdrawn and the rolled spiral is pushed into the centre hole marked X to secure. Glue the base of the rose to hold it together. Roses and leaves are then glued to lengths of steel garden wire and arranged within the wrapper. The rose clearly demonstrates the way in which the characteristics of the paper should be allowed to dictate the finished design. It seems more logical to take a rose to pieces, petal by petal, copy each piece in paper and then reassemble them to create a paper copy of a natural rose. But then, of course, the result would be an artificial flower and not an original paper sculpture.

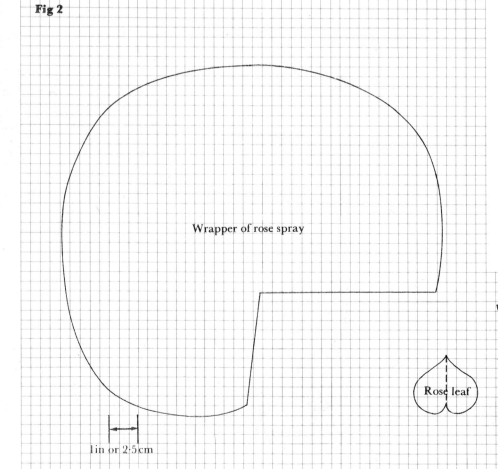

Fig 2

Wrapper of rose spray

1 in or 2·5 cm

Rose leaf

Rose flower

Paper Flowers

Paper can be used to make beautiful flowers – and you can fill the house with blooms throughout the year. Paper flowers will last well if they are not placed in direct sunlight and if moist conditions are avoided. All they need to keep them 'fresh' is an occasional dusting.

Materials

Paper Crêpe paper is by far the most versatile paper to use. Its silky finish and flexibility can create very realistic looking petals and leaves. The better quality papers have more sheen and greater stretch. Two-tone crêpe paper which has a darker tint of the colour on one side is particularly good for flower petals. Tissue paper produces a delicate looking bloom and is available in a wide variety of colours. It is crisp and twists and folds extremely well. Tissue paper should be handled with care and hands should be clean, dry and cool. Facial or paper tissues can also be used for flower making, and are particularly good for making balls for flower centres.

Wire Florists wire is ideal but it might be difficult to obtain. Any fine wire, plastic-covered garden wire or insulating wire can be used – or even medium weight galvanized wire.

Adhesives Several adhesives are suitable for glueing the papers used in flower making. Fabric adhesive, clear drying all-purpose adhesive, and wallpaper paste are the most useful. Instruc-

tions for making flowers of specific papers usually recommend one of these types of adhesives.

Techniques used in flower making

Cupping To produce a cupped petal out of crêpe paper, gently stretch the petal shape between the fingers.

Frilling By stretching a cut edge in crêpe paper, a frilled edge is obtained.

Curling Hold the petal or leaf in one hand. Use the blade of a pair of scissors or a blunt knife and gently stroke the paper between the thumb and the blade.

Veining Mark veins on a leaf surface by placing the leaf on a padded surface and drawing in the veins with a knitting needle or a thin wooden stick.

Christmas Roses

Real Christmas roses have delicately fringed centres and only five petals. But for a festive table setting, use a little artistic licence to create a spectacular interpretation of this lovely flower with a gleaming gold and pearl centre and

three times the correct number of petals!

Materials required:

White and deep cream two-tone crêpe paper

Mid and pale olive green two-tone crêpe paper

Small gold Christmas tree ball approx. $\frac{3}{4}$in *(2cm)* in diameter

Medium-sized pearl beads

Olive green drawing ink

Transparent adhesive tape

All-purpose clear drying adhesive.

To make one flower

Cut a strip of white crêpe paper about 4in *(10cm)* long by 2in *(5cm)* wide with the grain running lengthwise. Gather together lengthwise between the fingertips and then fold over at the centre. Remove the wire loop hanger from the neck of the Christmas ball and push the folded end of the paper right up inside. Secure at the neck with a narrow strip of sticky tape to hold firmly, if necessary. Trim off the paper $\frac{1}{2}$in *(1cm)* above the neck of the ball. Cut a 2in *(5cm)* square of crêpe paper and fold it into three

18

across the grain. Wrap this strip neatly around the paper protruding from the ball level with the lower edge, glueing to hold it in place. This will provide a firm base around which to stick the petals. Trace the petal from the trace pattern (see Fig 3) onto thin cardboard and cut out a template. Use this pattern to cut fifteen petals in white/cream crêpe, with the grain running as the arrow indicates. With the white side uppermost, 'cup' each petal at A by holding it in both hands, with the thumbs in the centre, and gently stretching the paper so that it forms a cupped, petal shape. Then turn the petal over and lightly cup it again at B, so that the tip curls back. Spread adhesive over the end of a petal, below the broken line, and press against the base of the centre, lower edges level, gathering the bottom of the petal slightly. Add four more petals equally around the centre – making five in all – each new petal half-overlapping the previous one. Glue another set of five petals equally around the flower, each falling exactly between those of the first row. Then glue the third row of petals so that they are positioned just behind the petals of the first row.

To give the middle of the centre petals a greenish tinge, moisten a facial or paper tissue with olive green ink and dab it on waste paper until it is almost dry. Then wipe it over the surface of the petal until the correct depth of colour is obtained. Although this colouring can be applied to the individual petals before making up the flower, the effect is more satis-factory if it is done at this later stage, as the ink will pick out slight creases in the paper, and give the impression of veins on the petals.

The leaves

Trace the leaf pattern (Fig 3) onto thin cardboard and make a template. Cut five leaves in two-tone green crêpe paper, the grain running as the arrow indicates in the diagram. Cup these at A and B as for the petals, but begin with the pale underside of the leaf, turning over to the darker top side to cup B, so that the leaf is shaped in the opposite direction to that of the Christmas rose petal.

Spread adhesive over the end of the leaves below the broken line, and glue equally around the base of the flower. Spread out the petals, re-cupping where necessary, and arrange the leaves – glue-ing lightly together where they overlap to hold in shape. Stroke the tips of the leaves between the thumb and the blade of scissors or a knife, to make them curl up slightly.

String pearl beads onto thread in a circle so that they fit exactly around the widest point of the Christmas ball. Tie the ends securely and slip the circlet over the ball to nestle underneath it.

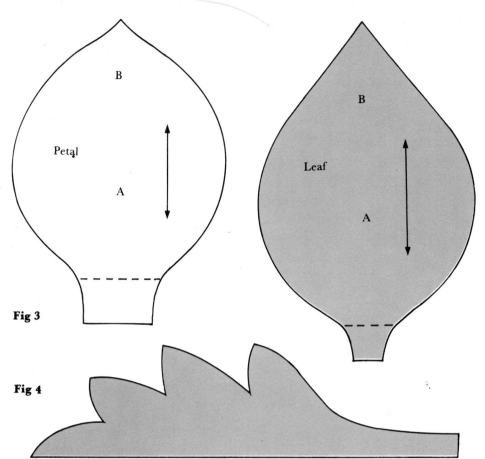

Fig 3

Fig 4

Autumn Glory

A bowl or vase of these glowing autumn blooms will add colour to your home throughout the winter.

Materials required:
Yellow-bronze shaded tissue paper
Clear adhesive
Plastic covered garden wire
Olive green crêpe paper
Clear drying all-purpose adhesive.

To make the flowers

Cut a 30in *(75cm)* long strip of tissue paper 5in *(12.5cm)* deep. Fold in half lengthways. Now fold the strip in half in the other direction, then in half again – and finally again, to measure 3¾in x 2¼in *(9.5cm x 6cm)*. Holding the folded edges together, cut down from this edge to within ¾in *(2cm)* of lower edge, making cuts fairly close together. Unfold and cut the strip into four equal lengths. Then on each piece, carefully open out the fringed fold and smooth it gently to flatten, then bring the lower edges to-gether again against the previous fold, without re-creasing, to form a looped edge. Having done this, glue the four sections together along the lower edges, one on top of another – darker side of each uppermost. Now, with the lighter side inside, roll the strip up loosely, glueing the lower edge and keeping it absolutely even, as the centre tends to ride up inside: if the centre does get lost, rescue it with the point of the scissors and

pull it down before squeezing the base together firmly. Cut a 36in *(90cm)* length of wire and bend it in half. Fix this loop around the base of the flower, close under the petals, then twist the wire until the flower is tightly gripped. Bring the two ends of the wire down to form the stalk.

Cut a 1in *(2.5cm)* wide strip of green crêpe paper and bind base of flower and then stem. Cut a crêpe paper leaf from the pattern (Fig 4) and glue around stalk. Add more leaves if desired for effect.

Paper Decorations

Many other types of decorations can be made using a combination of the techniques and materials described. The four following designs are simple to make and may give you ideas for other original designs that can be used to decorate your home, or given away as unusual gifts and presents.

Pixie Wreath

Materials required:

Wreath:

9in *(23cm)* diameter lampshade ring
Crêpe paper olive, emerald, leaf green
8 small Christmas tree balls
Tinsel gift-tie or fine cord
Curtain ring.

Pixies:

Medium weight assorted coloured papers
$\frac{3}{4}$in *(2cm)* diameter papier mâché or polystyrene balls for heads
Brown knitting yarn
Large coloured and tiny black beads
Absorbent cotton wool
White paper or facial tissues
Pipe cleaners or matchsticks
Strong black thread or crochet cotton
Flesh coloured poster paint
All-purpose clear drying adhesive

To make the wreath

Trace the leaf pattern (Fig 5) onto thick cardboard and cut a template. Cut a strip of crêpe paper about $1\frac{1}{2}$in *(3.5cm)* wide along the grain, right across the roll. This should measure 20in *(51cm)*. Pleat the strip every 4in *(10cm)*, fold in half. Hold leaf pattern against last fold, and cut around. This will make five pairs of leaves. Cut 60 pairs in each colour. Attach the leaves to the lampshade ring as follows. Beginning with a leaf green pair, twist once at the centre, between the two leaves. Dab a spot of adhesive above and below the twist – and loop over the ring, bringing the two leaves together on the outside so that the top leaf points a little to the right and the one underneath a little to the left (Fig 6 diagram 1). Pinch neatly around the ring. Repeat with a pair of emerald green leaves, pushing the twisted centre close against that of the first pair, so that the emerald leaves overlap the lighter ones above and below (Fig 6 diagram 2). Add an olive green pair in the same way. Continue until whole ring is covered. Now make 16 sprays of leaves as follows. Place a leaf green, an emerald and an olive pair of leaves one on top of another, glueing together at the centre with adhesive. Twist the leaves as before, and then fold them over at the centre so that they are positioned as before but without the ring between. Make two more sprays, twisting the centre, but do not fold over. Put all the sprays aside.

Cut four 8in *(20cm)* lengths of gift-tie or fine cord to hang. Tie the ends securely to the ring so that the ring hangs correctly balanced. Knot ends onto the curtain ring.

Tie the Christmas balls between the leaves, spacing them equally.

To make the pixies

To make each pixie, cut two semi-circles for body and cap of coloured paper (Fig 7). Bend a 3in *(7.5cm)* length of pipe cleaner in half and push the ends firmly into a papier mâché or foam ball for the head. Paint the head with poster paint and leave to dry. Make up the two cones, curving the paper around so that point B is level with C. Glue tiny black beads down the front of the bigger cone for buttons.

Thread a needle with a 4–5in *(10–13cm)* length of black thread and tie a small bead at one end. Pass the needle up through the hole in the top of the cap and through the large bead. Tie a knot in the thread exactly 2in *(5cm)* above the bead. When the head is dry, add the hair. Cut a piece of cardboard 2in *(5cm)* deep by about 3in *(7.5cm)* wide. Wind the yarn evenly around it 20 times. Cut along the edges. Remove the strands carefully from the cardboard and tie tightly together at the centre. Pin the tied centre to the crown of the head, then spread the strands out evenly all around. Glue to the top, sides and back of the head. Trim the ends neatly all around. Push the pipe cleaner or matchstick down into the body cone and glue it securely to the back of the cone with a small piece of sticky tape.

Wind a wisp of absorbent cotton wool around the neck to form a collar. Glue the cap firmly on top of the head.

Mark the features with a felt tip pen. Fold a paper or facial tissue into four and cut a $3\frac{1}{2}$in *(9cm)* diameter circle with pinking shears. Spread a generous blob of glue around the centre point, and push it well up inside the cone. Attach pixies to wreath between Christmas balls. Glue spray of leaves over pixies and balls. Push the last two sprays through the curtain ring.

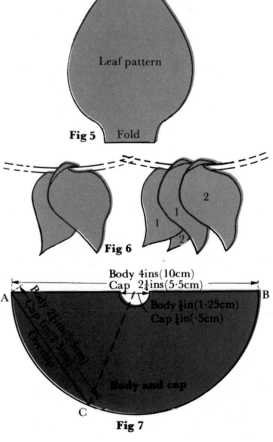

Leaf pattern

Fig 5 Fold

Fig 6

Body 4ins(10cm)
Cap 2¼ins(5·5cm)

A   B

Body ½in(1·25cm)
Cap ¼in(·5cm)

Body 2½ins(6·5cm)
Cap 1in(2·5cm) Overall

Body and cap

C

Fig 7

Bride and Groom

Cylindrical dolls are great fun to make – the body is nothing more than a tube of card or paper.

To make the basic doll

The bridegroom is made on a tube 1½in (3·5cm) in diameter and 8in (21cm) tall. The bride's tube is 6½in (16·5cm) tall and 1½in (3·5cm) in diameter.

Mark the face areas first: the bridegroom's is 1½in (3·5cm) down from the upper edge and 1¼in (3·25cm) deep. The bride's face is simply 1½in (3·5cm) down from the top edge. Paint the face areas pink with poster paint. Paint some white paper pink to match for the hands.

Bride's clothes The bride's dress is made out of a paper doily. Use pattern E (Fig 8) for the overskirt. Her veil is a square of white tissue paper edged with scraps of silver doily. The coronet is the decorative edge of the doily. Make the hair from brown crêpe paper, curled between thumb and knife blade. The bouquet flowers are made of pink crêpe paper.

Bridegroom's clothes Glue grey paper round the tube above the face area for the hat crown. Cut a 2½in (6cm) diameter circle for the brim and cut a 1½in (3·5cm) hole in it. Fit the brim on to the tube. Cover the tube with a similar grey for the trousers, drawing vertical lines with a felt tipped pen for the stripes. Choose a patterned gift wrap for the waistcoat, (pattern A, Fig 8). The jacket (B) is cut from mid-grey paper. A piece of plum coloured paper napkin makes the cravat and the carnation is made of white crêpe paper. Cut the bridegroom's shoes out of shiny black paper.

Features The bridegroom's hair, whiskers and moustache are cut from brown paper (pattern D, Fig 8). The eyes etc. are marked on the faces with felt tipped pen.

Arms Cut four hands from pink paper. Cut the bride's arms in white paper and the bridegroom's arms in mid-grey paper. Cut white paper cuffs for the groom and scraps of doily for the bride's cuffs. Glue the cuffs over the hands. Fold the arm piece as shown (C, Fig 8) and glue a hand between the ends. Round off the arm top. Punch a hole and fix the arms to the body with pronged paper fasteners (F, Fig 8).

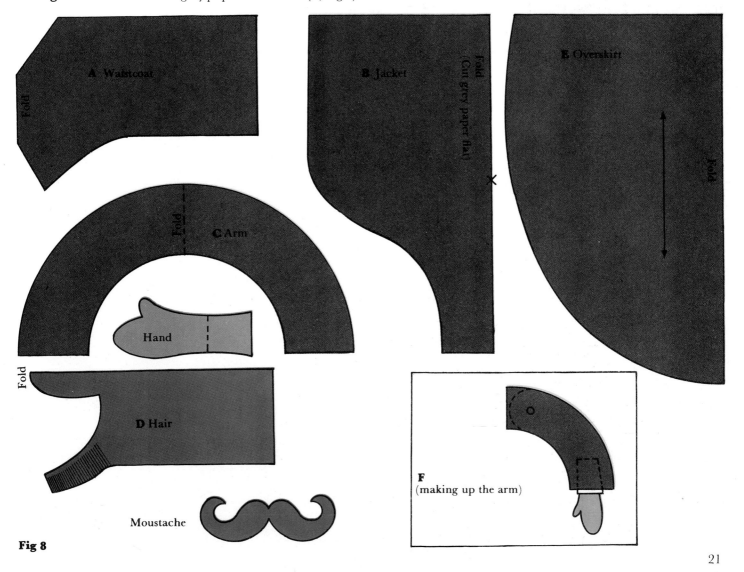

Fig 8

A Waistcoat — Fold

B Jacket

Fold (Cut grey paper flat)

E Overskirt — Fold

C Arm — Fold

Hand

Fold

D Hair

Moustache

F (making up the arm)

21

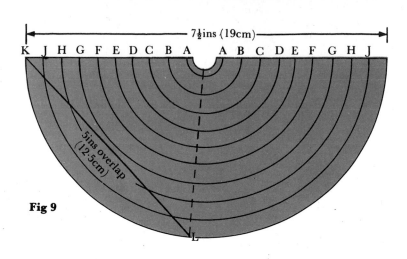

Fig 9

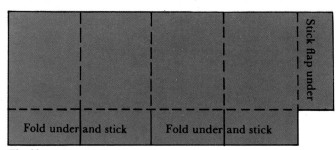

Stick flap under

Fold under and stick   Fold under and stick

Fig 11

Fig 10

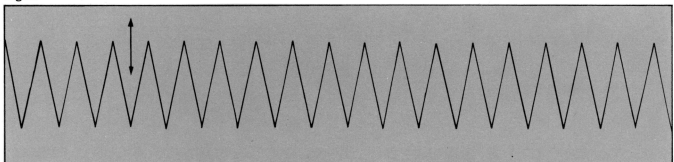

Christmas Trees

Make diminutive paper trees for table decorations. Green foliage and beads with a foil tub looks traditional or a monotone colour scheme looks smart and simple. The tree illustrated above is made in soft, brown coloured paper.

Materials required:
9in *(23cm)* square of cartridge or construction paper
Coffee or emerald and leaf green two-tone crêpe paper
Tissue paper
Small wooden beads, in pink, cyclamen and purple, tiny gilt beads
5in *(12.5cm)* thin dowel or plastic drink-

ing straw for the trunk
Plasticine or modelling clay
Thin cardboard
All-purpose clear drying adhesive
Coloured foil or brown paper for tub

To make the tree
Draw a 7½in *(19cm)* diameter semi-circle on the brown paper, with another ½in *(1cm)* diameter semi-circle at the centre. Mark into divisions as shown in Fig 9. The first line, A–A is ¾in *(2cm)* in diameter, and the second, B–B is 1½in *(4cm)* in diameter. Each subsequent semi-circle increases ¾in *(2cm)* in diameter. Mark point L 5in *(12.5cm)* from K, to indicate the overlap. Cut out, cutting away the small area at the centre.

Curve the paper around into a cone and glue the overlap. Cut a strip of crêpe paper 7in *(17.5cm)* long by 1⅝in *(4cm)* wide with the grain running widthways. Trace down the foliage (Fig 10) and cut backwards and forwards on the lines on pattern, to make two jagged strips of foliage. Cut more lengths of paper in the same way–making eight jagged strips in all.
Curl each fringe of foliage between the blade of a knife and the thumb, the blade against the darker side.
Beginning at the base, glue a crêpe paper strip all around the cone, the straight edge of the strip exactly even with line J–J. Repeat with another strip, level with H–H.

22

Thread purple and gilt beads onto black thread, alternating the colours. The string should be long enough to fit around the cone over the crêpe paper strip, and so that it falls level with the inner points of the jagged edge all around. Tie thread ends securely.

Glue another strip of crêpe paper around the cone level with G–G. Make a circle of cyclamen beads and slip over the cone. Repeat with another strip at F–F, followed by a circle of pink beads. Glue two more strips of crêpe paper around the cone–at E–E and D–D– then repeat with another set of purple, cyclamen and pink beads between strips of foliage. Glue a strip of crêpe paper level with A–A and a final strip overlapping the top edge of the cone, gathering it together neatly to form a point.

Push a pin into the tip of the tree, allowing the point to protrude enough to hold two or three graduated beads for the top decoration. Make a tiny circle of gilt beads to put on the tip of the tree. Slip beads of graduating size onto the pin. Glue them to hold securely.

Tub for the tree

To make the tub, cut a piece of thin cardboard as shown in Fig 11. Cut on the straight lines and score the broken lines. Fold under and glue the side flap. Fold and glue lower tabs to make base. Cover with foil. Half fill the tub with Plasticine and push in the straw. Fix a small knob of Plasticine or modelling clay on top of the straw and shape it into a point. Lower the cone onto the point pressing down firmly. Make the tub for the monotone tree in the same way.

Scrolled Candlesticks

Made in minutes, this decorative candle holder which looks like wrought iron-work will set off the glowing colours of party candles to perfection. Use a heavy, cylindrical candle with a broad base, so that it stands steadily.

Materials required:

Black cartridge or construction paper
All-purpose clear drying adhesive.

To make the candlestick

Measure the base circumference of the candle. The smaller of the two candles illustrated measures 5in (12.5cm) and the diagram (Fig 12) is based on this. Draw a rectangle 4in (10cm) deep on the black paper, the width equal to the circumference of the candle. Add a 1in (2.5cm) deep strip along the bottom for the base, adding ½in (1cm) at one side

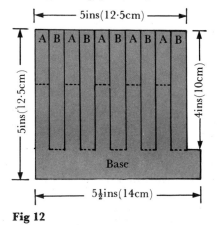

Fig 12

for the overlap as shown in the diagram. Divide the original rectangle into an even number of vertical strips, as shown (these measure ½in (1cm) wide). Score along the base of every other strip (B) as indicated by the broken lines. Cut out carefully, dividing the strips as far as the base. Turn the paper over and mark each un-scored strip (A) with a horizontal line 1¾in (4.5cm) from the end, as indicated by the dotted lines. Turn the paper back again and bend strips B back along the scored line so that they hang down below the base. Stroke each strip A between the thumb and the blade of a knife or scissors, so that it curls backwards, and stroke the hanging strips B so that they curl forwards. Roll the tip of each strip A around and glue so that the cut end of the strip is even with the marked line. Curve the base around into a circle and glue the overlap (strips B hanging down inside). Curve each strip A smoothly over and down and stick the scroll at the end against the base, so that the cut end of the strip inside the scroll is even with the lower edge of the base.

Then fold each strip B outwards over the lower edge of the base, and curl it around to glue the cut end of the strip even with the lower edge of the base.

These instructions are for the smaller version of the candlestick. The stand on the taller candle is made in exactly the same way, but 18 strips are used because the candle is fatter. The strips are also narrower, measuring ⅜in (1cm) to give a more delicate effect. It is most important to draw out the shape very accurately so it is wise to use a ruler.

Corn Weaving

In ancient times, corn dollies were made in England by pagan farmers to ensure the continuance of life. They believed that if the corn spirit was not captured before she left the field, the crops would not grow again the following year. The spirit was believed to move through the corn field ahead of the reapers to come to rest in the last sheaf to be cut. The effigy or dolly, made from this last sheaf, was hung in the farmhouse until the following spring, when it was taken into the field and planted along with the seeds. The harvest festival, in its present form, was introduced by the Reverend R. S. Hawker, vicar of Morwenstow in Cornwall during the late 19th century. He asked his local parishioners to receive the sacrament 'in the bread of the new corn'. Thus, the old-established pagan festival of 'Harvest Home' took its place in the calender and corn dollies were revived as a country craft. It is not certain how the corn dolly achieved its name. It may have been because they were made as effigies or idols to Demeter, the goddess of Agriculture, and it is therefore quite possible that 'doll' evolved from the word 'idol'.

MATERIALS

Straw Much of the wheat grown today is unsuitable for corn dolly making. Modern farmers prefer short, stiff-strawed varieties which resist weather battering and are suitable for the combine harvester. It is essential that the straw used for weaving is long down to the first node and hollow throughout. Some farmers in England still grow the long hollow varieties of wheat for thatching straw, and will usually allow a sheaf or two to be cut from along the headland of their fields.

Some of the best wheat straws for dolly-making are Maris Widgeon, Flamingo, Elite le Peuple, Eclipse, Cardinal and Squarehead Master. Most of these can be located quite easily except Squarehead Master, which is only grown in parts of the English counties of Somerset and Essex. Probably the best way to find a farmer who is growing a suitable variety of straw is through a local thatcher. In the US, brown corn cultivated mainly in the central West is good material to use. Alternatively, it may be possible to find a crafts supplier who cuts and sells straw specifically for the craft.

Sheaves should be cut approximately three weeks before the farmer puts his combine into the field. It is important that the ears are pointing skyward, the stems just turning gold and the nodes still green. Once the ears have begun to bend the straw is often too brittle, causing splits and cracks when plaited. Obtaining straw at times other than the harvesting period can be a little more difficult. The straw has by this time had the grain combed out, which can be a disadvantage if wanting to make a dolly decorated with grain. The straw alone is still suitable for weaving.

Wheat This is the straw most used for plaiting but oats, rye and barley are also useful as decorative heads and for tied work. (Stars, angels and animals etc.) The dollies in this chapter were made from spring wheat, pale gold in colour with a fine, long straw.

PREPARING THE STRAW

Make sure that the sheaves are dry throughout before setting about stripping them down. A sharp pair of scissors is necessary to strip the straw. This is a messy job and it is better to work in an uncarpeted room or in a garage or shed. Cut the string from around the sheaf, pick up a straw and cut about ½in *(1cm)* above the first node. Holding the top, pull off the outer sheath and discard it along with the straw from below the first node. Continue through the sheaf until every straw is cleaned. Now grade the straw.

Grading means sorting the straws so that thick, medium and fine straws are separated. It is possible to grade further until there are at least six grades, but three are usually sufficient to begin with. Dampen the straw prior to beginning work, either by submerging it in hot water for five minutes or for 20 minutes in cold water. The bathtub is the most suitable place for this process called 'tempering' as the straw can lie flat. Weight the straw down so that it is evenly tempered. Straw, when tempered, should have the same consistency as when growing in a field, when the stem has turned yellow but the node is still green. After tempering, roll the straw in a towel and leave it until needed, but do not leave straw damp overnight as it will discolour and mildew. After working, lay the remaining unused straw out to dry. Avoid oversoaking straw because it will not produce work of a high standard.

Straw is a strong medium. Always let the straw do the work, finding its own fold. Never flatten folds with the thumb nail but simply roll the straw in the direction of working and the result will be neat close work.

5-Straw Plait

This basic weave should be mastered before attempting the corn knack or other dollies.

Method

1 Tie five straws tightly onto a dowel or pencil with twine using a clove hitch (Fig 1). Tie them in the following positions around the dowel–12 o'clock, 9 o'clock, 6 o'clock and two straws at the 3 o'clock position (See Fig 2a).

2 Hold dowel firmly between the left forefinger and thumb and bend the straws down at right angles from it.

3 Take straw 1 from underneath straw 5, bring forwards again, then up and over straw 5 to rest on top of straw 2 (see Fig 2b).

4 Hold these two straws together with the right hand, letting go with the left and turn the work clockwise so that the straws being held are in the starting position.

Fig 1

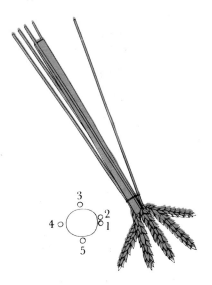

Fig 2a

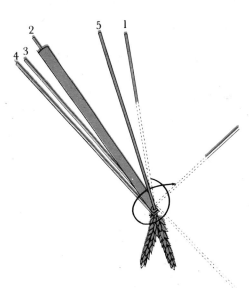

Fig 2b

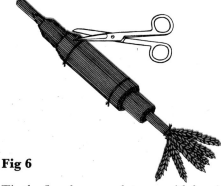

with heads tightly together with a clove hitch about ⅜in *(9.5mm)* below the ears. Measure 12in *(30.5cm)* from this first tie and cut the remaining straw away. Place the second tie 1in *(2.5cm)* from the end. Take half of the waste straw and cut it into 10in *(25.5cm)* lengths. Lay this around the core already started, 1in *(2.5cm)* from each end. Tie on securely with a clove hitch, 1in *(2.5cm)* from the ends. Cut the remaining bunch of waste straw 6in *(15cm)* in length and arrange around the centre of the core. Tie in the same way as before. With sharp scissors, cut the ends of the waste straw to taper it so that it is cigar shaped. (See Fig 6).

Fig 6

5 Continue actions 3 and 4 and the weaving action is in progress. Continue up the dowel until the weave has been mastered.

JOINING STRAWS DURING WEAVING
Cut off the straw when it becomes thick and coarse approximately 7in *(18cm)* from the end. The new straw to be inserted should have its head cut off at an angle to make the insertion process easier. (See Fig 3). Care should be taken to see that all the straws in use are of the same grade as this controls the neatness of the work.

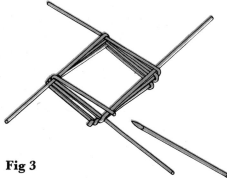

Fig 3

CONTROLLING THE SHAPE
Increasing To expand the dimensions of the work, lay the moving straw called the worker, to the right of the next straw, and hold it in that position while the same movement is made. Following this

Fig 4
26

process the work will expand. For a more gradual expansion, place the straw half way between the normal weaving position and the extreme right (Fig 4).

Fig 5

Decreasing To taper the work inwards, place the worker to the left of the next straw until the desired shape has been achieved. The decrease obviously is governed by the extent the worker is moved to the left. (Fig 5).

Traditional Knack

The Devon knack or neck was ritually tied and bound at harvest time to the joyful cry of 'Wee-en, Way-en'.

Materials required:
15 straws with heads
120 weaving straws of the same grade and colour
A 2in *(5cm)* diameter bunch of waste straw
Sharp scissors
Strong thread
A needle

Method
Temper the 120 weaving straws and five headed straws. Tie the ten dry straws

Tie the five dampened straws with heads in with the other heads of the core at the clock quarter positions, with two straws at the 3 o'clock position. Weave as for the traditional five-straw plait, being careful that the work is a perfect square formation around the core. Continue weaving up the core allowing the straws to rest gently against the core all the way. When the top of the core is reached the work will have become progressively narrower. Allow the work to taper off till there is no centre hole. Keeping to the square pattern, continue for a further 3in *(7.5cm)*. Draw the straws together and tie with a clove hitch, leaving the thread ends long. Bend the flexible end of the knack around a finger and position the end 1in *(2.5cm)* down the dolly. Thread the needle with one of the thread ends left on the dolly and sew through one of the folds of the weave. Tie the two thread ends together. Cut the ends of the straw off diagonally. (Fig 7).

Fig 7

Welsh Fan

An ancient ritualistic harvest thanks-giving offering now makes an attractive ornament.

Materials required:

25 tempered straws of the same size and grade with prime ears
Strong thread
Paper
Raffia
Newspaper

Method

Tie three straws securely $\frac{3}{8}$in *(9.5mm)* below the ears in a clove hitch, using strong thread, making sure the wheat husks are to the fore.

Lay the work flat on the table with the ears pointing away, and spread the straws, two to the right and one to the left as shown in the diagram (Fig 8). Do not allow the work to slip from the four to the five position as this will spoil the dolly. It is often helpful to mark a large piece of paper with drawn lines and to use this as a guide.

*Lift the top straw on the right (lying at four on the clockface). Insert a new straw between this top straw and the one below so that it lies along the inside of the L.H. straw. (The left hand straw is the one lying at eight on the clockface). Lift the outside L.H. straw and insert a new straw beneath to lie along the inside of the R.H. straws. (Fig 9).

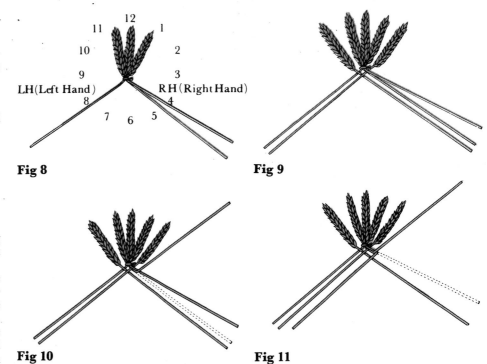

Fig 8   Fig 9

Fig 10   Fig 11

Lift up the second straw from the outside on the right and pass the outside R.H. straw across the inside R.H. straw, to lay at the inside position of the L.H. group. Then pull the second straw from the R.H. down in to its new position with a short sharp tug. (See Figs 10 and 11). Work this same action on the L.H. side, then once more on both sides, working from right to left and left to right

alternately. Repeat the actions from * until all 25 straws have been used. Put six of these locking stitches alternately on each side and cross the two inside straws over one another. Tie one side with raffia. Take the raffia to the other side and tie again, thus making a hanger. Lay the work flat on newspaper, arranging the ears evenly and press under a weight overnight.

Mordiford

This dolly derives its name from the English village where it originated.

Materials required:
23 tempered straws of the same grade with well matched ears
Strong thread
Raffia

Method
Prepare and tie seven straws securely ⅜in *(9.5mm)* below the ears using a clove hitch. Spread the straws out in a circle, holding just below the tie between the index and middle finger of the left hand, and using the left thumb to hold the straws in position. With the right hand take the straw that is nearest and place it over the top of the two straws to the

Fig 12

right. Miss the next straw to the left, and take the next one over two, working counter-clockwise (Fig 12).

Continue over two, skip one, making sure to go across the centre of the work each time, until only 4in *(10cm)* of the straw ends remain. Tie off close to the work with thread using a clove hitch. Prepare and tie another seven straws and work in exactly the same way taking

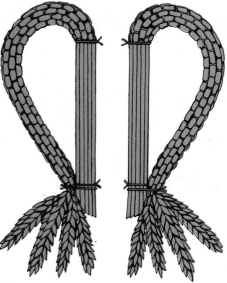

Fig 13

care that the finished plaits are exactly the same length. When completed, roll the plaits in the palms of the hands and then gently stretch by pulling away from the ears. Bend the plaits around to the unwoven straw and tie the plaits 3in *(7.5cm)* from the last tie (Fig 13).

Assemble these two ear-shaped plaits by tying together on top of the previous knots. Lay the remaining straws, five to the front and four behind, with the ears arranged neatly in with those of the plaits and tie on top of the two existing ties with thread. Put a raffia tie at the bottom with the knot at the back and another at the top, leaving the ends long enough to make a loop as a hanger.

Cornucopia

This is the horn of Amalthea, which in legend promised an abundance of fruit and corn to whoever owned it.

Materials required:
200 tempered weaving straws of medium thickness
Scissors
Dried flowers, cones etc.

Method
Tie six straws together with a clove hitch. Hold the straws with the longest part downwards ⅜in *(9.5mm)* from the end. Spread the long straws out in a circle at right angles to the short ends

Fig 14

(Fig 14). Work with an increasing weave for five complete circles, remembering to keep the five spaces between the straws even. Change to the straight weave, this time placing the worker on top of the next straw, for three complete circles, and then work around six times using the decreasing method with the worker

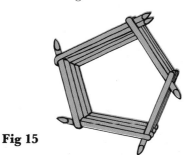

Fig 15

to the left of the next straw to move. From this point the worker is slightly to the right of the next straw to move, giving a gradual increase in the dimension of the work. Continue until the work is 14in *(33cm)* long and the mouth of the horn

is 5in *(13.5cm)* in diameter. Work around six times using the decreasing method and finish off by tucking the worker straw under the next straw (Fig 15).

Tie in position and trim off the ends of the straws ⅜in *(9.5mm)* diagonally. With a needle and thread, catch one of the folds in the top of the cornucopia and again at the mouth, and gently pull the thread until the horn is the required shape. Tie and cut off the thread ends. Leave this temporary tie on overnight so the straw will dry in the correct position. When the straw is dry the tie is discarded and the shape of the horn is then permanent.

To fill the cornucopia one of two methods can be used. Either place a piece of plastic foam which is available from most florists inside and push the dried material into this, or arrange the material into a pleasing bunch, making sure the stems are long, then, tying the flowers together, insert them into the horn. The method depends on the filling.

Rugmaking

Rug making is a community craft like quilting and several people can work on a project together, particularly if the latch hook method is being used, as then the work will be uniform throughout. Rug-hooking is methodical and soothing to do and the work grows quite quickly, producing a thick luxurious pile. When the project is finished you have a quality rug in exactly the colour and design you wanted for a fraction of the price it would have cost to buy!

As an alternative to hooking, try making an embroidered rug. Only one simple cross stitch is used producing a finished surface which is smooth and hardwearing. Three embroidered rug patterns are given here, one a traditional flower design, one a bright soldier motif, and lastly a dutch tile design.

MATERIALS AND TOOLS

Canvas Hooked and embroidered rugs are made on rug canvas which is available in widths from 12in *(30cm)* to 48in *(1.2m)* wide. The canvas is white and made of the best quality cotton, with a selvedge down both sides. Coloured lines in blue, red or brown divide the canvas into squares, to make it easier to count the holes when working a pattern. The most used size has nine holes to the square inch *(2.5cm)*. Rug patterns usually specify a little extra canvas than required for the finished rug because the canvas is turned over at both ends. Circular, semi-circular and oval rugs are usually worked on square or rectangular canvas and cut to shape after the rug is hooked.

Wool The correct wool to use for hooked rugs is a coarse 6-ply rug wool. This is available ready-cut and packaged in round bundles or in skeins which can be cut to the required length.

Tools A rug hook or latch hook is the only tool required if you are using pre-cut wool. These are obtained from handicraft shops. If skeins of wool are being used, a wooden gauge and a sharp knife or razor blade will be needed to cut the wool. These are available from shops selling rug wool and canvas. For making embroidered rugs, a rug needle is required.

USING THE LATCH HOOK

A latch hook is simple to use but it takes a little practice to get into the rhythm of working.

Work with the rug lying flat on a table. Have a few strands of each yarn colour on hand ready to pick up. Follow Fig A for the technique of working the knot. Work in one direction only or the pile will not lie evenly.

1 Double the yarn around the shaft of the latch hook and push the head of the hook under a double thread. The hook is open and faces left.

2 With the fingers of the other hand, pull the two ends across behind the latch and under the hook.

3 Pull the hook through the loop. The latch closes and the cut ends are pulled through.

4 Pull the ends gently with the fingers to tighten the knot.

WORKING CROSS STITCH

Fig B shows how how to work cross stitch. Work the first stitch right across the pattern from left to right, then cross them on the return journey. Cut lengths of yarn 12–14in *(30–36cm)* long. If longer lengths are used, the yarn tangles. It also frays on the canvas as work progresses and the later stitches do not cover the mesh. Never tie a knot to begin, but leave an end about 1½in *(3cm)*

on the wrong side and work the first few stitches over the end. To finish, run the end under the backs of stitches and then clip off the short end that remains.

Marrakesh Rug

The design of this luxurious pile rug was inspired by North African tile motifs. The brilliant colours of a burning sun combined with white give the rug the look of a traditional Arab design. The rug is worked with a latch hook but, if preferred, the chart could be used for making an embroidered rug in cross stitch. The finished size of the rug is 54in x 27in *(137cm x 69cm)*.

Fig 1 Marrakesh rug

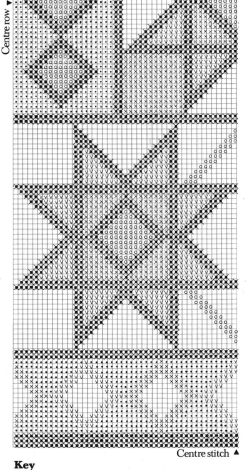

Centre stitch ▲

Key

Cream background
✗ Burnt orange
✶ Dark tan
∨ Old Gold
• Beige
○ Scarlet

Fig A

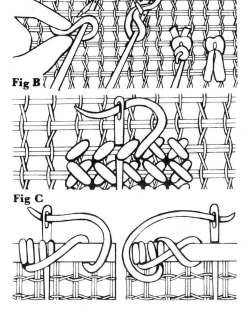

Fig B

Fig C

Fig D

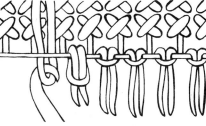

Fig E

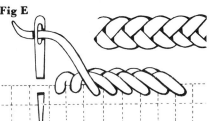

A Latch technique
B Single cross stitch
C Binding stitch
D Fringing
E Braid stitch

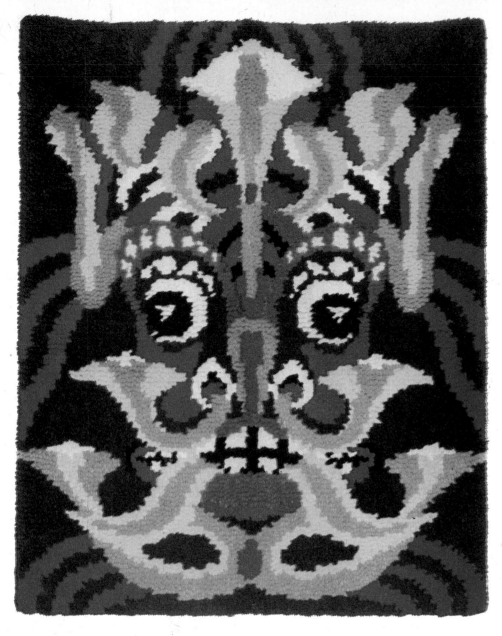

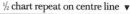

Key
Dark plum background
- × Scarlet
- ● Mimosa
- ╱ Marigold
- ◆ Pale purple
- + Black
- ■ White

Fig 2 Oriental mask

Materials required:

60in *(152cm)* of 27in *(69cm)* wide rug canvas
Pre-cut packs rug wool in the following colours and quantities: 16 packs dark tan; 14 packs cream; 8 packs beige; 6 packs burnt orange; 5 packs old gold; 3 packs scarlet; 3 skeins dark tan
Latch hook
Rug needle.

To work the rug

Turn under about 3in *(8cm)* across one cut end of canvas and skipping spare thread on folded edge, work first few rows through the double thickness of canvas. Fig A shows the technique for using the latch hook. Work each row of the design from left to right, making a knot in every hole of canvas. The chart (Fig 1) gives a quarter of the design and each square represents a knot on the canvas. The colour key shows the wool colours. For each row, work from the edge to the centre stitch arrowed on the chart. Note that there will be one hole of the canvas left unworked at the edge of every row. These will be taken in with the edging or binding stitches later. Work to the central row to complete one quarter.

When a quarter of the rug is completed, work back from the centre stitch to the other edge to finish each row and complete the second quarter.

Repeat the design from the centre row to the edge for the second half of the rug. When the rug is almost complete, count off the number of rows to be worked to finish the design and, allowing the spare thread on the folded edge, fold over the surplus canvas and work the few rows through double thickness last, as at the beginning.

Work binding stitch (Fig C) over the selvedge edge down each side using dark tan. Oversew both short ends of the rug using dark tan wool. An alternative edging can be worked using braid stitch (see Fig E).

Oriental Mask

Work this wonderfully fierce Chinese theatrical mask with the latch hook method for an unusual rug, or display it for dramatic effect as a wall panel. The finished size is 36in x 27in *(91.5cm x 69cm)*.

Materials required:

42in *(105cm)* of 27in *(69cm)* wide rug canvas

Pre-cut packs rug wool in the following colours and quantities:
13 packs dark plum; 6 packs scarlet; 5 packs mimosa; 6 packs marigold; 2 packs pale purple; 1 pack black; 3 packs white; plus 2 skeins plum for binding
Latch hook
Rug needle.

To work the rug

Turn under 3in *(8cm)* across one cut end of the canvas.

Leaving the spare thread on the folded edge, work the first few rows through the double thickness of canvas.

Refer to Fig A for the latch hook method, and remember to work from left to right, tying a knot in each hole.

The chart (Fig 2) gives one lengthwise half of the design. Follow the colours as indicated and repeat from the centre, marked with an arrow for the second half of the design.

When the rug is almost complete, count the number of rows to be finished and, allowing for the spare thread on the folded edge, turn under the surplus canvas and work through the double thickness.

Work binding stitch (Fig C) over the selvedges using the plum yarn. Oversew both shorter ends or alternatively edge with braid stitch (Fig E).

Rose Rug

This pretty rose-patterned rug is worked in cross stitch on rug canvas. The colour scheme shown would look attractive in both modern and traditional surroundings but if it is intended to work the design in different colours, plan out the proposed new scheme on graph paper using coloured felt tip pens. Copy the pattern square for square but make sure that the colour changes are noted on the chart colour key. The finished size of the rug shown is 51in x 24in *(130cm x 61cm)*.

Materials required:

58in *(148cm)* of 24in *(61cm)* wide rug canvas

Rug wool in the following colours and quantities:
7 skeins each old gold, white; 5 skeins moss green; 4 skeins black; 3 skeins light green; 2 skeins pink; 1 skein each cardinal, dark rose, dark tan
Rug needle

To work the rug

The rug is worked in cross stitch throughout, over one double thread of canvas. Each square on the chart represents one stitch. One-third of the design is given.

Turn under 2in *(5cm)* on one cut end of

Fig 3 Rose rug

Key   White background
× Cardinal   • Moss Green   ∨ Light Green   ■ Dark rose
∕ Old Gold   ▲ Black   ○ Pink   ⤬ Dark tan

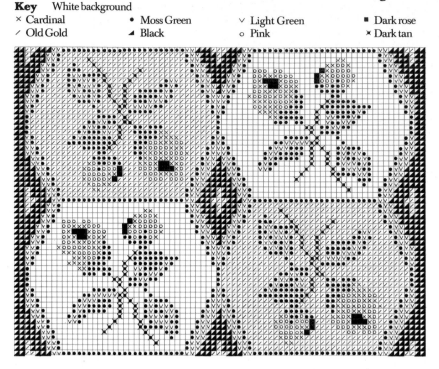

felt wall hanging of one soldier to match –just draw out a pattern onto squared paper from the chart using each square on the chart to represent ½in *(1cm)*.

Materials required:
40in *(102cm)* of 18in *(46cm)* wide rug canvas
Rug wool in the following colours and quantities:
6 skeins white; 5 skeins medium blue; 4 skeins each black, scarlet; 1 skein each pink, gold
Rug needle.

To work the rug
Fold under about 1½in *(3.5cm)* across one cut end of the canvas and skipping spare thread on folded edge, work first few rows through double thickness. The design is worked from the chart (Fig 4) in cross stitch throughout, and each square on the chart represents one cross stitch. The key shows the wool colours. Work the design from the chart across the width of the rug. One repeat consists of 20 rows. When one repeat has been completed, work five rows in medium blue. Repeat the 20 rows of design followed by five rows of blue three times more, finishing with 20 rows of the design making five soldier panels in all. When the rug is almost finished, count the number of rows required to finish the design. Fold under the surplus canvas and, allowing the spare thread on the folded edge, work the last few rows through double thickness as at beginning.
Work the details shown by heavy lines on the chart in back stitch, over two threads of the canvas, using a split length of black wool.
For the features, work the mouth in scarlet and the eyes in blue. Using white, work binding stitch (Fig C) over selvedge edges down both sides.
Cut the remaining white wool into 6in

the canvas matching the holes and baste. The first rows are worked through both thicknesses of canvas. The fringe is later worked onto the folded edge.
Work the first row of stitches over the first double thread from the folded edge, following the chart (Fig 3). Work the 59 rows of the first section. Then work the second repeat, but omitting row one. Work the third repeat, again omitting row one. When nearing the completion of the third repeat, count the number of rows still to be worked and fold under the cut end, matching holes. Work the last few rows through double thickness.

Finishing
Using black wool, work binding stitch

(Fig C) over the selvedges down both sides. Cut the remaining black wool into 7in *(18cm)* lengths and knot a fringe at both ends onto the thread on the folded edge (Fig D). Press the rug on the wrong side under a damp cloth with a warm iron.

Soldiers all in a row

Here is a nursery favourite–a bright needlemade rug with a row of soldiers marching across it. The design is worked in cross stitch and the finished size of the rug is 18in x 36in *(46cm x 91cm)* plus the fringe. It would be a nice touch to make a

(15cm) lengths and fringe the ends (see Fig D for knotting technique). Press the finished rug on wrong side under a damp cloth with a warm iron.

Fig 4 Soldiers rug

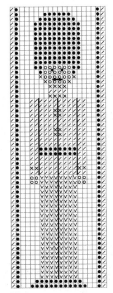

Key
White background

∨ Medium	• Black
blue	○ Pink
/ Scarlet	× Gold

Dutch-tile Rug

This pretty blue and cream rug design is based on an old Dutch tile pattern. The rug is worked in cross stitch on rug canvas.

Materials required:

Fig 5
Dutch-tile rug

60in *(153cm)* of 27in *(69cm)* wide rug canvas, for an eight-square rug.
Rug wool in the following colours and

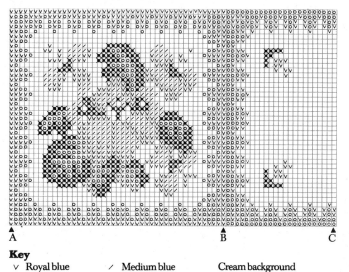

A   B   C

Key

∨ Royal blue	/ Medium blue	Cream background
○ Marble	✗ Light blue	

quantities for eight-square rug:
14 skeins cream; 7 skeins royal blue; 6 skeins marble; 4 skeins medium blue; 3 skeins light blue
Rug needle.

To work the rug

Turn under about 2in *(5cm)* across one cut end of the canvas and skipping the spare thread on the folded edge, work the first few rows of the design through double thickness. The rug is worked in single cross stitch throughout and each square on the chart (Fig 5) represents one cross stitch. The chart gives one and a half motifs and the key shows the wool colours. Work from arrows A–C on chart, then work back to point B to complete the two tile motifs.
Note: The last stitch on the right hand side of the rug is omitted at the end of every row. Alternate the motifs, as shown, until eight have been worked. Finish end as at beginning.
Using medium blue wool, work binding stitch over the selvedge edges down each side (Fig C). Oversew both short ends with medium blue wool. Braid stitch (Fig E) can be worked all around the rug instead of binding stitch if preferred.
Press the rug on wrong side under a damp cloth with a warm iron.

35

Jewelry

Jewelry, even costume jewelry, is expensive to buy. It is simpler and more fun to make your own attractive and inexpensive designs. Using ordinary metal wire, a wide variety of shapes can be achieved.

Ropes and Chains

Twisted Metal Ropes

These ideas for ropes are all traditional designs and make lovely necklaces and bracelets to wear at any time.

Materials required:

Any soft metal wire such as copper, silver-plated or aluminum
Hook

To make the rope

Cut a long piece of wire, bend it in half and secure the loose ends in a table vice. Take the hook, (or one can be made by bending a piece of wire with pliers), place it through the wire loop, and turn it so that a wire forms a twist (Fig 1). To twist up a long length of wire, place the hook in the hand drill, and use the drill to revolve the wire. Make sure that the wire is taut as you twist it; if it is allowed to go slack, the spiral will be uneven.

By using different thicknesses of wire together, many different effects can be achieved. Five pretty designs are shown in Fig 2.

1 The bracelet on the left is similar to the central twist No. 3. It is a thick twist with fine wires wound into the grooves.
2 To achieve this effect, twist together two strips of flat wire and then wind a fine twist in the groove.
3 This rope is made with a twist of thick wire and another of thin wire. Twist the thin one into the groove of the thicker one.
4 Here is a plain twist of two lengths of round wire.
5 The bracelet on the right is made with a tight right hand twist, doubled back on itself, and twisted in reverse direction. Silver plated spheres finish the ends.

To make the bracelets

Bend the finished rope around a solid cylindrical object, such as a wooden rolling pin or a tin can filled with earth. Do not attempt to do this with very thick rope or a very tight twist.

Finish the bracelet with hollow silver-plated spheres, purchased from a jewelry supply shop. Saw off or drill an opening in the ball large enough to take the thickness of the bracelet and glue the bracelet ends into the spheres with an epoxy adhesive. To wrap the ends with wire, allow ½in (1cm) wire to align with the twist and bind the wire back over this ½in end to secure. To fasten the other end, thread it back under the bound section. Cut off the excess.

Chains and Links

There are endless possibilities for creating different patterns and designs using chains. Different materials can be used together for exciting effects and the links themselves made in a wide variety of shapes and sizes. Beads and shells can be incorporated to make attractive necklaces and bracelets. The materials and tools are similar to those required for the ropes.

To make the links

Fix the hand drill in the vice as shown in

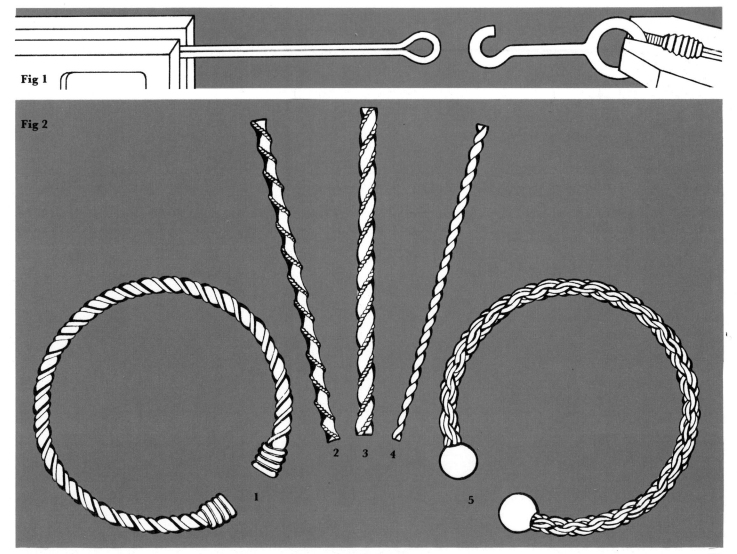

Fig 1

Fig 2

1 2 3 4 5

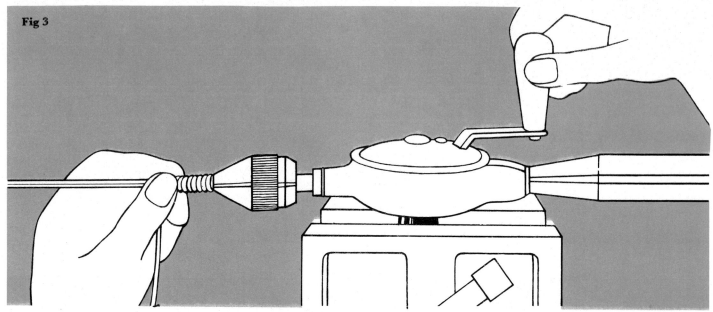

Fig 3

Fig 3. Secure a rod or dowel and one end of the wire in the chuck of the hand drill. Turn the handle of the drill to wrap the wire around the rod to form a coil or 'spring'. Hold the wire steady so that the coil is regular and tight. When all the wire has been wound, remove the rod and the coil from the drill. Slide the wire off the rod. If a long coil is made wrap a piece of damp tissue paper around the rod before turning the drill. To remove the coil from the rod, burn the paper when it has dried which will leave a tiny gap, and enable the wire to be removed more easily. To cut the links, hold the coil between the thumb and index finger of the left hand. Hold the hand against a firm surface and with the coil almost vertical, carefully cut a straight line down the coil with wire cutters or the jeweler's piercing saw.

To join the links

Grip one link in two pairs of pliers as shown in Fig 4a. The gap should be at the top. Gently twist the pliers in opposite directions, so that the two ends meet and continue to twist gently until the two ends overlap, then spring back together. This should form a strong sprung joint, with no overlap (Fig 4b). Take another link, thread it through the first one and join it in the same way as before. Finished links are called jump rings. Different shapes and sizes of link can be made according to the shape and diameter of the dowel or rod used to wrap the wire around. In oval or oblong links, cut the links in the middle of one of the long sides. This will be stronger than a join made in the short side.

Kinds of chain

Fig 5a. Use an oval metal rod and a rectangular wood strip to coil the links, then assemble the chain with oval and rectangular links alternating.

Fig 5b. To make the figure eight links,

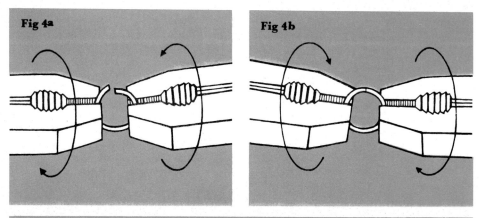

Fig 4a

Fig 4b

Fig 5a

Fig 5b

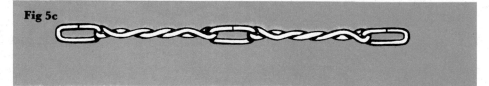

Fig 5c

Fig 5d

38

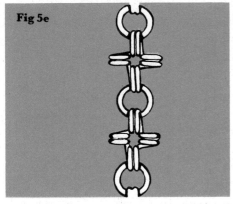
Fig 5e

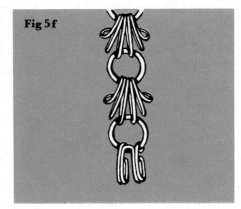
Fig 5f

Working in Silver

hammer two nails into a piece of wood ¾in (2cm) apart. Wind the wire around the nails in the form of a figure eight. Each link should be made separately and then joined with round links to make the chain.

Fig 5c. For the twisted rope links, bend a piece of wire approx. 2½in (7cm) long, and twist it as described for twisted ropes. Bend the open end into a link with the pliers, and attach this to a plain link.

For the more complex chains it is advisable to start with aluminum wire and big links. Aluminum can be anodized in many colours.

Fig 5d. To make the first chain cut off a piece of coil ten links long. Gently bend it around into a flower shape, easing the links apart with the back of a knife if necessary. The ends should meet. Join the flower shapes together with plain links threaded through two turns of the flower shape.

Fig 5e. The second chain is another version of the same idea. In this case, cut off a piece of coil eight links long. Bend it open into a cross shape, each arm of the cross made of two links. Use a second pair of pliers to keep the sets of two links together.

Fig 5f. The third chain is again the same technique, this time using six rounds of coil. Hold one side of the spring together and gently open the other side. Tuck in the ends so that they do not catch.

To make chain mail

Fig 6 shows how to assemble traditional chain mail using round links. For necklaces, bracelets and chain belts, bend up a fastening with the pliers as illustrated.

Bead and Tube Necklace

Mark a length of copper or silver-plated tubing into equal sections of ½in (1cm). Cut the tube into lengths with a saw. If the ends are rough, smooth them off with a metal file or sand paper. To make the wires from which the beads hang, cut a length of suitably thick wire into 1in (2.5cm) lengths. Curl up a tiny circle at one end to hold the beads on the wire. Thread on the bead and then turn up a curl at the other end. This end will be threaded onto the necklace. Tie one end of strong thread securely to a jump ring. Then thread the tube, the beads and the metal wires and finally secure a bolt ring to the other end (Fig 7).

Materials:
Sheet silver: This is sold specially for jewelry work in flat sheets of standard gauge thickness and it is usually priced by the weight; 12 or 14 gauge is adequate for rings, and 14 or 16 gauge for bracelets, unless very heavy pieces are required. The backing for brooches and pendants is usually made from thinner silver of 8 or 10 gauge. For the band which holds in the stone or bezel use 6 gauge silver.

Silver wire: Used for making chains, loops, narrow bracelets, neckbands etc, silver wire is sold in a wide variety of standard gauge sizes, and can be round, half-round or square in section. Round and square hollow tube is also available.

Jeweler's findings: This is a term used to describe ready-made fittings for all types of jewelry, such as brooch pins, earring hooks and screws, cuff link ends, jump rings for links, and bolt rings for clasps. A selection of these is very useful, especially for beginners.

Gemstones: For beginners, cabochon cut stones are recommended. These are gemstones which have been polished and shaped for setting but have not been faceted. They are much easier to set than faceted stones. Faceted stones require a delicate claw setting, but cabochon need only a simple setting.

Solder: This can be bought in strips or in sheet form and is graded by its melting point into hard, medium and easy.

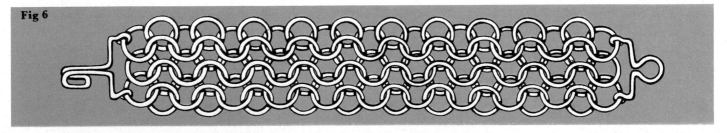
Fig 6

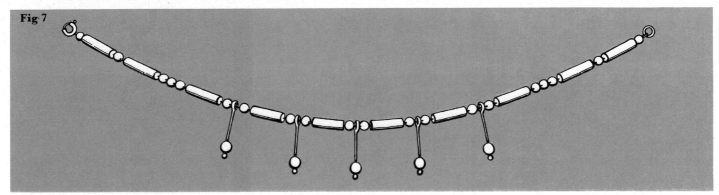
Fig 7

For cutting: A piercing saw with adjustable saw frame, jeweler's saw blades, a V-block and clamp, a 3–4in *(8–10cm)* vice, and a wire cutter.

For filing and shaping: Fine sand paper, at least two large files, half-round and flat and at least four needle files round, half-round, triangular and flat, a triblet or tapered steel spike also known as a ring mandrel, and a vice large enough to hold it, small round-nosed pliers, small flat-nosed pliers, jeweler's ring pliers with one jaw round and one flat, a wooden mallet, a jeweler's hammer, a hand drill with drills, a ring clamp.

For annealing and soldering: A piece of asbestos sheeting, a charcoal block, a gas/air blow torch, pointed tweezers, paint brushes, flux (traditionally a flux paste is made by rubbing a lump of borax in a little water in a rough-textured borax dish, but ready-made liquid flux is available), iron binding wire.

For cleaning and polishing: An acid solution made from one part sulphuric acid to ten parts distilled water (both available from pharmacists). Make this by adding the acid to the water, *never* the other way around as water added to acid gives off chemical heat and can even cause an explosion; keep the solution in an ovenproof glass or pottery container with lid. You will also need brass or copper tongs, tripoli polish, jeweler's rouge, a set of polishing buffs, and a flat or curved burnisher, Water of Ayr stone.

Top, Fig 8: making a ring shank. **a** bend ends of shank back and forth and over and under each other. **b** File join so that the edges fit evenly. **c** Flux and solder the join together. Bottom, Fig 9: making the bezel. **a** Measure circumference of stone. **b** If the bezel is too low or too high it will either not hold stone or will buckle. **c** Bezel should fit stone.

Note: A complete set of tools could be an expensive outlay for a beginner. If you want to try out the craft first of all before committing yourself to too much expense, it is a good idea to enroll for a day or evening class at a local school or college. Most of the equipment will then be provided at the class–cutting and filing can be done at home in your own time, soldering and polishing at the class. If you do intend to buy a complete set of tools, equipment and materials, most of the specialized equipment can be bought from jewelers' supply companies by mail order. Other items can be bought from hobby shops or do-it-yourself suppliers.

Basic techniques

To cut sheet silver Mark and lightly score the line to be cut. Always cut on the outside of the marked line. Fine gauge silver can be cut with wire cutters but for heavier gauges and thick wire use a piercing saw. When fitting the blade make sure that the teeth face outwards and down towards the handle. To obtain the correct tension first loosen the nuts at both ends of the frame, then insert the blade in the top and tighten it. The blade should make a 'ping' when plucked. Compress the whole frame slightly by pressing the top edge against the workbench. Keeping it compressed insert the loose ends of the blade and tighten the bottom nut. Release pressure on the frame gradually. Always keep the blade perpendicular to the sawing surface and cut on the downward stroke. Heavy pressure is not necessary and will break the blade. To support the sheet silver while cutting, a hardwood V-board clamped to the table or workbench is useful. For cutting thick wire or tube use a small vice to hold it, first lining the jaws with leather so that they do not mark the silver.

To anneal Sheet silver cannot be shaped

without first being heated and then rapidly cooled–a process known as annealing. This softens the metal so that it can be hammered or bent more easily. Put the silver on an asbestos sheet and heat it quickly with a blow torch until it turns dark red. If it turns yellow-red it is a danger sign, showing that the silver is on the point of melting. Try to avoid overheating when annealing or soldering as this can cause dull grey firestains which become visible after polishing and are difficult to remove.

Pick up the hot metal with tweezers and hold it under cold water. The silver will harden as it is hammered and when it becomes difficult to work, repeat the annealing process.

Silver wire is not always annealed. A round-wire neckband such as could be used with a pendant should be hard and springy. If the wire were annealed it would be too soft for its purpose.

To shape and file silver Sheet silver is shaped by twisting or curving it with pliers or beating it over the triblet. Pliers for bending silver must have smooth polished jaws as serrations will cause dents and roughness. Round-nosed pliers are used for curves, flat-nosed pliers for angles. When hammering silver over a triblet to bend it, use a wooden mallet–a metal hammer marks the surface. A metal planishing hammer is used to stretch and to thin silver. It is useful if a ring is too small and has to be enlarged. When using a file on straight edges, work at a diagonal to the filing surface with a long even stroke. File from the tip of the file to the handle.

To solder silver Solder will only flow into a join if it is clean and has been carefully fluxed. Apply flux to the surfaces with a paint brush, having first made sure that the surfaces are free from dust and grease by sanding them with clean sand paper. Always file joints to fit as

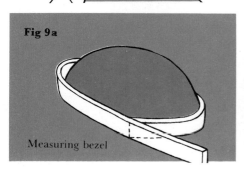

Fig 8 a — Bending the shank with round-nosed pliers

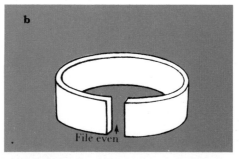

b — File even

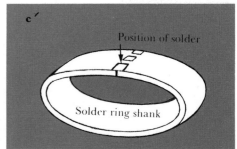

c — Position of solder / Solder ring shank

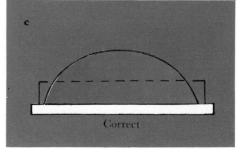

Fig 9 a — Measuring bezel

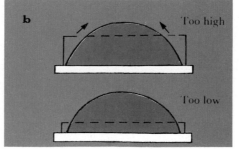

b — Too high / Too low

c — Correct

accurately as possible because if there are gaps, the solder can run between them onto the visible surface and the join will be lumpy or incompletely soldered. Choose the most appropriate type of solder for the design. If the design requires soldering a number of times begin with hard solder, go on to medium and then use easy solder. Clean the solder, cut it into tiny pieces about $\frac{1}{32}$ in (0.75mm) square and coat with flux by picking up and positioning with a brush moistened with flux. Several small pieces melt more easily than one large one. An even heat over the whole area to be soldered is essential for a successful result. Begin by quickly rotating the flame around the outside of the area without touching the silver. The flux will probably foam a little as it is heated which can dislodge the solder. Have a pair of pointed tweezers ready to re-position it if necessary. When white crust forms on the fluxed surface this indicates that the flux has hardened, and the area to be soldered can now be heated directly. Rotate the flame slowly over it until the solder melts and flows into the join. After soldering the metal will be discoloured and must be cleaned before further work can be done.

To clean silver after soldering The work is put in an acid solution or pickle to remove discolouring oxides and the remains of the flux. The acid is very corrosive so avoid splashing and keep it in a well-ventilated place to clear acid fumes. Leave the work in the solution until clean. It will then be a dull whitish colour. Rinse it in cold water when removed or the traces of acid will continue to eat into the metal.

Never use steel or iron tongs to put the silver into the acid as a copper deposit will form on it. Similarly if iron binding wire was used to hold the work together for soldering, it must all be removed before cleaning. If brass or copper tongs are not available, use bent pieces of strong silver wire.

To finish the surface A good machine polisher is an expensive piece of equipment, and not necessary for the beginner since it is possible to obtain a high degree of finish by hand-polishing.

Remove any scratches or dents by rubbing lightly with fine sand paper – a piece that has been worn almost smooth is ideal. Wash and dry the work and rub hard and evenly with a felt buffing stick charged with tripoli polish, changing the direction constantly. Any firestain will become noticeable at this point and should be removed with fine sand paper or Water of Ayr stone. Buff again and polish with jeweler's rouge. Places which cannot be reached by buffing can be polished by rubbing with a flat or curved burnisher and cake rouge. Alternatively, use a piece of soft string coated with rouge.

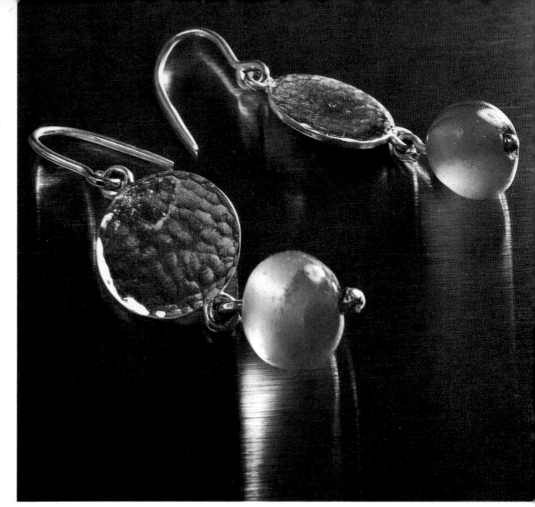

Silver and Agate Earrings

An attractive pair of earrings for both day and evening occasions.

Materials required:

2in x 1in (5cm x 2.5cm) strip 10 gauge sheet silver
Round silver wire
Agate beads
Earring screws or hooks

To make the earrings

Mark out two circles clearly on the sheet silver. The earrings illustrated are made from circles with $\frac{3}{8}$in (1cm) diameter. Cut out the circles with a piercing saw, keeping outside the marked line. If possible cut the circles from a piece of sheet at least 2in (5cm) long, as it is easier to hold a large piece steady while sawing. True up the circle with a file, filing up to the marked line. To do this, avoid concentrating on one part of the circle; turn it, so that a curve is filed, not a series of facets. To ensure that the disc is flat, place it on a flat metal surface, and tap it with a wooden mallet.

Take a length of silver wire, and with the small round nosed pliers make a spiral of five to six rings approx. $\frac{1}{8}$in (4mm) in outside diameter using the hand drill method. Holding the coil vertical between the index finger and thumb, cut through it with the piercing saw. Join

the ends of the links as described on page 38 to form jump rings.

Place the rings on a flat metal surface, and tap them flat with a wooden mallet. Hold each link, join uppermost, in the flat nosed pliers and file a small facet through half the thickness of the wire with a flat needle file. Keep the join in the middle of the facet. Place both discs on the charcoal block. Place two links opposite each other, touching the edge of the disc. Solder the links to the discs, using tiny pieces of solder. Concentrate the flame on the discs, not the links, because the links will tend to melt more easily. Clean in acid, and file off any excess solder.

Place the discs on a flat surface, and tap with a hammer to produce the beaten texture. To attach the bead, take a piece of wire which will go through the hole drilled in the bead. Cut off two pieces, long enough to thread the bead, plus $\frac{5}{8}$in (1.5cm). Hold one piece of wire by one end with the tweezers, put borax on the other end and heat it until the end melts into a small sphere. Repeat this with the other piece. Clean in acid.

Thread each bead onto each piece of wire, where it should be held by the melted sphere.

With the round nosed pliers, bend up a ring at the other end of the wire, and attach this to one of the links on the discs. Attach an earring screw or hook to the other link on the discs.

41

Cornelian Ring

This striking ring is lovely on its own or with the bracelet that follows.

Materials required:

Cornelian
⅜in *(1cm)* wide strip 8 gauge sheet silver
⅛in *(3mm)* wide strip 14 gauge sheet silver
⅜in x 2½in *(1cm x 6cm)* 12 gauge sheet silver
⅛in *(3mm)* square copper wire
Silver wire
Plasticine or modelling clay
Plaster of Paris
Water of Ayr stone.

To make the ring

Cut a strip of 8 gauge sheet, ⅜in *(1cm)* wide, and long enough to go around the stone, plus a fraction. Anneal it and bend up a band to fit tight around the stone. Cut off the excess with the piercing saw. Solder it and clean off any excess solder. Take a piece of 14 gauge silver and cut a strip ⅛in *(3mm)* wide and long enough to go around the setting already made. (Figs 9a, b, c.) Repeat the process, so that the thin metal circle fits tightly inside the thicker one, with enough of the inner setting projecting above the outer one to be pushed over the stone, i.e. about $\frac{1}{16}$in *(1.5mm)*. Solder the two together. Then make a wire ring which will fit inside the inner setting, to provide a support for the stone. Solder this wire in place.

Check that the upper and lower edges of the setting are flat and parallel.

To make the silver balls, cut six equal pieces from a length of silver wire. Place the pieces on the charcoal block, dip in borax, and heat until they melt to form little spheres. Clean in acid, and file a small facet on each one.

To hold the balls in position around the setting for soldering, put a collar of Plasticine or modelling clay around the setting. Place the balls, flat side towards the setting and partially embedded in the Plasticine or clay. Mix a teaspoon of Plaster of Paris with a little water, and pour it over the setting and clay. When the plaster is dry, turn the mould upside down and remove the clay. To ensure that no clay remains to impede soldering, brush the silver with turpentine. Now solder the balls to the setting.

To make the ring shank, cut a strip of gauge 12, ⅜in x 2½in *(1cm x 6cm)*. Anneal it and turn up with the pliers to fit the finger. If a measuring device is not available, use a piece of paper to measure the finger size. Solder the ring, clean it in acid, and line up the shape by tapping it with the wooden mallet. Before soldering the setting and the shank together, file a curve in the base of the setting. When this curve fits the curve of the shank, solder together, keeping the flame away from the fine setting edge. (Figs 8a, b and c).

Clean up and polish the ring. Finally set the stone, using a copper pusher, made of ⅛in *(3mm)* square copper wire, or a burnishing tool. Hold the ring in a ring clamp and with the pusher or burnisher press the metal against the stone at opposing points in at least eight places. Now move the tool slowly around the bezel, pressing the metal firmly against the stone. If the setting edge does not move easily over the stone, file it thinner with needle files and sand paper. Remove any scratches in the setting with Water of Ayr stone, and give the ring a final polish.

Cornelian Bracelet

Simple yet sophisticated this piece is of a classic design with a modern touch.

Materials required:

10 gauge sheet silver strip, long enough to go around both stones
8 gauge sheet silver for the base plates of both stone settings
7½in (19cm) silver wire
Cornelians

To make the bracelet

Make the stone settings by turning up two strips of 10 gauge to fit around the stones using the half round pliers. Allow enough metal to set over the stone. Solder the strips, file them flat, top and bottom, then solder them to a flat sheet of 8 gauge. Cut around the bezels with the piercing saw, and file the sheet flush with the bezels.

To make the bracelet, take a 7½in (19cm) piece of silver wire. Anneal it, making sure it is straight, and scratch a mark at the centre, and 2in (5cm) from each end. Place it on a flat surface, protected with a piece of leather or thick paper. Beat the centre flat, working outwards to the two marks, and gently spread the metal at each end. Avoid beating the edge of the wire as this will distort it, and do not beat it any thinner than 1/16in (1.5cm). Clean with sand paper and a file if necessary.

File a curve at each end of the bracelet, to accommodate the stone settings. Place the bracelet and the settings flat on the charcoal block, and solder them together, the base of the settings in line with the flat beaten at each end of the bracelet. Clean in acid, and file off excess solder, then polish the piece.

Set the stones as for the cornelian ring and finally bend the bracelet into a round or oval shape by hand.

Pierced Silver Pendant

Unusual yet comparatively easy to make this pendant is an elegant piece of jewelery.

Materials required:

10 gauge sheet silver 1½in x 1½in (5cm x 5cm)
Silver wire
Silver chain.

To make the pendant

Trace the design from Fig 10 onto paper. Mark the circle clearly on 10 gauge sheet silver. Trace the pattern onto the circle using carbon paper. Retrace over the carbon line with a sharp nail to mark the metal. Cut out the circle with a piercing saw and clean it up.

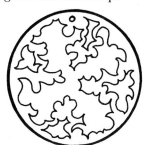

Fig 10

Drill a hole in the silver disc where the design is to be cut out. Fix a fine saw blade in the upper clamp of the piercing saw, then pass the blade through the drilled hole, and fix it in the lower clamp. The blade must be taut, with the teeth facing the handle.

Cut the design out carefully and clean up the cut edge with a half round needle file. Put the pendant on a flat metal surface, and cover it with a thick sheet or block of metal, then strike the block of

metal in to flatten the pendant. Place some sand paper on a hard flat surface and rub the pendant on this to remove any scratches. Repeat this process with progressively finer sand papers, until polished.

Drill a hole at least 1/16in (1.5mm) from the edge and put in a jump ring. Bend the ends of the ring together to form a tight joint and thread the pendant onto a chain.

Molten Silver Pendant

A more modern-looking piece which will look lovely on day or evening clothes. Wonderful shapes can be produced at random by melting silver and dropping it into water. For this, a bucket of water, a piece of asbestos, a small pottery crucible, and a pair of tongs and source of intense heat are required. Bottled gas torches are more suitable than ordinary jeweler's blowtorches because they are more powerful. Place clean silver scraps in the crucible and cover with either borax powder or paste. Heat the metal until it becomes molten, then holding the crucible in the tongs, pour the liquid silver quickly into the bucket of water from a height of 9–18in (23–46cm). The shapes which result are varied and can be soldered together or used separately to make pendants or earrings. They can also be used to design and make modern looking rings.

Toymaking

Soft toys have been favourites with children for many centuries. Traditionally mothers made them for their children from scraps of fabric found around the home such as left-overs from clothes and furnishings. Today, there is a wide range of washable fabrics and fillings available as well as lifelike glass eyes, plastic noses and joint units. The toys in this chapter are simple and comparatively quick to make and the techniques described can later be used and adapted for creating original soft toys designs.

If a rag-bag of fabrics is available, ideas for toys will soon occur as the different materials are handled and sorted. Some will suggest the fur of an animal or perhaps a pattern will resemble scales or feathers. All kinds of materials are suitable for toymaking–velvet, corduroy, silk, satin, cotton, tweed–and sometimes there will be opportunities for mixing two unlikely looking fabrics to achieve an interesting effect. When making toys for young children, only washable fabrics and fillings should be used. Printed fabrics should be colour fast and, if scraps of felt are used for features, these should be pre-shrunk by pressing them with a damp cloth and a hot iron.

STITCHES AND SEWING SEAMS

For a strongly made toy, two rows of machine stitching, worked on the wrong side, are recommended. Hand sewing can also be used if the stitches are kept small. Felt or suede toys are stitched by hand on the right side, working about $\frac{1}{8}$in (3mm) from the edge. Back stitch, stab stitch, oversewing or overcasting are suitable stitches for hand-sewn seams.

FILLINGS

Pre-cut foam chips are really only suitable for fur fabric toys or those made in thick textured fabrics. The chips tend to give a bumpy appearance to toys made of thin fabrics like cotton.
Kapok is the best all-purpose filling. It is soft and light and it is easy to achieve a smooth appearance in the finished toy. For an economical stuffing, cut-up nylon stockings make a good washable filling, and if the pieces are cut very small the finished surface is quite smooth.

MAKING PATTERNS

The patterns in this chapter are given as graphs where the scale is one square to 1in (2.5cm). To use these, re-draw the outlines from the graph onto squared paper to make paper patterns that can be used over and over again. Squared paper can be bought from needlecraft shops or graph paper, obtainable from most stationery stores, can be used. If both kinds of squared paper are difficult to obtain, draw out a squared 1in (2.5cm) grid on a large sheet of brown paper.
Copy all the instructions on the graph pattern onto the paper patterns. Cut out the paper patterns and glue the pieces to thin cardboard to make a template for each pattern piece. By making such templates, the pattern will last indefinitely. The template is held down onto the wrong side of the fabric and the outline traced around with a soft pencil or chalk. Seam allowances of $\frac{1}{4}$in (3mm) are included in all the patterns but add $\frac{1}{4}$in (3mm) extra for toys in thick fabrics. See page 169 for knitting abbreviations.

Green Elf

Materials required:

Lister Lavenda DK or Sport yarn: 3oz (75g) in green, 1oz (25g) in red, 1oz (25g) in white, 1oz (25g) in pink.
Small quantity black for hair
Scraps of felt in red, white, black and green
Kapok or other suitable filling
1 small golden bell
1 pair No. 3 (US) or No. 10 (UK) knitting needles.

Gauge (Tension)

6 sts and 6 ridges (12 rows) = 1in (2.5cm) on No. 3 (US) or No. 10 (UK) needles.

Size

Approx. 12in (30cm) high

Body: Cast on 20 sts in green. Work in g st and shape on the following rows: Row 5: * K1, inc 1 st in next st, rep from * to end (30 sts). Row 9: * Inc 1 st in next st, K4, rep from * to end (36 sts). Row 15: * Inc 1 st in next st, K5, rep from * to end (42 sts). Row 19: * Inc 1 st in next st, K6, rep from * to end (48 sts). Attach white and work six rows even. K10 rows green; 2 red, 4 white, 6 red, 3 green. Row 51: With green * K2 tog, K6, rep from * to end. K3 rows green. Row 55: With green * K2 tog, K5, rep from * to end. K2 rows green; 1 white. Row 59: With white * K2 tog, K4, rep from * to end. K3 rows white. Row 63: With white * K1, K2 tog, rep from * to end. Fasten off white. Row 64: Work with red. Row 65: With red, K2 tog, all across row. K2 rows red. Fasten off red. K2 rows green. Fasten off green. Attach in pink. Row 71 and all odd numbered rows: Purl. Row 72: * K1, inc 1 st in next st, rep from * to end. Row 74: * Inc 1 st in next st, rep from * to end. Row 76: * Inc 1 st in next st, K3, rep from * to end. Row 78: * Inc 1 st in next st, K4, rep from * to end. Row 80: * Inc 1 st in next st, K5 rep from * to end. Row 94: * K2 tog, K5, rep from * to end. Row 96: * K2 tog, K4, rep from * to end. Row 98: * K2 tog, K3, rep from * to end. Row 100: * K2 tog, K2, rep from * to end. Row 102: * K1; K2 tog, rep from * to end. Row 103: Bind (cast) off.
(Work a second identical piece for the back).

Assembling the Body

On WS of work seam the two sides (back and front) together leaving top of head (bound-off (cast off) edges) open. Turn. Stuff firmly. Push stuffing well out each side of the face. Close opening. For eyes cut out two white felt circles, two slightly smaller green ones and two even smaller circles of black felt. Make up circles and sew to face as shown in the illustration. (Approx. 2$\frac{1}{4}$in (6cm)

from start of pink and approx. 1$\frac{1}{2}$in (3cm) apart at centre of face). Cut out a tiny red circular nose, and crescent-shaped mouth and sew to face. Using lipstick pencil mark the cheeks and blend in well. With pink embroider two buttonhole stitch loops for ears and stitch on black loops of yarn at centre of forehead for 'forelock'.

Legs

Cast on 28 sts in green. Work in g st and shape on the following rows: Row 9: Bind off 5 sts at beg of row. Row 10: Bind off 5 sts at beg of row. Work even on 18 sts for 26 rows. Row 37: Bind (cast) off. Work a second identical piece. On WS, fold leg in half and seam all around leaving top of leg open. Turn. Stuff firmly with kapok. Sew each leg to base of body.

Arms

Cast on 20 sts in pink. Work in st st and shape on the foll rows: Row 3: Inc 1 st at each end of row. Row 9: K2 tog each end of row. Row 11: Break, attach green and work in g st for 21 rows. Row 33: Bind (cast) off. Work a second identical piece. Fold arms lengthwise, and on wrong side seam all around leaving bound-off (cast off) edges open. Turn. Stuff firmly. Close opening. Sew arms to either side of body.

Collar

Cast on 40 sts in red and work in loop st (Row 1: K. Row 2: K first st, then insert needle into next st in ordinary way, putting left index finger alongside left-hand needle wind wool around index finger and right-hand needle three times, pull all loops on right-hand needle through st on left-hand needle and put on to left-hand needle. Now finish knitting stitch with loops as one st in usual way. Cont in this way to last st which is knitted). Work 2 rows. Bind off. Fit collar around neck and secure.

Cap

Cast on 34 sts in green. Work in g st for 6 rows. Row 7: Attach red and K 3 rows. Row 10: Attach white and K 1 row. Row 11: With white, K2 tog each end of row. K 4 rows white; 1 green. Row 17: With green, K2 tog each end of row. K 4 rows green; 1 white. Row 23: With white, K2 tog each end of row. K 2 rows white; 1 red. Row 27: With red, K2 tog each end of row. (26 sts). K 3 rows red. Row 31: As row 27 (24 sts). Now K2 tog each end of every other row and work 6 rows green, 4 white, 2 red, 4 white and 4 green (4 sts). K 2 rows green. Bind off. Work a second identical piece.

Assembly of cap

On WS, sew the two pieces tog leaving straight cast-on edges open. Turn and sl st to head all around. Sew bell to tip.

Little Lamb

A very attractive knitted toy to find a place in any child's heart. He stands approximately 13in (32.5cm) high.

Materials required:

10oz (285g) washable double knitting yarn or Sport yarn in white; 2oz (57g) in black
10oz (283g) approx. kapok or other suitable stuffing
Strip of ribbon or felt for collar
3 bells
Scraps of felt or thread for features
1 pair of No.3 (US) or No.10 (UK) knitting needles.

Gauge (Tension)

6 sts and 8 rows on specified needles = 1in (2.5cm) over st st.

To make the lamb

Side of body Beg with front leg, cast on 14 sts in black. Work 8 rows st st. Row 9: Change to white and knit. Row 10: K1, k1 winding yarn twice around needle and first finger, then around needle only, draw loops through, slipping original st off left hand needle. Holding loops at back of work, slip loops back onto left hand needle and knit them together through back of loops. Repeat these loop sts to last st, k1. Repeat last two rows until 42nd row has been worked. Leave sts on a spare needle. For back leg work as for front leg until 30th row has been completed. Row 31: Inc 1 st at end of row. Work three rows even. Row 35: K2 tog at beg of row and inc 1 st at end. Rows 36 and 38: Loop row. Rows 37 and 39: As row 35. Work three rows straight. Row 43: K2 tog, k to end of row, turn and cast on 10 sts, then knit across the 14 sts on spare needle. Cont to work row 44 and every even row in loop stitch.
Row 45: Inc 1 st into first st, work to end. Row 47: Inc into last st. Row 49: As row 45 (41 sts). Row 50: Loop st. Repeat rows 9 and 10 three times. Row 57: K2 tog, work to end. Dec in same way on odd rows three times more. Row 65: K2 tog at each end. Row 67: As row 57. Dec at each end of next odd row. Row 71: Bind off 18 sts at beg of row. (14 sts). Row 73: As row 57. Row 75: as row 57. Bind off.
Make another piece to match but reverse shaping and working the back leg first, row 43 will read: Knit to end of row, turn and cast on 10 sts, knit across back leg sts to last 2 sts, k2 tog.

Underbody (first side) Work as for first body side but in st st only. Work to completion of row 44 (38 sts). Row 45: Bind off 6 sts, work to end. Row 47: Cast 6 sts, work to end, inc at end of row. Row 49: As row 45. Row 51: As row 45. Row 53: Cast off 7 sts at beg of row, work to end. Row 55: Cast off. Work second side to match reversing shaping, as for second body side but in st st to end of row 42. Row 43: Knit to end of row, turn and cast on 10 sts, knit across back leg sts, to last 2 sts, k2 tog. Row 44: Cast off 6 sts at beg of row. Row 46: As row 44. Row 48: Bind off 6 sts, work to last st, inc into last st. Row 50: As row 44. Row 52: Bind off 7 sts at beg of row. Bind off.

To make up body Join two underbody pieces along upper bound off edge. Place the joined pieces between sides of body, matching the legs and seam into place. Sew body sides together above front and back legs along back but leave bound off edge open. Stuff evenly and firmly.

Tail With white yarn, cast on 8 sts. Row 1: Knit. Row 2: Loop st. Cont in this way and inc 1 st at each end of next row, then work even until 26 rows have been worked. Cast off and make another piece to match, but in st st for underside of tail. Join pieces, ws tog, leaving bound off edge open. Turn to r s, join open end and sew firmly to back.

Side of head With white yarn, cast on 18 sts. Work six rows st. st. Row 7: Inc into first stitch, k to end, turn and cast on 3 sts. Row 8: P to last 8 sts, loop st 7, k1. Row 9: Inc 1 st at each end of row. Row 10: Inc into first st, p to last 8 sts, loop st 7, k1. Row 11: As row 9. Row 12: As row 10. Row 13: K. Row 14: P to last 8 sts, loop st 7, k1. Row 15: K. Row 16: P to last 7 sts, loop st 6, k1. Row 17: K. Row 18: P to last 6 sts, loop st 5, k1. Row 19: K. Row 20: P to last 5 sts, loop st 4, k1. Row 21: K. Row 22: As row 20. Row 23: Inc 1 st at beg of row (29 sts). Row 24: As row 20. Row 25: K2 tog at end of row. (Tie a coloured marker to first st.) Row 26: P2 tog, p to last 5 sts, loop st 4, k1. Row 27: K2 tog at end of row. Row 28: P2 tog, work to last 5 sts, loop st 4, k1. Row 29: K. Row 30: P to last 5 sts, loop st 4, k1. Row 31: K. Rep last two rows three times. Row 38: As row 30. Row 39: K2 tog at each end of row. Row 40: As row 30. Row 41: As row 39. Row 42: As row 30. Row 43: K2 tog across row to last st, k1. Row 44: As row 30. Bind off. Make another piece to match, reversing shaping so that loops will be at beg of rows.

Head gusset With white, cast on 4 sts and work six rows in st st. Row 7: Inc 1 st at each end of knit row. Row 8: P. Row 9: As row 7. Row 10: P. Row 11: As row 7. Row 12: P. Row 13: As row 7 (12 sts). Row 14: K1, loop st to last st, k1. Row 15: K. Rep these two rows to end of row 50. Row 51: K2 tog at each end of next and alt rows until 2 sts remain. Bind off.

To make up head Place the head gusset between sides of head, placing cast on edge of gusset even with the coloured marker on head sides. Sew gusset into place. Then sew head sides together from side to side, above and below gusset leaving cast on edge of head sides open. Stuff firmly and carefully. Sew head very firmly to body.

Muzzle With black yarn, cast on 12 sts and work in st st. Row 1: P. Row 2: Inc 1 st at each end of next row. Rep these two rows until there are 20 sts on needle. Cont in st st until 13 rows have been completed from beg. Row 14: K2 tog at each end of this and every foll alt row until 12 sts rem. Bind off. Run a length of yarn around edge of muzzle, pull up slightly and stuff lightly. Sew to head at nose, over base of gusset. Embroider on features or cut out in scraps of felt and sew to face.

Ears With black wool, make 4 pieces as for tail. 2 in st st for inner ear and 2 in loop st. Join the pieces together and attach to head. Join three bells to collar and fit round neck.

Princess Pig

This flowery little pig looks very smart indeed. She is about 8in *(20cm)* high and 10in *(25cm)* long.

Materials required:

18in x 24in *(46cm x 61cm)* printed cotton
9in *(23cm)* square pink felt
1in *(2.5cm)* square brown felt
Scraps of white yarn
10oz *(283g)* approx. kapok, or other suitable filling
Matching thread
Graph paper
Thin cardboard and paste
Fabric adhesive.

To make the pig

Draw the patterns onto squared paper from the graph pattern (Fig 1). Paste each pattern piece onto thin cardboard and cut out for templates – ¼in *(6mm)* seams are allowed throughout. Mark all appropriate letters and notes.

Hold each template in turn on the wrong side of the fabric indicated for that part of the body and draw around it. Mark and cut out all pieces required.

Body With right sides facing, baste and stitch back end of underbody gusset to back end of head gusset, matching EE, forming one long strip. Then, starting under nose at B, and with right sides facing, baste in one side of whole gusset to one side of body piece, working around legs, feet, up and across back and down to top of nose at A.

Leave open from A to B for insertion of felt nose-piece. Repeat with other side of

gusset and other body piece, this time leaving an opening along back for turning and stuffing. Clip all curves and corners carefully and turn to right side. Working on right side of pig, turn under ¼in *(6mm)* all around nose opening and tack down. Baste the felt nose circle into the opening, easing it around as the work progresses. Stitch firmly by hand with a small, neat running stitch about ⅛in *(3mm)* from edge. This will form a realistic ridge around the snout. Stuff the pig with kapok until full and firm, but be careful not to push the nose out of shape; it should look flattish from the front. Stitch neatly across opening and brush off excess stuffing.

Nostrils and cheeks Using a little adhesive, glue each brown nostril and pink cheek piece in position as shown and oversew all around each piece.

Eyes To make each eye, cut 13 or 14 lengths of white yarn about ¾in *(1.5cm)* long, and stick one end of each along one edge of the felt eyelid piece. Glue completed eyelid and lashes in place from D to D as shown in diagram, curving centre of felt strip slightly downwards. Back stitch along centre of felt lid. Repeat for other eye, and glue and stitch to other side of face. Trim eyelashes to shape.

Ears Spread a thin line of glue along top edge of ear, and glue to top of head in position matching F, G with K, J. Oversew all along the top edge, using small, neat stitches.

Tail Fold felt tail in half lengthwise, then run a double gathering thread all along the edge, leaving thread loose at one end. Stitch other end of tail firmly to pig at E. Pull up gathering thread until tail curls and twists around. Fasten off thread and coil the tail around.

Fig 1

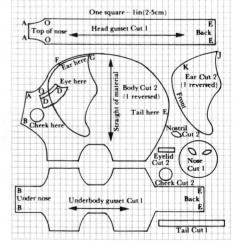

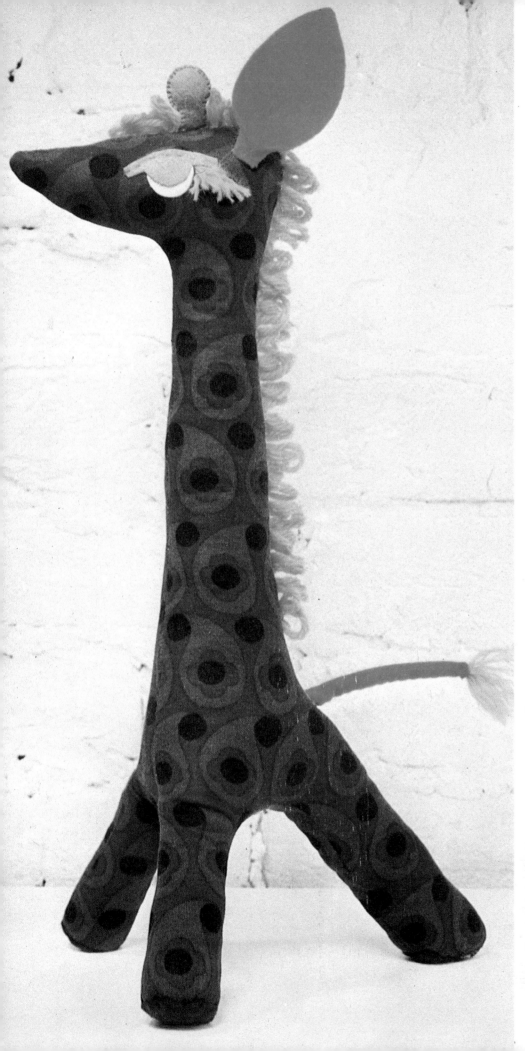

Angel Giraffe

Giraffes are rather unusual creatures, and this three-legged beauty is no exception. Angel is 19in *(48cm)* high.

Materials required:
20in x 28in *(50cm x 71cm)* brown printed sturdy cotton
7in *(18cm)* square turquoise felt
5in x 6in *(13cm x 15cm)* yellow felt
3in x 4in *(8cm x 10cm)* brown felt
Approx. ½oz *(14g)* thick turquoise yarn
10oz *(283g)* approx. kapok
Matching thread
Graph paper
Thin cardboard and paste
Fabric adhesive.

To make the giraffe
Draw the pattern onto squared paper from the graph pattern (Fig 2) where one square equals 1in *(2.5cm)*. Paste each pattern piece onto thin cardboard and cut out for templates. Note that ¼in *(6mm)* seams are allowed throughout. Mark on all appropriate letters and notes. Hold each template in turn on the wrong side of the fabric indicated for that part of the body and draw around it, close against the edge of the cardboard. Mark and cut out all pieces required.

Body On the underbody gusset, baste darts from O to P, working on wrong side of fabric. Stitch along the dotted lines, then snip along the fold carefully to allow the fabric to give when turned. With right sides facing, baste and stitch one side of underbody gusset to one body piece, starting at the front at C, and working down leg to D. Ease fabric gently around the curve at O to avoid puckering. Then baste and stitch from E around to F. Repeat with other side of underbody gusset and other body piece. With right sides of fabric facing, baste and stitch upper body pieces together, starting at C and working around head from B to A and then to back at J. Leave J to H open for turning and stuffing, but stitch seam together down the back from H to G. Clip curves and corners. Turn toy right side out, and fit in the three foot pads. Turn in ¼in *(6mm)* all round

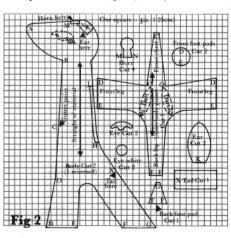

Fig 2

opening at bottom of each leg, and baste foot pads in place. Stitch around each pad by hand, using a small running stitch, about $\frac{1}{8}$in *(3mm)* from edge. Keep edge of felt even with edge of leg fabric. Stuff the toy until full and firm, being careful not to overstretch or twist the neck. Stitch up opening and brush off excess stuffing.

Eyes Glue three strands of yarn about 1$\frac{1}{4}$in *(3cm)* in length underneath back end of eyelid. Glue down one eye white, then stick complete eye in position as shown, and back stitch all along eyelid. Repeat for other eye.

Ears Fold lower corners (K and L) of one ear piece to meet in the centre of the bottom edge, and use a little fabric adhesive to hold the folds in place. Glue lower edge of ear to head, in position KL shown on pattern diagram, and stitch on firmly, with the folded tucks facing outwards. Repeat for other ear.

Horns Place two felt horn pieces together and oversew all around edge, pushing a little ball of kapok inside before stitching is complete. Stitch to top of head at MN as shown. Repeat for other horn.

Mane Fold 6yd *(5·5cm)* of the yarn into four strands about 1$\frac{1}{2}$yd *(1·37m)* long, (Leave about 40in *(1·02m)* spare for tail.) Start attaching to back of neck at H, and stitch in place. Make a series of loops, about $\frac{3}{4}$in *(1.5cm)* high and $\frac{1}{2}$in *(1cm)* apart, and stitch the bottom part of each loop securely to neck seam. Continue up and over head between ears and horns to finish in front of horns.

Tail Make a tube tail. Glue about eight strands of yarn lengthwise onto the tail piece, allowing it to protrude about 1$\frac{1}{4}$in *(3cm)* at one end. Roll up the felt, with the yarn inside. Glue and stitch edge. Stitch felt end of tail to body at X. Untwist yarn at tip of tail and fluff out to make a tuft.

Sparkling Mobile

Babies love to watch a sparkling nursery mobile. The decorative sequins catch the light and glitter as the butterflies move with any gentle air current.

Materials required:
$\frac{1}{2}$yd *(0·5m)* organdie
Scraps of brightly coloured felt
Machine embroidery thread in shades pink and green
Sequins in assorted shapes – 12 large pink, 12 large green, a bag of small gold and a bag of sparkling flower shapes
Six sheets writing paper
Fabric adhesive
Plastic covered thin wire:
    1 piece 12in *(30cm)* long
    2 pieces 8in *(20cm)* long.

To make the mobile
Cut 12 organdie pieces each measuring 6in *(15cm)* square. Place two organdie squares together over a piece of paper the same size and baste around the edge. Repeat the process with the other pieces of paper and organdie squares. The paper gives more body to the embroidery and prevents the light organdie from ruckling in the sewing machine.

Cut out a cardboard butterfly shape

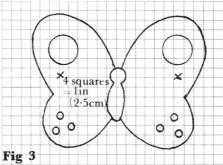

×4 squares
= 1in
(2·5cm)

Fig 3

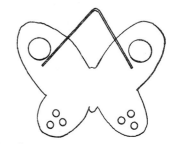

Fig 4

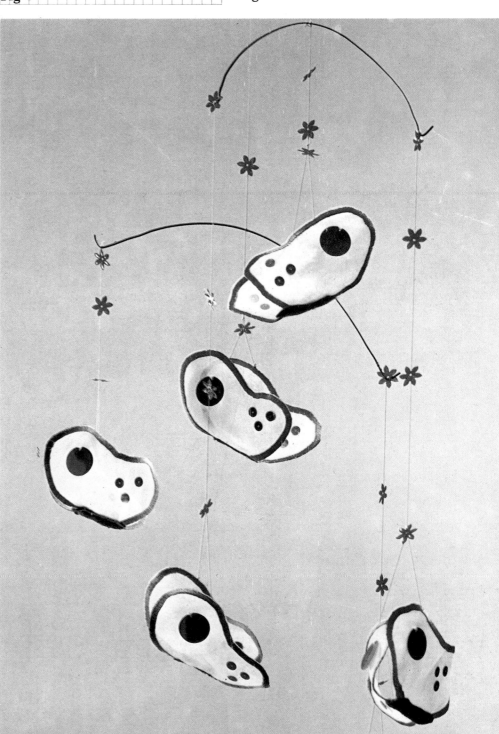

from the pattern (Fig 3), and draw around the shape with pencil, transferring the design to each of the six prepared organdie squares.

Stitch around the butterflies' wings, one at a time, using a wide machine zigzag stich with the stitches close together. If the butterflies are to be hand-made, use buttonhole stitch. Stitch three pink butterflies and three green ones.

Remove paper and basting. Trim away spare material outside sewing line.

Cut out the butterflies' bodies from the felt (Fig 3) to make six pairs.

Sandwich each butterfly between two felt shapes. Baste in position and machine stitch with a narrow zigzag stitch around the edge of the felt shapes. If hand sewing, use buttonhole stitch for this. Stitch the large circular sequins to the wings. Use the point of a pin to attach small ones with adhesive. See Fig 4.

Sew a 4in *(10cm)* long 'handle' of thread to each butterfly (Fig 4), to support the wings. Attach thread to points marked x in Fig 3. Twist a small circle in the centre of the longest piece of wire. Thread flower-shaped sequins at intervals onto long pieces of thread. Attach these to the 'handles' and then to the shorter pieces of wire. Tie to ends of long wire and adjust threads of butterflies for correct balance.

Solemn Owl

A small solemn owl to make in soft fur fabrics and felt. The finished toy is approximately 9½in *(24cm)* high.

Materials required:

15in x 24in *(38cm x 61cm)* brown fur fabric
14in x 16in *(35cm x 40cm)* white fur fabric
12in *(30cm)* square red felt
2in x 4in *(5cm x 10cm)* brown felt
8oz *(227g)* approx. kapok
Fabric adhesive.

To make the owl

Draw a pattern on squared paper from the graph pattern (Fig 5) where one square equals 1in *(2.5cm)*. Glue the pattern pieces onto thin cardboard and cut out for templates. Cut the pieces from the fabrics indicated in the pattern.

Body With right sides facing, baste and stitch front and back body together from A around top and down to B. Baste and stitch in bottom gusset, matching AA and BB. Leave gap open from C to D for turning and filling. Turn to right side and fill carefully so that the toy is a good shape but light and soft enough for a small child to hold. Close the gap with small neat stitches.

Face Spread a little fabric glue on eyes and pupils and glue in position on face as shown on pattern. Oversew each piece neatly. Spread a little glue all around edge of back of face and glue onto body in the position on pattern. Oversew all

50

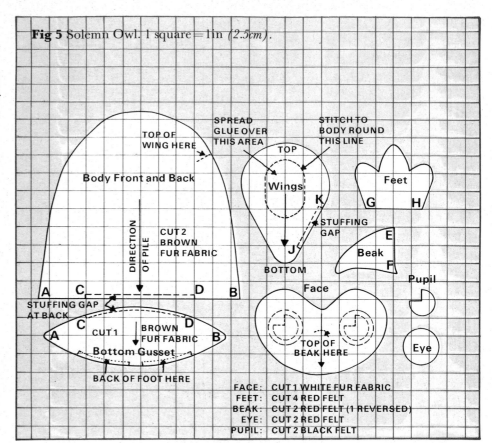

Fig 5 Solemn Owl. 1 square = 1in *(2.5cm)*.

FACE: CUT 1 WHITE FUR FABRIC
FEET: CUT 4 RED FELT
BEAK: CUT 2 RED FELT (1 REVERSED)
EYE: CUT 2 RED FELT
PUPIL: CUT 2 BLACK FELT

around carefully, using small stitches. With wrong sides facing, stitch both beak pieces together ⅛in *(3mm)* from edge. Leave open from E to F. Fill carefully with stuffing. Pin in position indicated on face and stitch all around very firmly with tiny stitches.

Wings With right sides facing, baste and stitch two wing sections together, leaving gap open from J to K. Turn to right side and insert enough filling to puff the wings out a little. Stitch gap closed. Spread a little glue on inside of wing and hold in place on body, as shown in picture. Stitch on firmly, carefully picking up body fabric and wing fabric alternately with the needle. Repeat for other wing.

Feet With wrong sides facing, stitch two feet sections together ⅛in *(3mm)* from edge. Leave open from G to H. Stuff. Apply a little adhesive along from G to H, and glue to body in position on front seam of bottom gusset as shown in pattern. Stitch firmly in place. Repeat for other foot.

To finish

Using the eye end of a needle, go over all fur fabric seams, picking out any fur pile that has become caught in the stitching. Brush the fur pile of the forehead downwards to fall over the edge of white face piece. Brush over rest of owl to fluff up the pile and plump him into shape.

Pop-up Puppet

Pop-ups are delightful toys for children of all ages – even the very small. Here is a clown that is sure to get a laugh.

Materials required:

Length of cardboard tube approx. 4in *(10cm)* long, 2½in *(6cm)* in diameter
13in *(33cm)* length ½in *(1cm)* dowel
7in x 13in *(18cm x 33cm)* striped cotton fabric
5in x 13in *(13cm x 33cm)* blue felt
3in x 5in *(8cm x 12cm)* white felt
Scraps of black, red and cerise felt
1½in x 6in *(4cm x 15cm)* yellow cotton
Approx. ¼yd *(23cm)* yellow yarn
Small amount kapok or other filling
Small button for hat
Approx. 12in *(30cm)* separate lengths of three fancy braids
Fabric adhesive.

To make the puppet

Body Draw the patterns onto squared paper from the graph (Fig 6) where one square equals 1in *(2.5cm)*. Glue pattern to thin cardboard and cut out for templates. ⅛in *(3mm)* seam allowance has been included on all pattern pieces. Cut out all parts of the puppet required in cotton and felt using the templates. Cut a notch all around the dowel rod about 1in *(2.5cm)* from one end. Stitch the

dress pieces together, right sides facing, down side seams and around the arms. Clip at curves and corners. Turn to right side and ease seams out carefully. Run a double gathering thread around neck. Insert dowel rod up into the dress from the bottom, until notch is even with gathering thread around the neck of dress. Pull up thread tightly and well into notch, bind around outside to secure and fasten off.

Head Stitch head pieces together on right side, leaving bottom open at neck. Stuff firmly and at the same time insert end of dowel rod into head as far as the notch. Run a double gathering thread around the felt neck, pull up tight, also well into the notch, and bind thread around outside to secure firmly. Fasten off thread ends neatly.

Stitch sides of hat pieces together and slip over head. Secure with a few stitches at each side. Stitch two or three loops of yarn at each side for the hair. Cut loops and fluff out. Make crosses for the eyes from black felt; each eye has two strips ⅛in *(3mm)* by ⅜in *(9mm)* long. Glue all the pieces in place.

Glue nose and mouth in place, and stick on hat button. Fold the frill piece in half lengthways and run a gathering thread along the fold edge. Place around neck, draw up thread to fit tightly and secure dress at the back. Fasten off.

Base Cut a piece of felt to fit all around cardboard tube, spread lightly with glue and stick on to cover tube. When glue is dry, spread a ¼in *(6mm)* band of adhesive all around top edge of covered tube, and press lower edge of dress onto it. Make excess fabric into a pleat at centre front of clown.

When dry, glue a length of braid all around to cover join of dress to tube. Glue more braid round the middle and bottom edge of tube to decorate. (See illustration) If necessary, smooth off any roughness at the lower end of the wooden dowel with fine sandpaper.

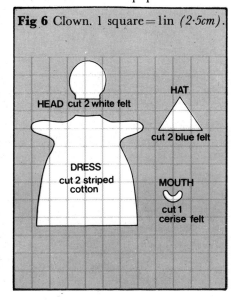

Fig 6 Clown. 1 square = 1in *(2.5cm)*.

HEAD cut 2 white felt

DRESS cut 2 striped cotton

HAT cut 2 blue felt

MOUTH cut 1 cerise felt

Appliqué

Appliqué is a fascinating needlework art form and has been practised for thousands of years. Although it probably originated as a method of repairing the worn parts of clothing, examples of decorative appliqué have been found in the tombs of ancient Egyptians. The technique consists of cutting fabrics into shapes and then stitching them onto a ground fabric. Decorative embroidery stitches are sometimes added to the applied fabrics afterwards. Almost any design can be translated into appliqué and embroidery, and it is this flexibility that is part of the craft's fascination and continuing popularity. Anyone who can sew can appliqué; the only expertise required is that of being able to cut out, to press with an iron and to hem neatly.

FABRICS AND TEXTURES

All kinds of fabrics can be used for appliqué but choice should be determined by the eventual use of the piece of work. A picture or panel to be framed under glass, for instance, could be worked in delicate organdie on silk but a wall hanging would need sturdier fabrics. For clothes and home furnishings, which will receive hard wear or need to be laundered, both applied fabric and background fabrics must be washable and colour fast. The applied fabrics should be of lighter or similar weight to the background fabric. Non-fraying fabrics are the easiest to use for appliqué because the edges can be used raw and need not be turned under. Materials which are likely to fray can be mounted onto an iron-on adhesive backing before cutting out.

THREADS IN APPLIQUÉ

For 'blind' appliqué, use a mercerised or satinised cotton sewing thread with a fine needle. Machine embroidery thread can also be used for machine stitched appliqué techniques. For embroidering appliqué, all kinds of threads are suitable – rug wool, tapisserie yarn, metallic threads etc., but the eventual use of the item must be considered when the final selection is being made.

USING A FRAME

Large pieces of appliqué are best worked in a frame so that the background fabric is held taut. A slate frame, obtainable from needlecraft counters, is the best kind of frame to use, but a wooden picture frame can be adapted and used. Very small pieces of appliqué can be worked in the hand without a frame but it is important that the applied fabrics are kept absolutely smooth on the back-

52

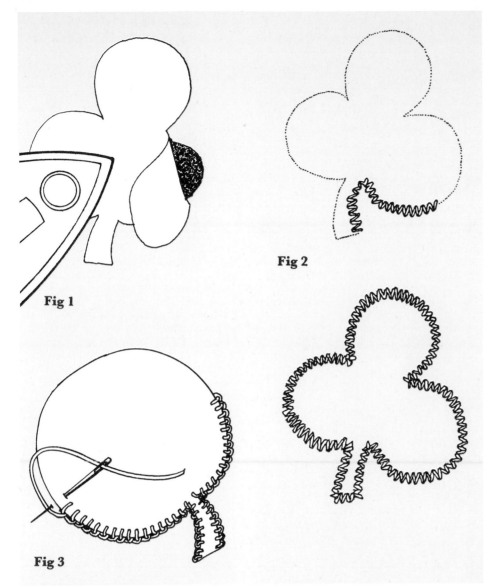

Fig 1

Fig 2

Fig 3

ground during working as differing tensions will cause puckering in the finished work. Match the grain of the applied fabrics to that of the background fabrics for a smooth finish. Non-woven fabrics such as felt, leather or vinyl can be applied in any position.

STICK-ON AND APPLIQUÉ
This is the easiest method of appliqué. Simply cut out shapes in a non-fraying material such as felt, leather or plastic and glue them down onto the background fabric. Finish the edges with zigzag machine stitching or blanket stitch.

IRON-ON AND STITCH
This technique uses a double-sided adhesive material which will cling to all kinds of woven and non-woven fabrics. First draw the design onto the adhesive material. Iron the material to the wrong side of the fabric to be applied. Cut out the design on the drawn lines and remove the backing paper. Press the shape down onto the background fabric (Fig 1). Finish the edges with zigzag machine

stitching (Fig 2) or with an edging stitch such as buttonhole or blanket stitch (Fig 3).

BLIND APPLIQUÉ
Draw the design on heavy paper and cut a template for each area of the appliqué. Hold the template down on the right side of the background fabric and draw lightly around the shape using a dressmaker's carbon pencil or tailor's chalk. Pin the template to the fabric to be applied and cut out the shape, allowing $\frac{1}{4}$in (6mm) turnings all around. Turn the edges to the wrong side and baste. Clip into curves and corners to make the turnings lie absolutely flat. Press. If the shape is a difficult one, keep the paper template pinned in position and follow the outline. Now baste and then sew the prepared shape to the background using slip stitch. The stitches should not show on the front of the work. Remove template.

APPLIQUÉ USING THE SEWING MACHINE
Appliqué can also be worked using zigzag machine stitch. Cut out the fabric

shape and baste to the background fabric. Set the machine stitch to a close zigzag and about $\frac{1}{8}$in (3mm) wide.

An alternative method uses iron-on adhesive fabric. First mount a piece of the fabric to be applied onto the adhesive stiffening. Cut out the shape around outline and baste to the right side of the background fabric. Zigzag around the outline with a narrow stitch, working on the wrong side. On the right side, trim away the surplus material close to the stitches. Re-set the zigzag stitch to a close satin stitch about $\frac{1}{8}$in (3mm) wide. Stitch around the shape again on the right side. This method is particularly suitable for clothes which have to stand up to a considerable amount of wear and laundering.

An alternative method of working this form of appliqué involves mounting the fabric on adhesive stiffening, drawing the design on the stiffening backing, stitching around with a narrow zigzag and then cutting out. Baste the cut-out piece onto the background fabric and zigzag stitch around again (Fig 2).

OTHER WAYS TO USE APPLIQUÉ TECHNIQUES
The appliqué techniques described can be adapted to all kinds of uses. Shapes crocheted in cotton thread can be applied to a variety of household furnishings. Lace motifs, cut from edging and stitched to a delicate fabric look pretty for lingerie and baby clothes. Braids and decorative ribbons can be applied to plain background fabrics in strips or to follow the lines of a design. Choose whichever of the techniques described seems most suitable for the project, and for the fabrics and materials being used.

Landscape in Felt
This delightful felt picture has an attractive simplicity about it and looks as though it might have been designed by a child. The picture illustrated is 15in (38cm) wide but plan the background and road to fit the size of frame you intend to use. You could also make an entire wall frieze from the design by continuing the undulating road left and right and adding more cars, and more houses to the background.

Materials required:
Blue felt for background in size required for finished picture
Scraps of emerald green, yellow, sand, scarlet, blue and orange felt
Stranded cotton
Scraps of white cotton fabric
All-purpose clear drying adhesive
Knitting yarn in brown and black.

To make the picture
Copy the outlines of houses, trees, cars, road, etc., from the illustration and then

enlarge drawings to size required. Using carbon paper, draw the outlines onto thin cardboard. Cut out each shape as a template. Use the templates to cut out the shapes in felt. Cut the blue felt to size required plus 2in (5cm) all around. Cut out the green felt grass, the yellow path and the sand coloured road. Using catch stitch or slip stitch, sew the grass to the background first, then the path and finally the road.

Cut out houses in felt and white cotton fabric. Glue the white fabric to the wrong side of the felt with fabric adhesive so that it shows through the cut-out windows. Cut out the trees. Pin trees and houses in position and stitch to the background. Embroider tree trunks in stem stitch using brown yarn. Embroider roof details in stem stitch using black yarn.

Cut out vehicles. Stitch to the road. Work details in stem stitch in stranded cotton using 2 strands. Alternatively, couch threads down onto felt as shown. Work car wheels in chain stitch or couch down threads.

To mount the picture

Cut a piece of hardboard or thick cardboard a little smaller than the size of the frame to allow clearance for the felt turnings. Place the appliqué picture face downwards and put the hardboard on top. Turn the felt over to the wrong side and glue down to the board with all-purpose adhesive, neatly mitring the corners.

Kitchen Wall Tidy

A cheery wall tidy to hang in the kitchen made from scraps of printed fabrics. The tidy could also be made for a work corner to contain sewing or writing materials or for a teenager's room to hold brush, comb, ribbons, hair bands etc. The tidy illustrated makes clever use of printed fabrics for the strawberry and little girl motifs, but these designs can be made up in appliqué using whatever fabrics are available and a suitable appliqué technique for your materials and design.

Materials required:

Coarse cream-coloured linen 38in x 24in (95cm x 60cm) wide
Blue bias binding 7½yd (6.75m)
Assorted fabrics for pockets
Iron-on Vilene (Pellon) interfacing
22in (55cm) length of dowel.

To make the tidy

Unravel all four edges of the linen fabric for about six threads to make a fringed edge. Fold sides to right side of fabric, 1in (2.5cm); fold bottom edge 1in (2.5cm). Press and baste. Apply and machine-stitch blue binding to the turned hems so that the fringed edge shows. Mitre the corners. Turn the top edge down 1¾in (4.5cm) and baste. Stitch binding across as before, so that there is sufficient space above the top row of stitching to make a casing for the dowel.

Pockets Draw up a pattern from the diagram where one square equals 1in (2.5cm). Trace down the outlines of the pockets onto iron-on Vilene (Pellon).

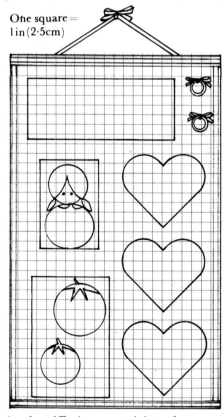

One square = 1in (2.5cm)

Apply stiffening material to the wrong side of the fabrics, following manufacturer's instructions. At this stage, make up the appliqué motifs and finish the edges using either zigzag machine stitching or blanket stitch. Apply the appliqué motifs to the right side of the pocket sections. Cut out pockets and bind edges with blue bias binding. Machine stitch to tidy using thread matching bias binding. Hem two 10in (25cm) lengths of bias binding to make hangers. Stitch ends to the top of the tidy, on the wrong side. Tie a bow.

Bathset in Crochet

A pretty matching bathroom set to make in terry cloth towelling and appliquéd with circles of crochet. If preferred, apply circles cut from cotton fabric instead, or for quick appliqué, make motifs from a washable cotton braid.

Materials required:

1yd (92cm) pink terry cloth towelling
Crochet cotton thread in blue, orange, pink, white
Crochet hook.

To make the towel

Cut the towel to measure 31in x 21in (80cm x 53cm) and neaten all four sides.

To make the bath mitt

Make a paper pattern first. Place your hand, palm downwards, on a sheet of paper. Hold fingers together with your thumb along the index finger. Draw around roughly and then, on removing the hand, smooth out the line to create a shape that looks like the one illustrated. Cut out the pattern and pin to a piece of doubled towelling fabric. Cut out, allowing 2½in (6cm) all around, including the wrist edge. Remove pattern. Turn a hem on the wrist edge of both pieces. Pin front and back of mitt together right sides facing. Machine stitch all around

twice. Trim seam allowance and oversew to neaten. Turn mitt to right side and press.

Appliqué motifs

Crochet a strip 3½in (9cm) deep, width of the towel, in double (single) crochet using blue thread. Sew by hand to one end of the towel. Work circles in double (single) crochet in the colour sequences shown, to make discs 3½in (9cm) in diameter. Hand sew to the blue crocheted border.
Work a strip 2in (5cm) deep for the cut edge of the mitt in orange. Work six more circles 2in (5cm) in diameter in the colour sequences shown. Stitch strip to the mitt and circles onto the strip.

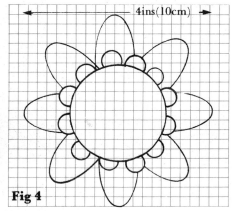

Fig 4   ◄──── 4ins(10cm) ────►

Sunflower Cloth

Here is an idea for quick appliqué. Work sunflower motifs in crochet cotton to match the colours of a tablecloth.

Materials required:

1¼yd (115cm) 48in (122cm) wide cotton fabric
Crochet cotton thread in colours chosen from fabric
Crochet hook.

To make the cloth

Cut the selvedges from the fabric and trim to make a cloth 45in (115cm) square.
Turn a narrow hem, press, and then turn a 1in (2.5cm) hem all around, mitring the corners neatly. Stitch. Following the flower shape in the diagram (Fig 4), work motifs in double (single) crochet. Work the circular centres first and then the petals. Position and stitch the motifs in the four corners of the cloth. Work a crocheted edging to the cloth, or, if preferred, edge with ric-rac braid.
The flower pattern can also be used for fabric appliqué.
Cut out the circle, the stamens and the petals in fabric, adding ¼in (6mm) seam allowance all around. Using one of the appliqué techniques described, prepare the motifs and stitch to the tablecloth.

Name Belt

Here is a novel idea for an appliqué design—work initials or the whole of your name onto a belt. Choose a variety of textured fabrics for the best effect. Whether you have a short name, such as Pat, or a longer name such as Veronica, the finished appliqué design will be unique and very effective.

Materials required:
Fabrics for appliqué in a mixture of textures
Lining fabric
Fabric adhesive
Eyelet holes and insertion tool
Leather thongs or cords.

Making the belt design
To create a design from a short name, reverse the letters mirror-wise and position both versions back to back; or alternatively the name can be repeated all around the belt (Fig 5).

Fig 5

For a long-name design that is likely to fit the waist measurement, use the first or last letter again at the other end so that the name is complete when the belt is fastened (Fig 6).

Fig 6

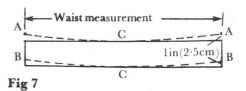

Fig 7

Making the belt pattern
Measure the waist and mark out the measurement on a large sheet of paper. Mark the depth of the belt 2½in (6cm). Now make a mark 1in (2.5cm) above the line at the top corners (A). Make marks on both short sides 1in (2.5cm) from the bottom corners (B). Make marks on the middle of the bottom and top line (C). Join up the lines as in Fig 7, to make a curved belt. Take a tracing of the shape and place this pattern on one

Braid Mats

Attractive place mats add distinction to the simplest meal and whether it is 'just the family' or a formal dinner party, it is important to set the table with style. By making sets of place mats in a linen-like woven fabric and decorating them with braids and ribbons, it is possible to change your table settings as often as you like. A set of six mats can be made from ½yd (46cm) of 36in (92cm) wide fabric.

Materials required:
For each mat use the following:
9in x 12in (23cm x 31cm) woven fabric
¼yd (23cm) of braid for each stripe.

To make the mats
Cut the fabric to size, following the thread. Draw three or four threads about ⅝in (1cm) from the edge, all the way around. Zigzag stitch the inner edge on the sewing machine—or hem stitch by hand. Pull away the remaining threads to form a fringe.
Cut the ribbon or braid into strips to fit the mat, allowing ½in (1cm) at each end to turn under. Baste into position making sure that the ribbon is lying quite flat and smooth. Hem stitch or machine stitch all around.

side. Trace off the letters of the name from Fig. 8 (1 sq = 1in *(2.5cm)*). Cut out and arrange them on the belt shape. Do not try to get the letters evenly spaced because in design, the spaces between the letters can be as decorative as the letters themselves. It is interesting to try the effect of having some letters touching, if the letters are suitable. Glue the

Fig 8

letters onto the belt outline. Cut out the belt shape and then cut out the letters and the spaces in between carefully. Keep the letters and the space pieces separate.

Preparing the fabrics

Choose fabrics of strongly contrasting textures but in a toning or matching colour scheme. Any type of fabric or material can be used; thin cotton, coarse linen, chunky tweed, glazed furnishing fabric, velvet, corduroy, suede, leather or vinyl. Cut out the pieces roughly and stiffen them by ironing Vilene (Pellon) onto the wrong side. Pin or tape the spaces-between shapes to the right side of fabrics and cut out, but this time allowing $\frac{1}{2}$in *(1cm)* allowance all around, except on those parts of the shapes which will lie on the edges of the belt.

Fig 9

Working the appliqué

Using the tracing of the belt pattern, draw the shape onto a piece of firm fabric such as curtain lining.

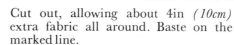

Cut out, allowing about 4in *(10cm)* extra fabric all around. Baste on the marked line.

Baste the spaces-between shapes onto the background fabric. Now stitch the letter shapes over the spaces, taking the stitches over the edges of the letters as shown in Fig 9. Use a matching thread for the stitching and keep the stitches small. Set the sewing machine to a fairly wide satin stitch and zigzag over all the raw edges of spaces and letters.

Making up the belt

Trim the background fabric to within $\frac{1}{2}$in *(1cm)* of the appliqué edge. Clip into curves and clip the corners diagonally. Turn and press the turnings onto the

wrong side so that none of the background fabric shows on the right side.
Stiffen the back of the belt with iron-on Vilene (Pellon). For the belt lining, if a non-fray material such as leather, suede, vinyl or felt is being used, trim the paper pattern $\frac{1}{8}$in *(3mm)* all around. Cut out the lining to this size and glue to the wrong side of the belt. To make a fabric lining, cut out the shape using the paper pattern, adding $\frac{1}{4}$in *(6mm)* seam allowance all around. Clip into curves and turn $\frac{3}{8}$in *(9cm)* to the wrong side. Stab stitch the lining to the wrong side of the belt using closely matching thread.
To make the fastening, insert eyelet holes on both centre front edges. Lace up with leather thongs or cords.

Beadwork

Bead Weaving

Beads are fascinating in their variety and colour, and weaving with them is an absorbing and creative pastime.

Although beadweaving is one of the traditional crafts of the North American Indians, it has been adapted to suit many tastes and beautiful and decorative things can be created using very simple techniques. Beadwork woven on a loom produces a most attractive flat, closely-woven texture with the beads lying in neat parallel rows. The finished work is identical on the back and front surfaces, and therefore reversible.

EQUIPMENT AND MATERIALS

Beadweaving requires very little equipment and the few things needed are inexpensive and easily obtained.

Loom A loom of some kind is essential. These are available from craft shops in various sizes and designs and are fairly inexpensive. It is a simple matter to prepare them for working and instructions for setting up are usually supplied with the loom. Alternatively, a loom can be made easily from an old picture frame (see Fig 1) which has the advantage that it will take work of wider measurements, such as a picture, a hanging or even a handbag.

Large wooden table looms, manufactured for fabric weaving, are a good investment if you plan to make a number of beadwoven articles. Several pieces can then be worked at one time by setting up warp threads of different widths for the different items being made.

Buckled belts can be woven without a loom (see Fig 2). The warp threads are attached to the buckle bar at one end, and are then kept taught by tying the free ends in a bunch to a heavy weight or to the handles of a sturdy piece of furniture.

Needles Beading needles are used for beadweaving. These are very fine and long, and slightly flexible. Beading needles are available in sizes 10–14 from craft and needlework shops.

Before starting work check that the needle, threaded with double thread, will pass easily through the beads.

Thread The colour, strength and thickness of the thread used must be appropriate to the beads and to the purpose intended for the finished article. The thread must be strong; polyester threads are the most suitable because various thicknesses are available and there is a very wide range of colours. Whenever possible, match the colour of the warp threads to the background or main colour of the beads.

Avoid using pure nylon thread as it stretches too easily and is difficult to fasten off securely. Linen beading thread is strong and wears well but can only be obtained in its natural colour.

Beads Generally speaking, very small beads are used for beadweaving. Craft shops and needlework counters usually have a good selection to choose from, under such names as china and glass rocaille, 2 cut and 3 cut glass and lustre, and bugle beads. Larger beads can be used for beadweaving, although the work will naturally be bolder and heavier. Articles such as bags and hangings can be most effective woven with wooden beads and the work is completed more quickly. Always use beads of uniform size in a piece of work or the result will be uneven and unattractive.

Designing patterns Creating original designs on squared paper is really very easy. Aim first for a simple symmetrical pattern. Use felt tip pens to mark the colours of the beads.

Leaflets and books on needlepoint and cross stitch embroidery provide endless suitable designs. Simply substitute a bead for each stitch.

Usually, it is necessary to draw out only half of a graph design, the second half becomes a repeat. Most beads are slightly longer than they are wide, so that the finished work is a little longer than the graph will indicate. When planning a piece of beadweaving to a specific size, it is worth measuring the beads first. To find the width, thread a few onto a needle and hold the needle against a ruler to count the number of beads to the inch. To find the length, lay the beads in a line on a piece of felt to prevent them from rolling around, touching each other and with holes uppermost. Measure with the ruler to estimate how many to the inch or half-inch. With the longer shaped beads, it may be necessary to pin them to keep them upright. It is helpful to keep beads separated into colours in containers. The knack of picking up several beads at one time on the needle can soon be aquired.

SETTING UP THE LOOM

The warp threads are those which run the length of the loom from front to back. Cut the threads to the length of the finished work, plus about 20ins *(50cms)*. Allow one more thread than the number of beads in the widest row of the pattern, as the beads fit into the spaces between each warp thread (i.e. a row of 20 beads requires 21 warp threads).

Tie one end of the bundle of threads to the back roller of the loom and roll the loose threads round and round it until the ends can be tied to the front roller. It is very important that the threads are kept very taut and evenly spaced while being rolled on.

Pass each thread through the toothed or notched reed, and tie them all to the front roller. Fig 1 shows how to set up a home-made loom.

STARTING TO WEAVE

Load the needle with a double thread, not more than 1½yd *(1.35m)* in length when doubled, and tie the ends to the warp thread on right hand edge at the front of the loom, leaving an end long enough for weaving in afterwards.

Thread a complete row of beads onto the needle (see Fig 3, step A). Count the beads from the pattern working from the right and pick them up in this order throughout. Pass the correctly strung beads underneath the warp from right to left. Now hold the needle in the left hand and use the right hand fingers to push the beads firmly upwards, with one bead between each warp thread. Each bead should lie about halfway up, so that the holes are clearly visible from the upper side of the work (see Fig 3, step B). Now take the needle up and over the end warp thread on the left side of work, and pass it back through the beads in the opposite direction, but above the warp threads (Fig 3, step C). The beads are now locked in position. The working or weft thread carrying the beads should be pulled firmly and eased down against the previous row to produce neat straight lines of closely-worked beads. Be careful not to pull the weft thread too tightly or the edge of the work will become distorted. The first two or three rows will set the spacing and the tension for the rest of the work. Special techniques are dealt with in the individual pattern instructions which follow.

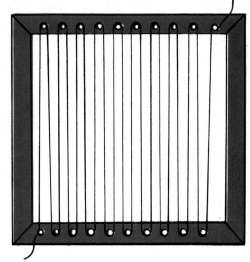

Fig 1 A bead loom can be made on a picture frame for work of wider dimensions than an ordinary loom. Fix small tacks into opposite sides of frame and wind warp threads round tacks as shown.

JOINING WEFT

Never use knots to join weft threads for they spoil the tension and can catch in a bead. Use the overlapping weaving method of joining instead. Leave a 6in *(15cm)* length of the old thread hanging from the work, and thread a new length alongside it through the beads. Leave a 6in *(15cm)* length of the new thread hanging loose too. Weave in the loose ends afterwards.

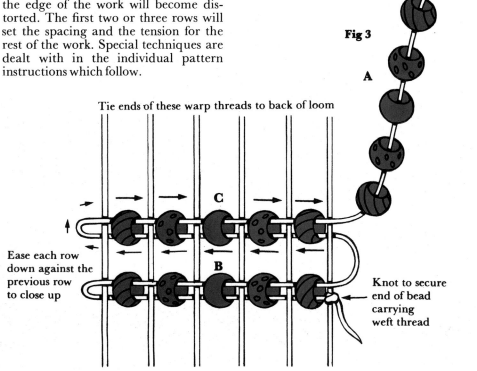

Fig 3

A

Tie ends of these warp threads to back of loom

C

B

Ease each row down against the previous row to close up

Knot to secure end of bead carrying weft thread

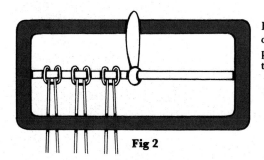

Fig 2

Tie ends of these warp threads to front of loom

FINISHING OFF

When the last row of beads has been worked, pass the needle with the weft thread around the right warp thread, back through a worked row of beads, around the left hand warp thread and back through a few beads. Snip off close to a bead. Do the same with the loose weft end at the beginning of the work. Remove the finished work from the loom and lay it flat. Thread one of the warp ends onto a needle. Darn this end back into the work for about 3in (7.5cm). Darn the end through a few beads to the left or right. Repeat for all the other loose ends of warp at each end of article. Special methods of finishing off work are given in the pattern instructions.

Napkin Ring

Weave a set of unusual napkin rings for your table.

Materials required:

Approx. ½oz (14g) china Rocaille beads in brown
Approx. ½oz (14g) china Rocaille beads in red
Approx. ½oz (14g) china Rocaille beads in white
Brown thread
Size 10 beading needle
Clear drying adhesive.

To make the napkin ring

Set up the loom with 22 threads 18in (45cm) long. Follow the graph pattern (Fig 4) and the colour key, always working from the right hand side of the pattern. Four rows complete the pattern and nine patterns complete the ring. Additional rows can be added to make a ring with a larger diameter, if desired, but it is important that the actual pattern repeat is completed before finishing off the work. Weave the end of the weft thread back into the work.

Finishing

Remove the work from the loom and lay it on a flat surface. Bring the two ends together and tie the warp threads together to form a ring. Each thread is tied to the thread opposite. The beads at each end should lie touching and the join should not show. With a needle, thread each pair of ends to the wrong side of the ring, pulling the knots through too. Snip off the ends close to the work. Spread a fine line of adhesive along the row of knots. When the glue is almost set, press it down with the fingers.

Fig 4
Key
· White
× Red
○ Brown

Fig 5

Key
· White
× Red
⁄ Yellow
● Black
Turquoise background

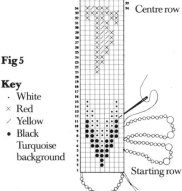

Bracelet

A lovely ornament for everyday or special occasions.

Materials required:

Approx. 1oz (28g) china Rocaille beads in turquoise
Approx. ½oz (14g) china Rocaille beads in assorted colours, white, red, yellow and black
56 larger china or plastic beads in turquoise
Thread

Size 12–13 beading needle
Large bead for fastening or a suitable button.

Making the bracelet

Set up the loom with 10 threads 20in (50cm) long. Work from the graph pattern (Fig 5) and the colour key, always working the pattern from the right hand edge. Half the bracelet design is shown in rows 1 to 34. Row 34 is the centre. The second half of the work is repeated in reverse i.e. Row 33 back to Row 1.

Finishing

Remove work from the loom. At one end, weave the six centre warp ends back into the work, leaving two loose ends at each side. Thread 15 beads onto one pair of these threads, and then take the strand across and tie the ends to the pair of warp threads at other side of work (see Fig 5). Make sure that the knot is very secure before threading the ends back into the beads.

At the other end of the work, weave in the end of the weft thread and then all the warp ends back into the work.

Attach the large bead or button for the fastening. Sew it into the centre of the work near the end. Tie the ends firmly together to secure them before threading into the beads.

Side fringes Tie the ends of a long double thread around the warp thread at one side of the bracelet. Thread a needle onto the other end. Thread beads on as follows: 16 small, 1 large, 2 small, 1 large then 16 small again. Take needle around selvedge warp thread two rows further along and repeat the threading sequence. Continue working along the edge, until desired amount of fringe is added. Tie off the finishing ends very securely, and thread back into the beads. Do the same with the starting ends of the fringe.

An assortment of colours was used for the bracelet fringe illustrated. The colours were picked up from the main design colours of the bracelet–red, yellow, black, white and turquoise.

Bead Picture

Here is an attractive decoration for your wall. Using the materials given, the finished work will measure 2¾in x 4¼in (6.5cm x 10.5cm).

Materials required:

Approx. 1oz (28g) lustre 2-cut beads in blue
Approx. ½oz (14g) lustre 2-cut beads in orange
Approx. ½oz (14g) lustre 2-cut beads in pale green
Approx. ½oz (14g) lustre 2-cut beads in silver
A few lustre 2-cut beads in red and pink.
Blue thread
Size 14 beading needle
Velvet
Clear drying adhesive
Small frame, if desired.

Working the picture

Set up the loom with 37 threads 17in (42.5cm) long. If the loom is not wide enough to take 37 threads, use a picture frame loom.
Follow the graph (Fig 6) and the colour key, always working the pattern from the right hand edge.

Fig 6	Key		
	× Silver	• Orange	All blank
	· Red (nose)	o Green	squares
		/ Pink	blue

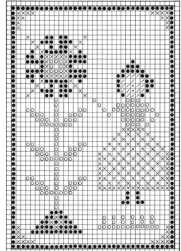

Mounting the picture

Remove weaving from the loom, leaving the warp ends free. Cut a piece of velvet to the desired size, leaving an allowance of ½in–1in (1cm–2.5cm) to show all around the woven picture.
Spread a very thin layer of clear drying adhesive over the back of the beadwork and glue it exactly in the centre of the velvet. Press down firmly until the glue has set and the work has adhered to the fabric.
Thread a needle onto the first warp thread at one end of the beadwork close to the last bead and pass this through the velvet to the back. Thread both ends of

all warp threads through to the back of the velvet in the same way. Pull all the threads firmly, without puckering the work at the front. Tie together in pairs. The completed picture can be fixed into a frame or mounted on cardboard.

Necklace

An Indian-style necklace in pastel-coloured beads (see page 58 and page 62).

Materials required:

Approx. 1oz (28g) pearly 3-cut beads in white
Approx. ½oz (14g) pearly 3-cut beads in blue
Approx. ½oz (14g) glass 3-cut beads in pink
Approx. ½oz (14g) glass 3-cut beads in green
8 glass 3-cut beads in yellow
White thread
Size 13–14 beading needle.

To make the necklace

Set up the loom with 20 threads 32in (80cm) long. Follow the graph (Fig 7) and the colour key, always working the pattern from the right hand edge. In this type of necklace, after a number of rows have been worked, the necklace is divided and the two sides are then woven separately. It is wise to work each side more or less at the same time, to ensure that the patterns are at the same level and that the tension is even. The centre front is slightly tapered. This is achieved by simply adding one more bead to each row, as shown in the pattern, until work has increased in width from 7 to 19 beads (see Fig 7).
The back of the necklace is narrowed by reducing the number of beads in the rows, as shown in the pattern. Leave the spare warp threads and weave them into the beads when work is completed.

Joining the centre back

Remove the work from the loom and lay it on a flat surface. There are now six warp ends at each side of the back. To join the sides together tie the opposite ends together very neatly, as for the napkin ring. Weave the ends back into the work. If required, a small piece of felt may be glued over the join on the inside, to prevent the beads and knots from rubbing the back of the neck.

Front fringes

Thread a needle onto one of the outside warp threads. Thread 15 beads then take the needle back into the 12th bead and then back through all the beads on the thread (see Fig 7). Work thread back through a few beads to fasten with a slip knot, and work into a few more beads to secure. Continue threading beads onto each warp thread in turn until fringe is completed. (See page 58).

Work
13 rows
only
5 beads
wide

Last row

**Fig 7
Key**
White pearly
background
• Blue pearly
／ Pink glass
o Green glass
· Yellow glass

Dividing row▶

Increase to
19 beads wide ▶

First row 7 beads ▶

Threading
the fringes

Threading Beads

Threading beads onto wire is a delight-ful Victorian handicraft and one which is enjoying a revival in popularity. Small, pretty fashion accessories such as pins, brooches, hair clips and earrings can be made with beads on wire—as well as beautiful pieces of bric-à-brac. Victorian ladies made fragile trees of silvery glass beads on which they hung their rings at night. Beautiful table centre-pieces of swans, mythical beasts and fairytale forests, made entirely of beads on silver wire still exist in collections of Victoriana.

The flower spray and the dragonfly are simpler to make than they appear on first glance. The technique is simple and easy to learn and adapts itself to producing a variety of shapes.

Basic technique

The only tools required for this work are tweezers with blunt ends and a small pair of pliers. Each petal or wing is made in the same way. Thread the first bead or beads onto a length of wire and slide them to the centre. Thread a number of beads for the next row on one end of wire, then push the other end of the wire through the beads in opposite direction (Fig 8). Pull both ends tightly, and while so doing adjust the position of beads in relation to the previous row. Repeat for each row.

Pearl Flower Spray

Pin this gleaming spray onto your lapel or into your hair.

Materials required:

1 packet each small beads in pearl (knitting beads are suitable), ⅛in (3mm)

bugle beads in pale pink, smaller bugle beads in silver, sequins in pale pink, 5 larger round pearl beads, 12 small dia-mante or glass silvery beads.
14ft (4.2m) thin silver wire
Clear drying adhesive
Pearlised hair clip or brooch fastening

To make the spray

Make five petals, starting each with a small round pearl bead (see Fig 9). To avoid petals splaying out too much, join each to its neighbour by a tiny twist of wire between each fourth row from bottom. For each stamen cut 3in (7.5cm) of wire and centre a small dia-mante bead on each. Bend ends around to meet and twist length together. Make 12 stamens and twist all ends together, all heads being at the same height. Place in centre of flower letting them project for 1in (2.5cm). Wind a short piece of wire around all ends to hold stamens and petals together.

Leaves Make four sprays of leaves to surround flower.
For first spray use a 14in (35cm) length of wire and work four leaves on each side. For second spray use 16in (40cm) and work four leaves on one side and five on the other.
The third spray takes 20in (50cm) of wire and has six leaves on one side, five on the other. Make fourth spray as first. Each leaf pattern consists of two pale pink bugle beads with a smaller silver one in between (see Fig 10). To make each spray, cut the length of wire and thread on three beads. Bend wire in half and twist together for ½in (1cm). On one end of the wire thread three more beads, then bend it so that there is a space of about ¼in (6mm) of wire between beads and wire already twisted. Again bend

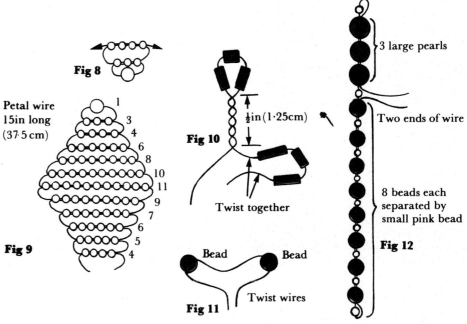

Fig 8

Petal wire
15in long
(37·5cm)

Fig 9

1
3
4
6
8
10
11
9
7
6
5
4

Fig 10

½in(1·25cm)

Twist together

Bead   Bead

Fig 11   Twist wires

3 large pearls

Two ends of wire

8 beads each
separated by
small pink bead

Fig 12

wire in half, back on itself and twist two lengths together for ¼in *(6mm)*. Join to first end of wire and twist two together for a further ¼in *(6mm)*. Repeat to make another leaf on the other side.

Assemble flower and leaf sprays and bind all ends together tightly. Cut off most of the ends, winding the few remaining tightly around the hinged end of the hairclip. Secure with a few dabs of adhesive.

Hold sequins with tweezers and apply a small dab of adhesive to the back of each, glueing them to the centre of the flower. Arrange stamens and leaf sprays.

Dragonfly Hairslide

This beautiful Victorian-style hair slide will catch many eyes.

Materials required:
1 packet ⅛in *(3mm)* bugle beads in silver
A few small beads in deep pink
3 large and 8 small beads in pearl
Approx. 8ft *(2.4m)* thin silver wire
Clear drying adhesive
Pearlised hair clip

To make the hair slide
Make two main wings and two smaller wings, arranging the beads as in the photograph. For this project it is simpler to follow instructions rather than a diagram or chart. The numbers of beads in each row are:

Smaller wings Row 1 (tip): 1 bead. Row 2: 2 beads. Rows 3–12: 4 beads each. Rows 13–16: 5 beads each. Row 17: 4 beads. Row 18: 3 beads. Row 19 (next to the body): 2 beads.

Larger wings Row 1 (tip): 1 bead. Row 2: 2 beads. Row 3: 3 beads. Rows 4–7: 4 beads each. Rows 8–12: 5 beads each. Rows 13 and 14: 6 beads each. Rows 15–17: 5 beads each. Rows 18–20: 4 beads each. Rows 21 and 22 (next to the body): 2 beads each.

Antennae As can be seen in Fig 11, each one of the antennae is approximately ⅜in *(9mm)* long, made of twisted wire and tipped with a small pink bead. Clip ends of wire in centre.

Body
Thread all beads for the body (Fig 12) on a 12in *(30cm)* length of wire, using pearl beads with smaller pink beads. Bend each end of wire back on itself, around the end of the beads, threading antennae into the head end. Then push back through the beads so that both ends emerge to meet at the centre of the body. Arrange wings in pairs so that the smaller are on top. Place body in the centre. Twist wing and body wires together and bind tightly. Wind onto hair clip as for the flower spray. Glue a few sequins on the top surface of the wings for additional glitter.

Apply a small dab of adhesive to hold antennae in position.

Patchwork

Patchwork is a fascinating and rewarding craft and those who like hand sewing will like patchwork. There are dozens of intricate patterns on record. Most of these were originated by the early American settlers, and 'Duck's-foot-in-the-Mud' and 'Goose Feet' are two of the more picturesque ones. 'Lincoln's Platform' commemorated a famous speech made by the president.

PATCHWORK SHAPES

Squares, triangles, diamonds, hexagons and pentagons are the shapes most commonly used in patchwork. Any of these shapes can be used to build up designs or can be combined for a more complex effect. Fig 1 for instance, shows three different designs which can be made using squares and triangles.

Hexagons can be combined to make rosettes, diamond shapes or stripes. A pretty quilt border can be built up using hexagon rosettes linked with a band of diamonds (Fig 2).

Diamond patches can be used to make six and eight-point stars. In Fig 3, an eight-point star has been finished off with squares and triangles to create a block motif which could be used for a quilt. A six point star can be finished with diamond shapes to make a hexagon. A popular early American box pattern called 'Tumbling blocks' is made entirely from diamond shapes (Fig 4). Fabrics in three different colours or shades are used. One of the colours must be dark to create the optical effect of cubes.

Star motifs, sometimes called 'Star of Bethlehem' or 'Sunburst' are created with diamond shapes. The beauty of the motif depends on the choice of fabrics. Built up from a central eight-point star, each band of diamond shapes is in a different colour or print so that the effect is shaded from the centre motif outwards (Fig 5).

Clamshell patchwork uses a different shape from the traditional geometric ones. The shape (Fig 6) resembles the overlapping scales of a fish when it is made up and differs from traditional patchwork in that the stitching is done on the right side of the work. The clamshell shape is used to make the teacosy on page 68.

TEMPLATES

These provide the master shape from which the fabric is cut. Template sets are sold at many needlecraft shops and consist of a solid template which is the size of the finished patch and which is used for cutting out paper linings and a 'window' or transparent template for working out the fabric. The window enables the sewer to experiment with the pattern of a fabric and choose exactly the piece desired before actually cutting out the patchwork shape.

MAKING YOUR OWN TEMPLATES

Templates can be easily and cheaply made from stiff, firm-textured cardboard, but they must be accurately drawn and cut out or the patches will not fit together neatly. *Diamonds, triangles and pyramids* are drawn as shown in Fig 6. To draw a *pentagon*, decide upon the length of one of the sides. Draw this on a piece of paper. Place a protractor so that the 90 degrees line is exactly on the left end of the line and mark a pencil dot at the angle of 72 degrees (Figs 7 and 8). Join the dot and the left side of the horizontal line and draw this line to exactly the length of one side as before. Turn the drawing and place the 90 degree line of the protractor on the end of the line and again mark 72 degrees. Continue in the same way until the pentagon is completed. This is the finished size of the patchwork shape and is the template which will be used to cut out the backing papers. Add $\frac{5}{16}$ in *(5mm)* all around to make the second fabric template, for cutting out fabrics. *Hexagon* shapes are drawn in the same way except that the angle is 60 degrees. *Octagon* shapes are drawn with angles of 45 degrees.

FABRICS IN PATCHWORK

Almost any kind of fabric can be used in patchwork provided that it does not fray too easily. Cotton, linen, velvet, silk, satin, wool and most of the man-made fibres are suitable. Fabrics should be pre-shrunk and be colourfast if the

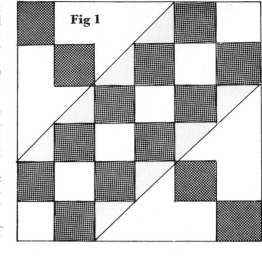

Fig 1

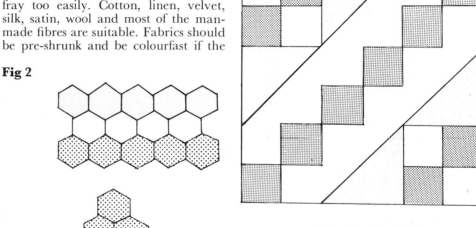

Fig 2

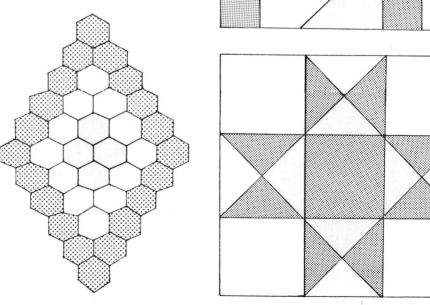

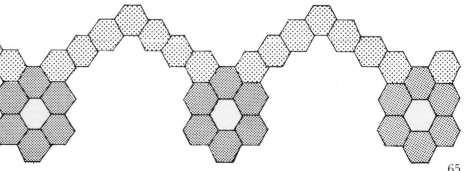

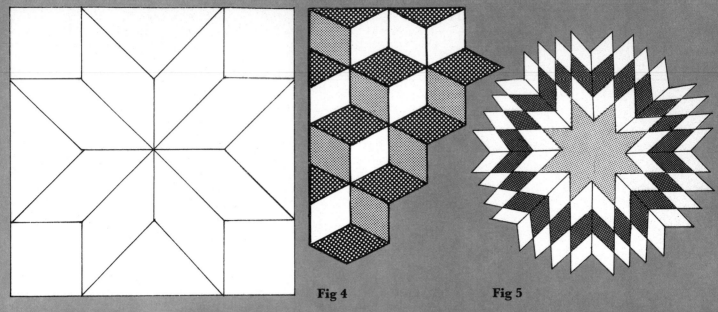

Fig 4

Fig 5

Fig 3

finished patchwork is to be laundered, but generally, it is better to have patchwork dry-cleaned to preserve the stitches and colours.

Generally, it is an unwise practice to mix different kinds of fabrics in a piece of patchwork unless one is absolutely sure that the weight and texture of the fabrics are similar. Patches of mixed fabrics are likely to pull apart with wear.

LINING FABRICS Thin and semi-transparent fabrics will need lining, and individual patches are worked into the patchwork with a muslin backing already basted to them. Cut these muslin shapes out using the fabric template. Most patchwork articles will need to be lined after they are completed. The fabric used for lining will depend on each article and the use to which it is put. Unbleached muslin is often used for quilts and similar large pieces. Cotton or dress lining fabric are used for smaller items and clothing.

BACKING PAPERS Paper is used to make temporary lining for each patch. Any paper will do as long as it is pliable. Index cards or postcards are ideal. The backing papers must be cut out carefully because they determine the accuracy of the finished shapes. Backing papers can be used several times before being thrown away.

OTHER EQUIPMENT The only equipment required for patchwork is a pair of sharp scissors, fine dressmakers' pins, needles and thread. The thread should be matched in colour and type to the fabric. Polyester threads are used with man-made fibres, and cotton or silk for fabrics made from natural fibres. A slim, strong needle with a small eye is used for sewing patchwork.

66

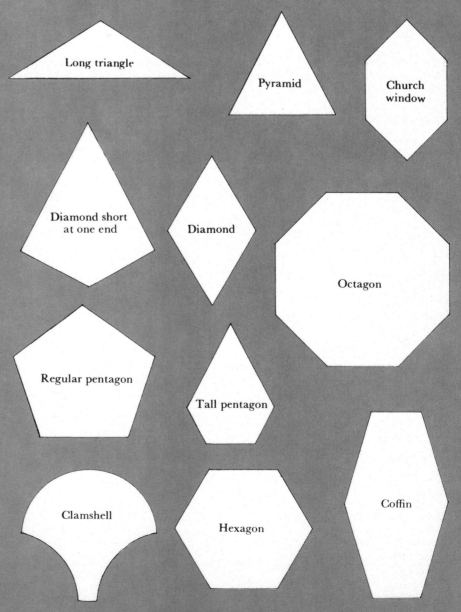

Fig 6 The traditional shapes used in patchwork.

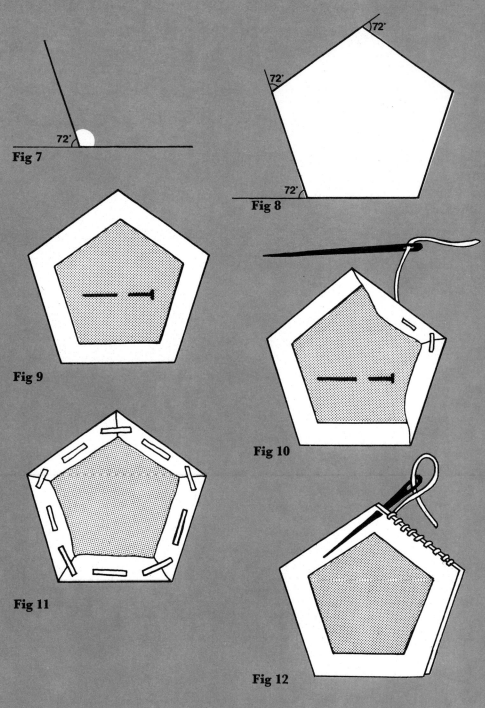

Fig 7

Fig 8

Fig 9

Fig 10

Fig 11

Fig 12

Cutting out fabrics and papers Press all the creases out of the fabric and lay it out flat. Place the fabric template on the wrong side and draw around the shape with a sharply pointed pencil. Draw and cut out as many shapes as required.

Hold the smaller template down on the lining paper and draw around the outline with pencil. Cut out a number of backing papers.

Making and joining patches Pin a backing paper to the wrong side of the fabric shape making sure that it is centred accurately (Fig 9). Fold the turnings to wrong side neatly (Figs 10 and 11), baste the fabric to the backing paper. When all the backing papers have been basted to the fabric shapes, it is time to start sewing. Do not tie a knot in the thread. Hold two patches together with corners exactly matching and right sides facing. Lay the end of the thread along the edges of the patches and oversew the end (Fig 12). Finish and begin with two or three stitches.

The needle is pushed through the fabric only making small and neat stitches. Several patches can be joined continuously but always strengthen the corners with three or four stitches. When the required area of patchwork has been stitched, press the patchwork under a dry cloth with a warm iron on the wrong side and then remove the backing papers by snipping the basting threads. The papers should come away easily unless the oversewing stitches have been taken through the edge of the paper by accident.

Figs 7, 8 How to draw a pentagon.
Figs 9, 10, 11 Basting the fabric to the paper.
Fig 12 Joining two patches with oversewing.

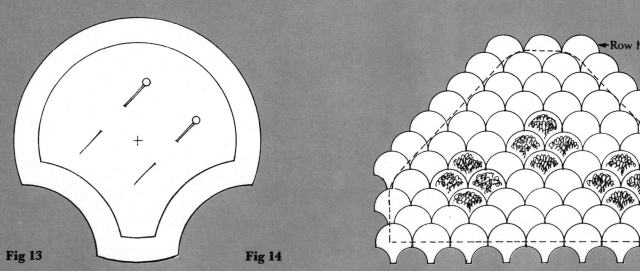

Fig 13

Fig 14

67

Tea Cosy

Before starting on this project check the size of your teapot. The finished measurements of this tea-cosy are: 16in x 9in *(40cm x 22.5cm)*. It was made to fit a long, low teapot; you may need extra depth and therefore extra patch-work pieces.

Materials required:

2in *(5cm)* clamshell template
Heavy paper
1yd *(1m)* solid colour cotton fabric
½yd *(0.5m)* patterned cotton fabric
½yd *(0.5m)* synthetic wadding
2yd *(2m)* piping cord
Sewing thread

To make the cosy

Prepare the material for the piping first. Fold patterned material diagonally across so that crossways thread lies parallel to lengthways thread and iron the fold. Open up material and cut along fold line. Using this line as guide, cut three strips of bias material 1in *(2.5cm)* wide by the entire length. Use these strips to enclose the piping cord.
Cut out 76 clamshell shapes in paper using the template.
Cut 11 clamshell shapes out of the patterned fabric allowing ¼in *(6mm)* seam allowance all round.
Cut 65 solid colour clamshells in a similar fashion.
Place paper pattern on wrong side of fabric and position two pins to stop material from slipping (Fig 13). Baste around top curved edges, using small stitches and making small pleats to ease the fullness. Remove pins and press lightly on wrong side. Prepare all paper patterns in same way.
Begin at the top of the tea cosy with row 1 (See Fig 14). Sew the patches together in rows, with the right side facing upwards. The top of the curve of the first row of three patches is placed against the edge of a ruler to ensure that they are even. Place the second row of four patches in position, overlapping the first row and baste in place. Sew these together using very small hemming stitches around the curves of the second row. Continue adding one row at a time, increasing each row by one patch. In the fifth row place one patterned patch in the centre (Fig 14). In the sixth row place two patterned patches directly underneath the first patterned patch. Make the seventh row as follows: two plain patches, one patterned, three plain, one patterned and finally two plain. The eighth row is worked as one plain, two patterned, two plain, two patterned and one plain. For the ninth row make two plain, one patterned, three plain, one patterned and two plain. The tenth row has 8 plain patches, and the final row has 9 plain patches.

Remove basting stitches and papers and press work lightly on right side.
Pin the lengths of prepared piping on the right side of the patchwork raw edges together on the dotted line (Fig 14). Trim off edges to ½in *(1cm)* all round and use patchwork completed thus far as a guide for cutting out back of teacosy in patterned material. Cut out two pieces of lining using remaining pieces of solid colour material allowing ½in *(1cm)* seam allowances all around.
Baste right side of patterned material to right side of completed patchwork and stitch together close to piping around sides and top. Pin and baste piping to right side of bottom edges. The seam can be machined but a small hemming stitch gives a more satisfactory result. Stitch piping round bottom edge. Turn teacosy inside out and use shape as guide to cut wadding to exact size allowing no seam allowance. Overstitch wadding around sides and top. Machine stitch lining together around sides and top. Turn patchwork right side out. Slip wadding inside, overstitched edges to inside edges of patchwork. Turn up edge of patchwork over wadding and catch the two together with large herringbone stitches. Place lining inside tea cosy, turn under ½in *(1cm)* seam allowance around bottom edge and hemstitch to edge of piping.

Pin Cushion

This makes an unusual pincushion that also serves its purpose particularly well.

Materials required:

½in *(1cm)* hexagon template
Scrap of flowered cotton fabric
½yd *(0.5m)* plain cotton fabric
1yd *(1m)* narrow piping cord
Sewing thread
No. 10 sharps needles

Small amount of Kapok.

To make the pincushion

Prepare hexagons in plain and patterned cotton fabric.
Make a rosette consisting of one plain fabric hexagon surrounded by six patterned hexagons. Sew 12 plain fabric hexagons around the rosette shape. Turn work wrong side and press lightly. Now find the centre point of the centre hexagon. Take a pair of compasses

and draw a circle so that the line touches the outer edge of every second patch of the outer 12 patches. This indicates where patches need to be filled in between each of these flat edges—an extra 12 patches will be needed. Sew these in. Draw another circle but this time draw it very lightly on the right side of the work. This is the line where you will be attaching the piping cord. If it is done on the wrong side you will not be able to remove the papers. Work the under-

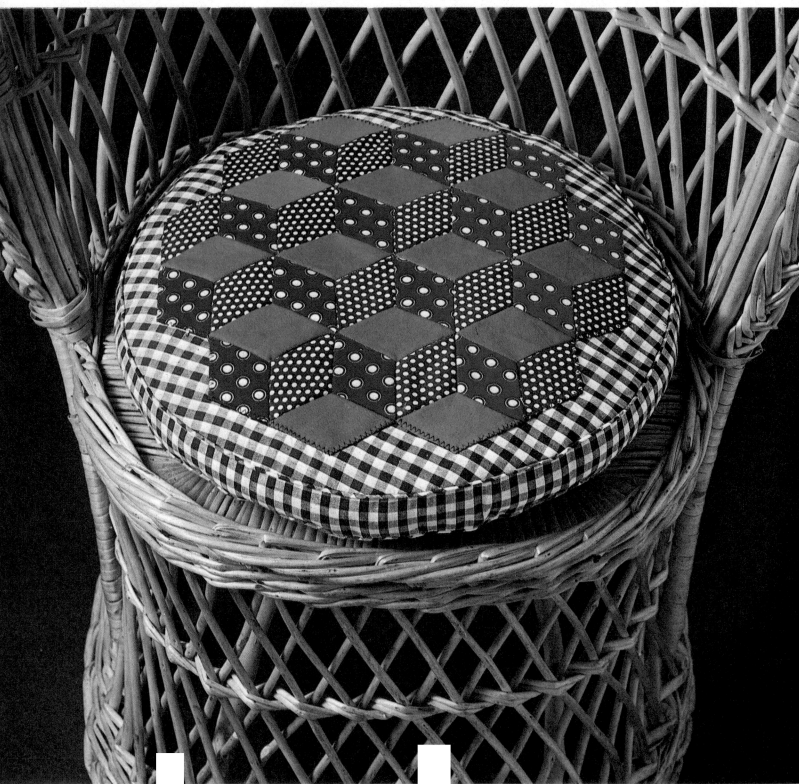

side of the pincushion in the same way. Press the work and remove papers.

Cut bias strips of plain material for the piping. Enclose piping cord in bias strips with a small running stitch fairly close to cord. Attach piping to top and bottom pieces of pincushion with tiny hemstitches, following guide lines.

Cut a piece of material $1\frac{1}{4}$in x 15in *(3cm x 37.5cm)* to go around the side of the pincushion. Press $\frac{1}{4}$in *(0.5cm)* seam allowance across top and bottom of length. Again using a small hemstitch attach one edge to top of pincushion until ends meet. Turn work wrong side out and sew together ends. Trim off excess material to $\frac{1}{4}$in *(0.5cm)*. Sew bottom of pincushion to remaining free edge, leaving 2in *(5cm)* open. Stuff carefully with kapok. Hemstitch opening together.

Round Cushion

An early American patchwork pattern called 'Tumbling blocks' is used for this bright cushion. Choose two geometric fabric patterns and one plain dark coloured fabric to achieve the three-dimensional effect.

Materials required:
$\frac{3}{4}$yd *(46cm)* 36in *(90cm)* wide cotton gingham for the cushion
$\frac{1}{4}$yd *(23cm)* each of blue and red geometric pattern fabrics
$\frac{1}{4}$yd *(23cm)* plain blue fabric
$1\frac{3}{4}$in *(4.4cm)* diamond template
14in *(36cm)* diameter round cushion pad

To make the patchwork
Prepare two diamond shaped patches from each of the three fabrics (six patches). Join these to make a star matching fabrics diagonally. Cut more patches from the three fabrics and stitch patches between the 'arms' of the star, making the 'cube' effect. When the 'arms' of the star have been filled with diamond patches the shape of the patchwork will be hexagon. Continue adding patches round the hexagon, keeping to the colour sequence until the patchwork is 12ins *(30.5cm)* in diameter. Press the patchwork on the wrong side and remove the backing papers.

To make the cushion
Cut two circles from the gingham, $15\frac{1}{2}$ins *(40cm)* in diameter. Pin and baste the prepared patchwork to the centre of one piece and stitch around the outside edge, securing it to the gingham, using either slip stitches or zigzag machine stitching. Cut a strip of gingham fabric 45in x 3in *(1.22m x 7.5cm)* for the cushion gusset. Cut bias strips from the gingham for the piping. Make up the cushion in the same way as for the pincushion.

Bedspread

This is a particularly beautiful covering which will become a principle feature in your bedroom. The finished size is 9ft x 7ft *(3m x 2.5m)*.

Materials required:
$1\frac{1}{4}$in *(2.5cm)* hexagon template
7yd *(7m)* patterned cotton fabrics in assorted colours
7yd *(7m)* brown cotton fabric
9yd *(9m)* cotton lining
Coloured threads
No. 10 sharps needles.

To make the bedspread
Prepare hexagon patchwork shapes in patterned cotton fabrics and brown cotton fabric. Make several flowers consisting of one hexagon of patterned cotton fabric surrounded by six hexagons of another colour cotton fabric. Take the flower which you want in the centre of the bedspread. Prepare hexagonal patches of the brown fabric and sew around flower shape. Now sew six more flowers around this piece. Sew 7 brown patches around each flower. No matter how many flowers you sew on, the work will still be hexagonal until your work is the width required for the bed. Now continue to sew flowers on four sides only so that work becomes rectangular. Be sure to continue the straight line of the free sides. Continue until work is the required length measuring from point to point i.e. the centre point of each of the two sides you have been working. Now fill in the triangles that you have left to square the shape using brown hexagons.

Make enough brown patches to go around the entire edge. With right sides together, attach them around outside edges of work. Press carefully and turn to the wrong side. Press again lightly. Remove the papers and the basting stitches.

Cut and seam lining material to the size of the patchwork. Place the first width down the centre and have a half width or more, depending on the required size, sewn to each side of this centre piece. Place wrong side down on the wrong side of the patchwork and pin to secure. Cut the lining, following the outline of the hexagons on the edges, leaving $\frac{3}{4}$in *(2cm)* seam allowance all round. Turn under seam allowance and hemstitch the lining to the patchwork all around. Turn work to right side. Working from top side, catch some of the patches to the lining. Use a small running stitch and go around one patch in the centre of the bedspread. Do this six more times half way between the centre patch and the outside edge of your work. This will stop the bedspread from ballooning when picked up.

Smocking

Smocking is a form of decorative embroidery worked on gathered fabric. It is featured on many national costumes–Russian, Albanian, Rumanian, Hungarian–usually around the neck and wrists of women's blouses. It also appeared on the work smocks of British workmen during the late 18th and early 19th centuries. These smocks were made of heavy linen and thickly gathered across the shoulders and back as protection against the weather. The gathers were embroidered with motifs and symbols indicating the occupation of the wearer. Smocking is now used mostly for small children's clothes – dresses and sun-suits for girls and smocked rompers and shirts for boys. In recent years it has also become fashionable as a way of decorating dresses, lingerie, blouses and evening frocks. Done properly, smocking gives a natural elasticity to fabric and this enables it to be used for a wide variety of garments.

PREPARING THE FABRIC

Smocking is worked with embroidery thread on gathered fabric, and it is absolutely essential to prepare the fabric correctly first. The gathers must be uniform, and are made in the ratio 2½:1, so allow 2½in (6cm) of fabric for every 1in (2.5cm) finished work. If working with plain fabric it is necessary to apply a smocking transfer first. These are sold in different widths, depths and spacing between the dots. The choice is determined by the required size of the finished work. After first pressing the fabric, pin the transfer in position on the wrong side of the material. Transfer the dots by pressing with a warm iron for most natural fibres or a cool one if the fabric is very delicate or synthetic. Finally, remove the paper. Dotted or checked fabrics can be gathered without the use of a transfer but they may have to be gathered on the right side of the fabric if the design is not printed through onto the wrong side. Each individual dot must be picked up on the needle. Use a fine sewing needle and bright or contrasting coloured thread, and as the running threads cannot be joined, each thread should be the width of the fabric. Knot the thread at one end, then make a back stitch to prevent the knot from pulling through and, working from right to left, put the needle in one side of every dot and bring it out on the other, carry the thread to the next dot and continue to the end of the row, being careful to put the needle in each side of the dot and not through the centre (see Fig 1). When all the lines have their running stitches, pull up the work carefully to the required width (with very deep gathers pull up a few at a time) and tie the loose ends to prevent the gathers from slipping. Even out the gathers carefully. An extra thread run in at the top of the design helps to keep the first row of stitches even and is particularly useful when smocking the neck of a child's frock, or the gathers for a yoke. In both these cases transfer an extra row of dots and leave the gathering thread in at the top after the smocking is finished as the yoke or neck band will be sewn to this line. The actual smocking is worked on the right side of the work. Do not draw up the stitches too tightly as the work should 'give'.

PLANNING DESIGNS

There are many beautiful smocking patterns available which show how to use the various stitches to the best advantage. When following a pattern notice how the rows of different stitches are placed to fit into each other, making a secondary pattern of the pleats. If the design is symmetrical work it out carefully first. Remember also that one more dot should be transferred than is required for the design. The reason for this is that the transfer is ironed off on the wrong side of the work and the extra stitch is needed to make the last pleat. If planning your own design, try to achieve a balance between the different types of stitches, interspersing straight stitches with those which form a diamond pattern. Try not to overcrowd the work by leaving a blank line here and there. Also plan for an attractive blending of colours which will tone or contrast with the fabric, such as red on white, autumn colours on cream, or turquoise, white and lilac on purple.

FABRICS

Almost any type of fabric can be smocked, but the lighter weight fabrics are the most successful; organdie, voile, lawn, fine cotton, poplin, silk, shantung and lingerie fabrics are all very suitable for smocking techniques. Heavier weights such as linen and some fine wool fabrics can be smocked successfully but avoid textured fabrics as they do not gather well. Garments in different fabrics will require slightly varying amounts of material; for example thin silks will take up more material than thicker fabrics such as linen. Also no two workers use exactly the same amount, as one will work more tightly than another. Stitches make a difference too, honeycomb smocking takes far less material than diamond stitch and wave stitch takes more than either. Sew a few practice pieces first to gauge your standard tension.

THREADS

Stranded embroidery thread is used for smocking and depending on the weight of fabric used, is split to make a thinner thread. Four strands are used for heavy fabric (wool, velvet, etc.), three strands for normal fabrics and two strands for light fabric (voile, organdie and fine lingerie materials). Linen can be smocked with linen thread and silk and shantung with silk thread. It is not wise to use wool or other yarn as this is too heavy and breaks too easily.

STITCHES

Smocking stitches are usually worked from left to right, with some exceptions. When working down, the thread must be over the needle. When working up, the thread is below the needle.

Outline stitch This stitch is used to start most patterns. Keep the needle level with the gathering thread at all times. Bring needle up on left hand side of a pleat, then pick up the next pleat to the right allowing needle to slant as shown in the diagram. The thread here is kept above the needle, it can however be kept below with needle slanting upwards (Fig 2).

Fig 2

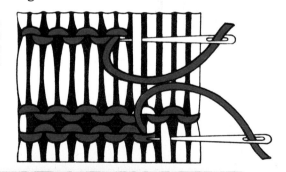

Cable stitch This is similar to outline stitch. Bring the needle through to the left of the first pleat on lower line. Take a stitch through second pleat with the

Fig 3

Fig 1

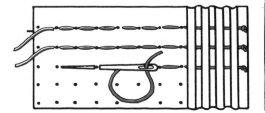

73

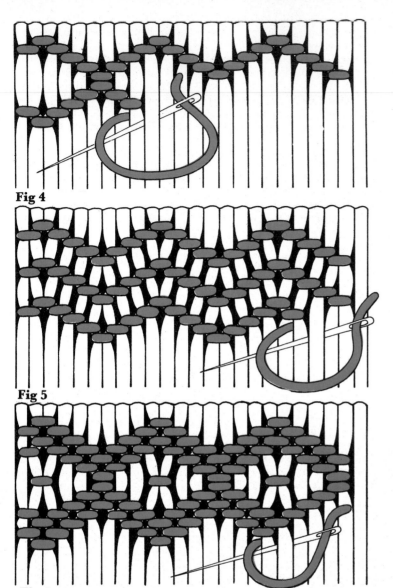

Fig 4

Fig 5

Fig 6

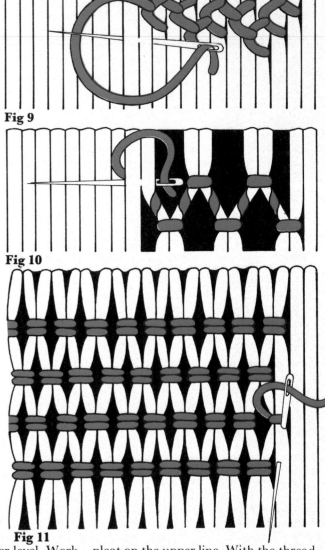

Fig 9

Fig 10

Fig 11

thread above the needle, take a stitch through the third pleat with the thread below the needle and continue (Fig 3). Lower section of Fig 3 shows a row of double cable stitch, which is two rows of single cable stitch worked close together, as used on the baby's dress illustrated on page 72.

Trellis stitch The trellis formed may be of different sizes: three, four or five stitches are the usual numbers for the side of each trellis. Bring up the needle to the left of the first pleat on a gathering thread. Take a small stitch through the second pleat at a lower level slanting the needle slightly and keeping the thread above it. Take a stitch in the third and fourth pleats in the same way, then one in the fifth pleat at the same level as the last but with the thread below the needle. This stitch should be halfway between two gathering threads. Work three stitches upwards on the next three pleats, always keeping the thread below the needle, the last stitch being on a level of the first gathering thread. Take a stitch in the next pleat at the same level but with the thread above the needle and work

downwards again to former level. Work alternately up and down until the end of the row is reached.

The second row is begun level with the second gathering thread and the stitches are worked upwards until the fourth pleat is reached and then downwards. The centre stitches of each row of zig-zags meet and form the trellis (Fig 4).

Wave stitch This is worked exactly in the same way as the first row of Trellis stitch. After working this row a second row or even a third row is stitched to fit into the zig-zags, either close together or spaced as shown in Fig 5. The Double Wave stitch is shown in Fig 6. In this instance the rows are grouped in pairs but for a heavier effect they could be in threes. To form the little dot in the centre of the wave take the two middle pleats together with one stitch over.

Diamond stitch Begin half way between two gathering threads and bring the needle through to the left of the first pleat. Take one horizontal stitch through the second pleat with the thread below, then take the next horizontal stitch with the thread below through the third

pleat on the upper line. With the thread above, take another stitch beside the third through the fourth pleat on the upper line and finally with the thread above, take a stitch through the fifth pleat on lower line. Continue in this

Fig 7

Fig 8

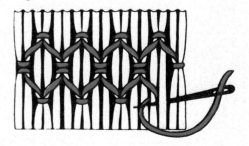

74

way to end of row, always remembering to take only one stitch in each pleat (Fig 7). The other half of the diamond is formed by starting immediately below the first stitches and arranging them as shown in Fig 8.

Feather stitch Bring needle up in first pleat on right side of material on first gathering thread. Take first and second pleats together, keeping thread before needle, then come down to quarter way between first and second gathering thread, and take second and third pleats together, holding thread as before; come down to halfway between first and second gathering threads, and take third and fourth pleats together, holding thread as before. Go up to quarter way again, and take fourth and fifth pleats together, and then up to first gathering thread and take fifth and sixth pleats together, and so on (Fig 9).

Vandyke stitch Bring needle up on first pleat on right side of material, halfway between first and second gathering thread, pass needle through first two pleats together and take another stitch over; then go up to second gathering thread, and take second and third pleat together with another stitch over, then down halfway between second and first gathering thread take third and fourth pleat together with another stitch over, and so on to end of line. This stitch should always start halfway between two gathering threads. A space of half the distance between two gathering threads should always be left after every line (Fig 10).

Honeycomb stitch This type of smocking is used where the gathers need to be held together but no design is required, as the thread shows only where the stitches are taken. Traditionally, it should be worked with embroidery thread just a shade lighter or darker than the material. Only a small stitch on the surface is seen and in

order to make a really deep honeycomb the pleats should be heavier and deeper than regular smocking. Gather up the work from left to right, start in the first pleat and take a stitch through the top of the second and first pleats together. Catch them together with a second stitch, but this time bring the needle down at the back of the second pleat to the second row of gathering, then bring it out. Catch together the second and third pleats with a stitch, make a second stitch over the top, and take the needle back under work to the first gathering thread. Catch together the third and fourth pleats with two stitches, taking the needle down at the back to the second row of gathering threads and catch together the fourth and fifth pleat (Fig 11). Continue in this way working up and down until the row is complete. Work a second row on third and fourth gathering threads and so on until the smocking is as deep as required. The thread, as in all smocking, is above the needle for the top level stitch and below for the bottom level stitch.

Practice Pieces

Here are two pieces of smocking which are ideal for the beginner.

Smocking on polka dot fabric

This uses only four basic stitches, but the combination of colours adds variety and creates a much more interesting design.

1st row: Outline stitch. **2nd row:** Cable stitch. **3rd row:** Outline stitch. **4th and 5th rows:** Diamond stitch. **6th row:** Outline stitch. **7th row:** Cable stitch. **8th row:** Outline stitch.

Red on white smocking

The right-hand side of the sample below

is worked in honeycomb stitch as described, with a row of chain stitch at the top. For a row of chain stitch, work from left to right and continue as for chain stitch in embroidery, picking up each pleat in the needle. Do not pull the work too tight or the gathers will not give and stretch. The left-hand side of the sample is as follows:

1st row: Outline stitch. **2nd row:** Vandyke stitch. **3rd row:** Cable stitch. **4th and 5th rows:** Diamond stitch. **6th row:** Trellis stitch. **7th row:** Cable stitch. **8th row:** Single row of Wave stitch. **9th row:** Outline stitch. **10th row:** Half the Diamond stitch.

Little Girl's Sun Dress

The instructions as given will make a dress to fit a 5-year-old, but these can be altered to fit other sizes. As with all smocked designs, the main fabric pieces are cut and smocked before the garment is made up (Illustrated on page 76).

Materials required:
1yd *(103cm)* 36in *(91cm)* wide cotton fabric
Sewing thread
Stranded embroidery cotton: 2 skeins blue (split and use three strands throughout)
Bias binding to match dress fabric (optional).

To make the dress
Cut two pieces from the fabric 21in *(54cm)* by 36in *(91cm)*, with the short side to the selvedge. Cut four pieces 12in *(31cm)* by 1½in *(3.5cm)* for the shoulder ties. Cut curves for armholes by cutting out semi-circles at the upper corners of the two large pieces of fabric about 3in

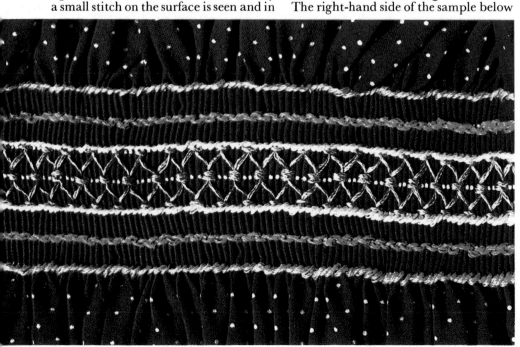

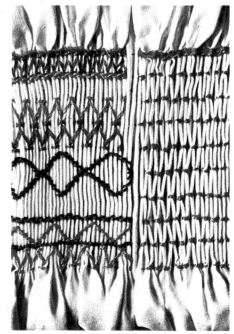

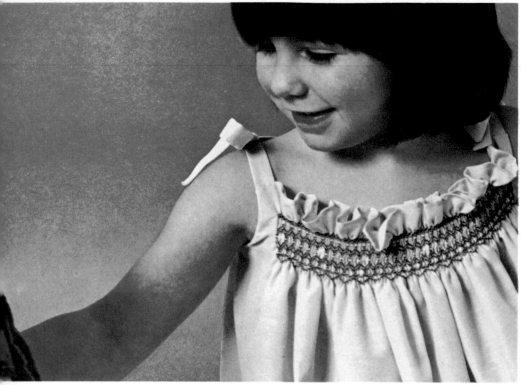

indicate the pleats of the material.
1st row: Double Cable stitch. **2nd row:** Work half a row of Diamond stitch and then work another similar row immediately beneath the first. **3rd row:** as for second row. **4th and 5th rows:** Cable stitch and Wave stitch.

To finish
Press the pieces of smocking lightly under a damp cloth. Smocking should never be pressed firmly or ironed as the pleats would flatten and the whole purpose of the work would be ruined.

To make up
Remove all gathering threads. Join the side seams with a French seam, face the armholes using the small remnants of fabric cut on the cross, or use matching bias binding. Turn up the hem and slip stitch. Press the hem, seams and armholes being careful not to flatten the smocking. Fold ties in half lengthwise, machine stitch the long side and one short side ½in *(1cm)* from edge, trim seams and turn up right side. Turn in raw edges and slip stitch, then press. Finally attach ties to dress at shoulders.

(7cm) in depth and 2in *(5cm)* in width. Leave edges raw at this stage. Make a small hem along the top edge of the fabric, either by hand or machine. Trace the section of the full-size drawing of the smocking dots (Fig 12) onto the wrong side of the fabric, 1in *(2.5cm)* down from the top edge, and ¾in *(2cm)* in from the armhole. Repeat this section as required across the fabric to within ¾in *(2cm)* of the other armhole. If preferred an iron-on smocking transfer to

the same scale can be used. Gather up and secure the pleats.

Fig 13 gives a section of the smocking which is repeated across the fabric; the dotted lines on the left-hand side indicate the rows of gathers and show the placing of stitches in relation to rows; the broken lines between the stitches

Fig 12

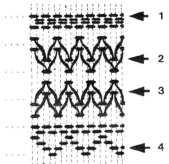

Fig 13

Baby's Dress

This little dress uses a variety of basic stitches and is a good introduction for a beginner. (Illustrated on page 72).

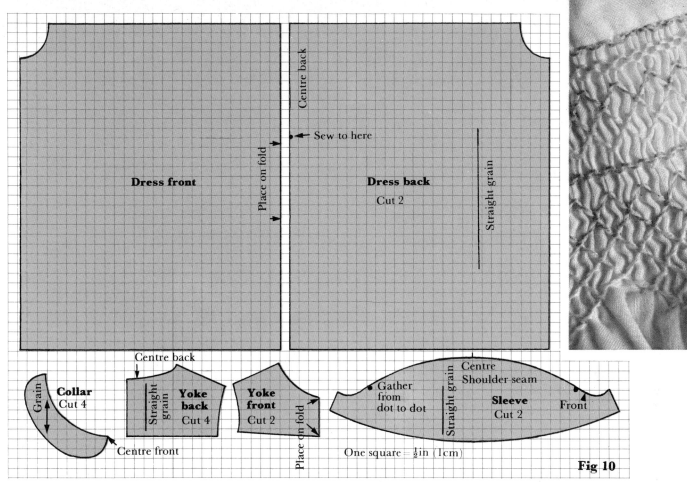

Figure labels (Fig 10):

- Dress front — Place on fold
- Dress back — Cut 2 — Centre back — Straight grain — Sew to here
- Collar — Cut 4 — Grain — Centre back — Centre front
- Yoke back — Cut 4 — Straight grain
- Yoke front — Cut 2 — Place on fold
- Sleeve — Cut 2 — Gather from dot to dot — Straight grain — Centre — Shoulder seam — Front
- One square = ½in (1cm)

Fig 10

Materials required:

1¾yd *(1.60m)* 36in *(91cm)* wide fine fabric

Smocking transfer with 30 dots per sq. 1in *(2.5cm)*

Stranded embroidery cotton (split and use 2 threads throughout): 1 skein each pale pink, medium pink, rose

Sewing thread.

To make the dress

Draw and cut out a paper pattern from the graph (Fig 10). No allowance has been made for seams on the pattern although 4ins *(10cm)* has been allowed for the hem. Pin the paper pattern to the fabric, placing pieces to fold where instructed and keeping fabric to straight grain marks on the pattern. Cut out pieces, allowing ¾in *(19cm)* all around for seam allowance. Join front to backs using French seams.

Smocking Transfer smocking dots to backs and front, on the wrong side of fabric. The first row of dots should be ¾in *(19cm)* in below top edge. Gather each row, picking up each dot. Tie off threads in pairs, pulling pleats out evenly. Work smocking as follows:

1st row: Cable stitch, rose. **2nd row:** Double cable stitch, medium pink, pale pink. **3rd row:** Diamond stitch, rose. **4th row:** Diamond stitch, medium pink. **5th row:** Diamond stitch, pale pink. **6th row:** Cable stitch, rose. **7th and 8th row:** Diamond stitch, rose. **9th and**

10th row: Diamond stitch, medium pink. **11th and 12th row:** Diamond stitch, worked into points, pale pink.

Collar and yoke Stitch one piece of front yoke to one pair of back yokes at shoulder seams. Stitch second yoke (for facing top yoke) in the same way.

Place two collar pieces together, right sides facing, and stitch around outside edge. Trim and clip seam allowance. Turn to right side and press. Make up two collars in the same way.

Baste the two collars to the top fabric yoke unit, right sides facing, making sure that centre fronts match and that the back collar is ½in *(13mm)* in from the centre back opening. Baste second unit facing on top of the collar, basting through all thicknesses of fabric. Collar is now 'sandwiched' between the right sides of yoke. Stitch to attach collar. Layer and trim seam allowances. Turn yoke to right side and press.

Attaching yoke Press seam allowance on skirt edge of top yoke piece. Having removed gathering threads from smocking, pin yoke to skirt front, distributing pleats evenly. Use tiny hemming stitches, picking up the top of each pleat. Do not machine stitch because this would distort the smocking pleats. Press seam allowance on inside yoke and stitch to skirt front in the same way. Stitch centre back skirt and press seam open. Make seam edges neat. Attach back yoke using the same method as for front.

Sleeves Join sleeves with French seams. Work two rows of gathering threads around bottom edge of sleeve and gather up to circumference of baby's arm, plus ½in *(1cm)* for ease. Cut two ¾in *(2cm)* strips of fabric on the diagonal for bias edging. Pin and baste to the right side of sleeve between rows of gathering stitches. Stitch. Press away from sleeve, turn under raw edge and slip stitch to wrong side of sleeve so that a neat edge ⅛in *(3mm)* shows. Remove gathering threads.

Gather up the head of the sleeves. Pin and baste sleeves into armholes, matching centre mark to shoulder seam, side seam to underarm seam. Distribute fullness evenly. Stitch. Remove gathering stitches. Trim seam allowance and cover with bias binding.

With back of dress facing, turn and hem back neck opening. Position three buttonholes, the top ½in *(1cm)* below collar line, the bottom ½in *(1cm)* above skirt and the third centred between them. Work buttonholes by hand or with machine zigzag stitch. Stitch on buttons to correspond.

To finish

Turn up hem 2in *(5cm)* and press. Turn hem a further 2in *(5cm)* and baste, thus forming a double hem. Work small running stitches to stitch hem, using the deep pink thread used in the smocking. Work running stitches around sleeve edging to match.

Quilting

In its earliest form, quilting was valued for warmth and protection, the purpose of the stitches being to secure padding between two outer layers of fabric. As the craft developed over the centuries the stitches were used increasingly to form patterns. Inspiration for these patterns came from everyday objects — flowers, leaves, shells and feathers. Patterns also acquired regional characteristics so that quilts made in the various parts of the country took on distinctive styles.

Many of the traditional British regional patterns crossed the Atlantic to America with the early settlers where the designs were adapted and given new names. Other new quilting patterns were developed and a rich heritage of American quilting evolved. Quilting bees were an important feature of the social life of 19th-century America. They were an occasion for the meeting together of women and girls who often lived in remote areas. Pieces of patchwork, enough for a large quilt, were stored away until the

day when a daughter was to be married. When the neighbours were invited to a quilting bee, it was tantamount to announcing a girl's engagement. The women would busy themselves around the quilt frame while the children played and the men gossiped and smoked. The gathering often extended well into the night enlivened with music and dancing. This communal quilting is still practised in rural America where it is a popular method of raising money for charity. But the days when most homes could boast a quilting frame are gone — there is seldom the space for it and the quilting of a whole coverlet by hand is hardly a practical proposition nowadays. Quilting can be done by machine — it's both practical and efficient — but lacks something of the charm and quality of hand stitching. Home quilting is now usually confined to small items which can be worked on an embroidery or tapestry frame. The methods described here are those traditionally used for quilting. Projects include hand and machine work.

EQUIPMENT

Quilting frame A traditional quilting frame consists of two long bars of wood called rails and two short pieces known as stretchers. The stretchers fit into slots in the rails and are held in place by wooden pegs fixed in holes. Occasionally the quilting frame rests on its own trestles but more usually it rests on the tops of two straight backed chairs. For a full sized quilt the frame should be at least 90in *(230cm)* long. A frame 36in *(92cm)* long is sufficient for making a smaller quilt for a baby and cushion covers. For small pieces of work a large embroidery frame can be used, provided that it rests on a stand as it is essential in quilting to have both hands free for the work. Machine quilting is worked without a frame.

Fabrics For the traditional wadded quilt where the sewn design is completely reversible, the top and backing should be of the same material. It should be soft and smooth. Sateen, poplin, silk, cotton, linen, cambric, satin, gingham, corduroy and fine wool are all good fabrics. If the top of the quilt is pieced patchwork or appliqué, then the backing can be made of lightweight muslin. This type of quilt is not reversible.

Filling The filling can be of well washed corded sheep's wool, absorbent cotton wool or any synthetic wadding such as Terylene (Dacron).

DESIGNS AND TEMPLATES

Patterns for quilting can be geometric or be inspired by natural shapes. Some traditional designs are on page 83. Draw designs out onto paper before transferring them to the template. Templates should be firm and can be made of cardboard, metal or plastic.

MARKING PATTERNS

Having decided upon the patterns to be used to build up the overall design, then mark these out on the top fabric before setting it in the frame. Spread the top fabric over a thick blanket on a table or on the floor. Mark the central line vertically and horizontally. Place the appropriate template in position and mark around it with the tip of the quilting needle which is held almost flat on the material so that it makes a slight crease. Tailors' chalk can be used for complicated shapes in the pattern but on no account use lead pencil as pencil marks are difficult to wash out.

SETTING UP THE WORK

If the quilt is being made from appliqué or patchwork all seams must be sewn and pressed flat before quilting. Do not have a seam down the centre of the work. If two widths are needed to make up the area, split one width down the middle and sew a half to each side of the centre panel.

Tapestry and embroidery frames can be used for quilting small items.

METHOD OF WORKING

The backing fabric is set in the frame first, wrong side upwards. The padding is laid on next. The top fabric with the pattern marked on it is laid on top of the padding. Baste the layers together securely along the front rail. Fasten them together along the far rail with a row of pins put at close intervals. Quilting is traditionally done in fine cotton thread or pure silk with a No. 9 needle.

Small, even running stitches are worked through all three layers of material.

Regularity of size is the most important thing in quilting. The most accurate way of working is to keep one hand beneath the work and push the needle vertically down through the layers of material from the top. The needle is then pushed back up through the work to complete the stitch.

Knots at the beginning and end of the thread should be drawn carefully through the fabric and into the wadding so that they do not show on either side.

FINISHING

There are three methods of finishing the edges.

1 The edges of the top and backing are turned in and a line of running stitch worked as near to the edge as possible. A second row of stitching is worked $\frac{1}{4}$in *(6mm)* inside the first.

2 A piped edge is used on cushion or pillow covers and sometimes on baby quilts.

3 On coverlets, the backing material is cut slightly larger than the top. It is then turned over the top and hemmed down. Alternatively the edges are trimmed and bound with a bias strip cut from the same fabric as the top or from a contrasting material.

QUILTING PATTERNED FABRICS

Look for fabrics with an interesting pattern and quilt along the outlines. Beautiful remnants of fabric can be made into unusual personal accessories with this technique.

Nightdress Case

This pretty quilted case will solve the problem of where to store your nightie.

Materials required:

14in *(36cm)* dia. circle printed fabric
½yd *(45cm)* nylon fabric
¾yd *(69cm)* synthetic wadding
½yd *(45cm)* backing fabric
Fine sewing thread
2yd *(183cm)* bias binding.

To make the case

Cut two circles each from the nylon and the backing and three circles of wadding. Cut the circles 15in *(38cm)* in diameter. Lay one circle of wadding between one circle of nylon fabric and one of backing. Baste and then machine stitch or hand quilt the three circles together in the square diamond pattern. (Fig 1). This makes one side of the case.

Fig 1

Make the other side in the same way. Pin the remaining circle of wadding to the wrong side of the printed fabric. Quilt along all the lines of the design. This is best done by hand using running stitches but machine stitching can be used. Trim the wadding to the outline of the print pattern (see illustration of the nightgown case). Turn in the edges and baste. Baste the quilted patterned fabric to the quilted side of one case piece. Machine stitch around the edge of the patterned fabric thus stitching it to the case. Now seam the front and back of the case together. Use a French seam so that the raw edges are concealed. Seam about two thirds of the circumference of the case, leaving one third open. Finish this opening with bias binding.

Child's Quilted Coat

Quilting can be worked on almost any garment and many commercial paper patterns can be adapted to this technique. Here a pattern for a zipper fronted jacket for a young child, has been quilted for extra warmth. When using commercial patterns for quilting, cut side seams, shoulder seams, armholes and sleeve heads ½in *(1cm)* larger. This extra fabric will be taken up in the quilting.
Measurements: Size 6:
Chest 25in *(64cm)*; Waist 22in *(56cm)*; Back length 10½in *(26cm)*.
Fig 2 (4 squares = 1in *(2.5cm)*)

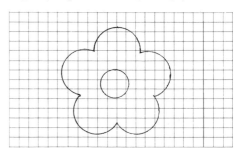

Materials required:
½yd *(45cm)* red cotton/wool blend
½yd *(45cm)* white synthetic fabric
½yd *(45cm)* synthetic wadding
½yd *(45cm)* muslin
Red sewing thread
White sewing thread.

To make the jacket

Cut out all pieces in both the outer and the lining fabric. Cut wadding and muslin from the pattern pieces for the fronts, back and sleeves. Cut out a template of the flower shape (see Fig 2) in stiff cardboard. Lay jacket fronts out side by side on a blanket and mark the flower shapes on the fronts so that the motifs are balanced on both pieces of fabric. Mark the back piece in the same way. Mark both sleeves, again so that they match. The collar and waistband are not marked for quilting. Mount wadding pieces onto muslin pieces. Baste the top pieces to the wadding. Hand quilt the lines of the design in white thread. When all quilting is completed, finish the garment according to the pattern instructions using red thread. Top stitch collar edge as shown.

Child's Quilt

A pretty washable quilt for a child to make from gingham, quilted in an easy square pattern. The frilled edge is stitched in before quilting. The stitching on the quilt illustrated (see page 78), was done by machine but could be stitched by hand.

Materials required:
1½yds *(135cm)* of 36in *(90cm)* cotton gingham ¾yd *(69cm)* of 36in *(90cm)* synthetic wadding
Fine sewing thread.

To make the quilt

Cut two pieces, top and backing from fabric 27in *(69cm)* by 19in *(47cm)*. These measurements include ½in *(1cm)* allowance. Cut and join pieces 4in *(10cm)* wide to make a strip 144in *(360cm)* long for a frill. Join strip into a circle. Baste the wadding to the wrong side of the base fabric piece. Fold the frill circle along the length and press the fold. Gather up the raw edges. Baste the raw edges to the raw edges of the base piece, on the right side, easing and gathering at the corners. Pin and baste the top piece to the bottom piece, right sides facing so that the frill is 'sandwiched' between. Stitch on the seam line on three sides and then on the fourth, leaving enough of the seam open to turn the quilt to the right side. Turn and close the seam by hand. Mark out the quilting pattern of squares 2½ x 2½in *(6 x 6cm)* 2in *(5cm)* in from frilled edge and quilt by machine stitching or by hand.

82

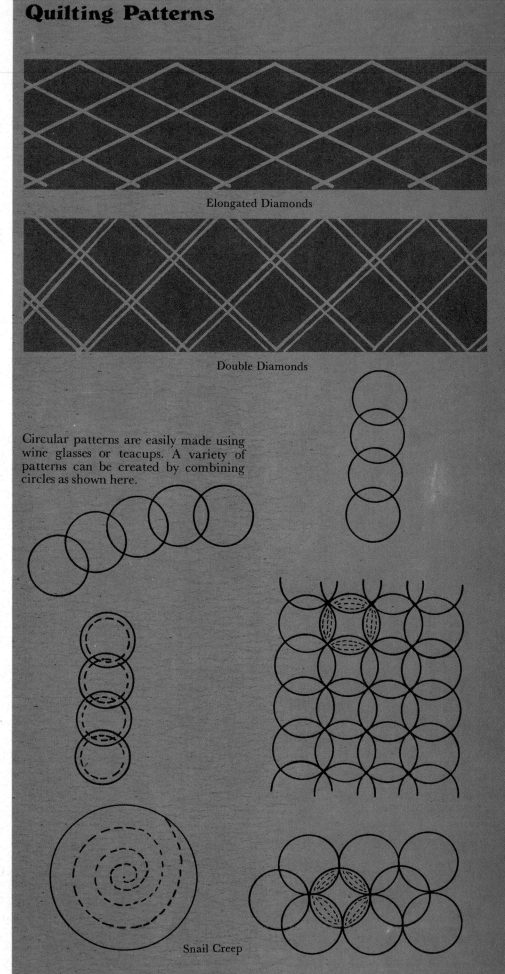

Quilting Patterns

Elongated Diamonds

Double Diamonds

Circular patterns are easily made using wine glasses or teacups. A variety of patterns can be created by combining circles as shown here.

Snail Creep

Here are some traditional quilting patterns. In every case the pattern outlines should be marked onto the fabric before stitching is begun. On the left are two patterns based on straight lines. The square diamond pattern, Fig 1, is on page 80. Use the patterns on this page same size or enlarge them. Mark only the outline on the fabric, the dotted lines are stitched while working.

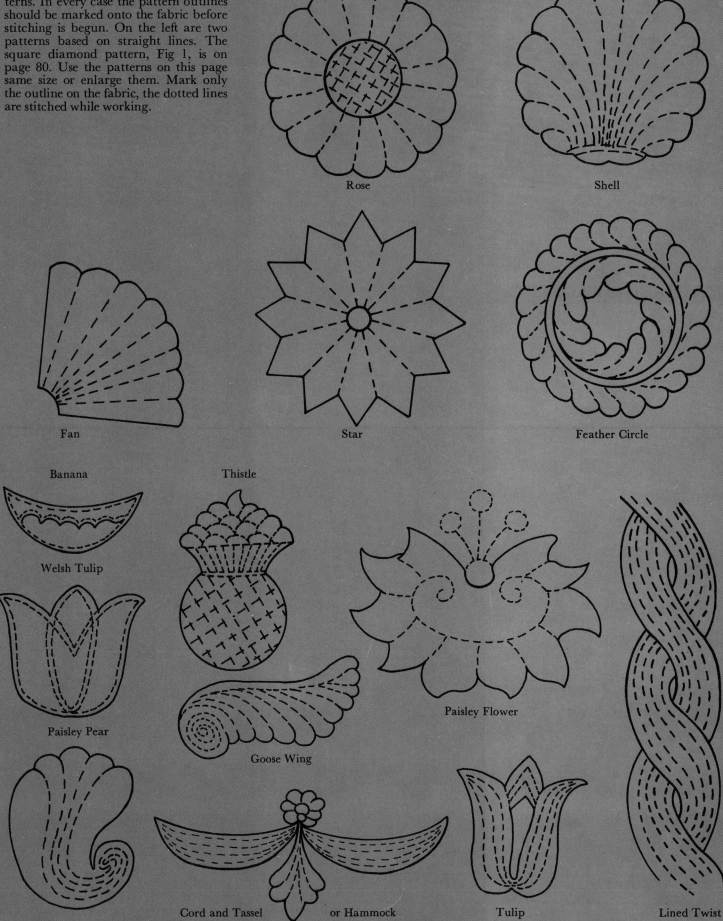

Rose

Shell

Fan

Star

Feather Circle

Banana

Thistle

Welsh Tulip

Paisley Pear

Goose Wing

Paisley Flower

Cord and Tassel   or Hammock   Tulip   Lined Twist

Festive Papercrafts

Here are a few new ideas for wrapping gifts to make them look really great! There are also designs for making novel greeting cards, and instructions for making a delightful nativity scene in cardboard, coloured paper and using two or three boxes.

DECORATING GIFT BOXES

Read illustrations right to left. Boxes 1–4 are illustrated on the opposite page, boxes 5–8 on this page. All diagrams are to scale 1 sq = $\frac{1}{2}$in *(1cm)*.

1 Wrap a square box in orange cartridge or construction paper. Make stars in foil by tracing the pattern (Fig 1) onto the wrong side of the paper. Fold on the dotted lines. Glue the short ends to make a star. Glue to the box.

2 Cover a cardboard tube with shiny black paper and leave one end open. Cut circles of silver foil and glue to the surface. Cut a piece of white crêpe paper 8in x 3in *(20cm x 8cm)*. Snip into one edge 2in *(5cm)* to make a fringe. Roll up and glue the uncut end of the crêpe paper into the open end of the tube.

3 Wrap a box in patterned silver foil. Fasten gift ribbon across the box diagonally with tape. Make a star shape in foil (Fig 2) and glue a large circle of coloured foil to the centre of the star.

4 Wrap a large square box in magenta crêpe paper. Decorate it with bands of gold ribbon and top with a large looped pompom made from strips of coloured foil. Fix loops together with staples.

5 Wrap a box in patterned silver foil and decorate it with little Christmas trees and a star. Cut the trees in green cartridge or construction paper (Fig 3). Cut circles of coloured paper for the decorations. Make a gold star (Fig 1) in foil, folding on the dotted lines and glueing the short ends.

6 Cover a cylindrical box in silver foil and make scalloped collars for both ends in blue foil. Use the pattern (Fig 4) to cut scallops, extending the pattern to fit the circumference of the box. Make a loop in pink ribbon.

7 Here is a beautiful wrap using coloured cartridge or construction papers. Wrap the box in silver foil and cut the shapes (Fig 5) in bright colours and mount them on cardboard. Cut out the cardboard shapes. Tie a length of ribbon around the middle of the box and slip the shapes under the ribbon.

8 Wrap a cylindrical box in a striped paper so that the stripes run in a spiral. Make a water lily in foil to go on top. Glue two sheets of foil together, blue on one side and a contrasting colour on the other. Cut out three 'petals' (Fig 6) and fold on the dotted lines. Glue the largest flower to the box first, then the next and finally the smallest. Top the flower with a gold glass ball.

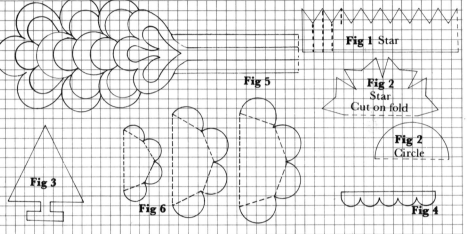

Fig 1 Star
Fig 5
Fig 2 Star Cut on fold
Fig 2 Circle
Fig 3
Fig 6
Fig 4

Greetings Cards

It is much more fun to receive bright original home-made cards – and more fun to make them too. The basic card is a single fold in stiff white paper. The designs use a variety of novelty papers and trims. All diagrams are to scale 1sq equals $\frac{1}{2}$in *(1cm)*.

Fruit tree

Enlarge the pattern from Fig 7. Cut the paper 17in x 11$\frac{1}{2}$in *(43cm x 25cm)*. Fold in half across the width. Cut out the tree shape in green felt and glue it to the card. Cut out the shape folded leaving the edge marked 'fold' uncut. Cut out the fruits in coloured paper and glue to the tree. (Illustrated below).

Hello twins

Cut a piece of white paper 22in x 6$\frac{1}{2}$in *(56cm x 1cm)*. Fold across the middle. Enlarge the pattern as in Fig 8. Trace the various shapes on coloured papers.

feathers are silver foil and the heart is pink foil. Cut card round wheels.

Snowman

Cut the paper 24in x 6in *(61cm x 15cm)*. Fold across the width. Enlarge the design (Fig 11). Cut the background in blue paper and the hat in black. Cut a pink face and red nose. Glue a piece of absorbent cotton wool to the card for the snow body. Cut small black squares for the eyes. Cut out the card leaving the fold at hat top intact. (Illustrated on page 85).

Bottle and trumpet

This card might be used for a party announcement. Cut the paper 16in x 8in *(41cm x 20cm)* and fold. Enlarge the design (Fig 12) and cut the shapes in foil, glue to card. (Illustrated left).

Cannon and hearts

An unusual card for an engagement announcement. Cut the paper 34in x 8in *(86cm x 20cm)* and fold. Enlarge the design (Fig 13) and cut the shapes in foil. (Illustrated left).

Soldier

Cut the paper 18in x 9in *(46cm x 23cm)*. Fold. Enlarge the design (Fig 14). Trace off the parts of the design and cut in coloured paper and foil. Mount the pieces against the folded edge. Trim the card to fit exactly when completed. (Illustrated left).

Top hat and flower

Cut the paper 12in x 14in *(30cm x 36cm)*. Fold. Enlarge the design (Fig 15). Cut

Cut the girl's collar in foil. Draw in the eyes and mouth in felt-tip pen. Glue the faces down first, the hair next and add cheeks, bows and collars last. The fold is on left. (Illustrated on page 85).

Rocking horse

This card will stand up and rock! Cut a piece of paper 17in x 8½in *(43cm x 22cm)*. Fold across the middle. Enlarge the design (Fig 9). Trace the shapes of the design in coloured papers and mount them onto the card. Glue the blue rock-

ing horse down first and then add reins, mane, saddle and tail. Cut out the rocker shape leaving the fold intact.

Chick on wheels

This would make a delightful Eas card. The card stands up on its wheels. Cut a piece of paper 23in x 7in *(58cm x 18cm)*. Fold across the width. Enlarge the design (Fig 10) and cut out the chick shape in flocked paper. Cut the wheels, wings, beak and tail in red and green felt and glue to card. The ribbon and

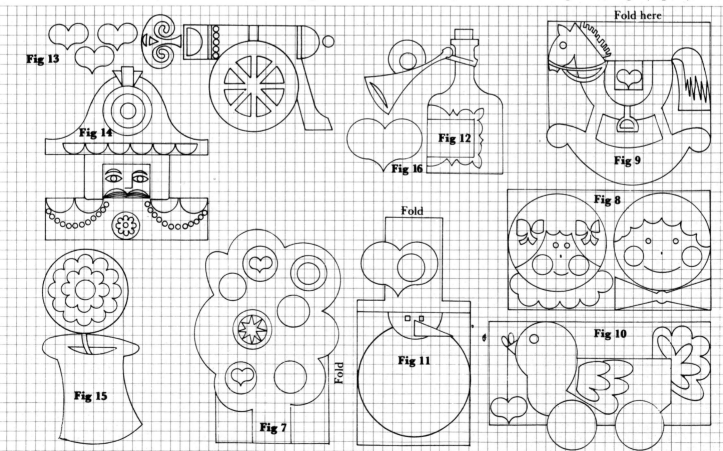

Fig 13

Fig 14

Fig 12

Fig 16

Fold here

Fig 9

Fig 8

Fold

Fig 11

Fold

Fig 15

Fig 7

Fig 10

out the hat in black paper and the flower in foil. (Illustrated left).

Nativity Scene

Here is a charming nativity scene to make in coloured paper and cardboard. The overall size of the set is 13in *(33cm)* and the height of the figures is approximately 9in *(23cm)*.

Materials required:
Stiff cardboard
Wood patterned paper
Cartridge or construction paper in assorted colours
Crêpe paper in blue and green
Gold foil
All-purpose clear drying adhesive.

To make the backdrop
Enlarge the design to scale, one square equalling ½in *(1cm)*. Trace the outline down onto stiff cardboard. The design shows only half the stable. Reverse the design for the second half and match at centre. Draw out the design again on wood patterned paper and draw the windows again on black paper. Cut out the windows and glue to the wood paper. Mount the wood paper on the cardboard and trim the edges. Score and fold on the dotted lines so that the back-drop stands firmly.

To make the figures
Each of the figures has a stand (D below). Enlarge the designs for the figures and trace onto stiff cardboard. Trace the design again and cut out the garments,

beards, faces etc., in coloured paper. Mount the shapes on the cardboard. Cut the figure out of the cardboard when completed. Cut out the stands in stiff cardboard and glue to the base of the figures. Fold on the dotted line so that the figure stands up.
Cut out and make the animals in the same way.
Cut out and make the crib.

Trees and grass
Only half of the palm tree is given. Reverse the pattern for the second half

and match at centre. Cut out and make the grass and palm tree as for the figures and animals.

To arrange the set
Line a big cardboard box with paper. Pleat blue crêpe paper for the sky and arrange green crêpe paper for the foreground. Position two long cardboard boxes under the green crêpe paper to make steps for the figures to stand on, so that each of them can be seen clearly. Cut out the star in yellow paper and gold foil and glue to the sky over the crib.

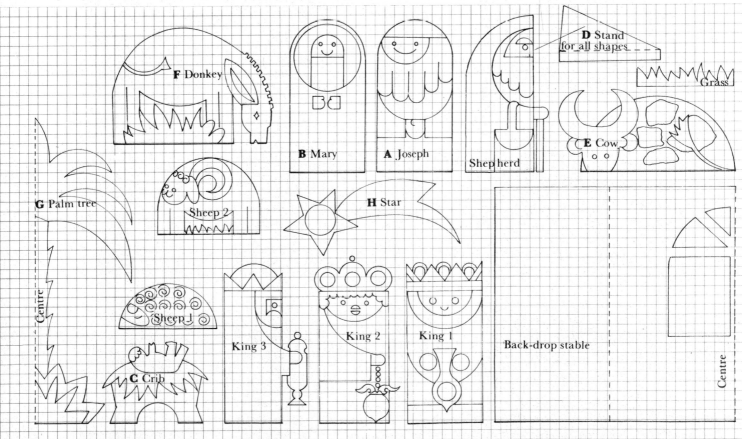

Candlemaking

Candles have been a source of light for thousands of years. Until paraffin was developed beeswax and tallow were used for this vital craft. In recent years, candlemaking has become a popular home handicraft and one which is so simple that even children can do it, as long as there is some adult supervision. Complete kits of all the basic materials are available at craft shops. Some include pre-formed moulds which enable even a beginner to make professional-looking candles.

Left to right: hexagonal candle; two marbled candles; appliquéd candle; rose-patterned pink candle; chunk candle cut back to show colours; tall blue chunk candle; purple bull's-eye candle; marbled candle in orange and yellow; red petalled candle, petals fixed to candle separately with hot wax; balloon candle on a glass stand.

Materials required:

Wax A fully refined paraffin wax with a melting temperature of 56°–60°C (135°–140°F) is recommended for candle-making. This is usually sold in solid blocks ranging in colour from cream to white. Weigh the wax and melt it slowly in a double boiler or in a saucepan over hot water. The wax is at the correct temperature for pouring at about 82°C (180°F).

Stearin This is a flaky wax substance which allows dyes to dissolve readily with perfect colour suspension and also helps to release the finished candle from its mould. Stearin is added to melted wax in a proportion of 1:10 (i.e. 1lb *(0.45kg)* of stearin to 10lb *(4.54kg)* of wax). Melt the stearin in another double boiler or saucepan and sprinkle the dye powder onto it. Stir the mixture gently until the dye is completely dissolved. Add the dissolved dye to the melted wax and raise the temperature gently to 82°C (180°F).

Dyes Wax dyes used for candlemaking are available in both powder and solid form. Powder dyes are very concentrated and a pinch is sufficient for 1pt *(0.571 litres)* of liquid wax. Wax crayons can be used for colouring candles but they are not recommended because they do not dissolve as readily and the pigment can clog the candle wick.

Perfumes Oil soluble perfume can be added to the wax after the colour for a scented candle. Use the oils sparingly for a delicately perfumed candle.

Wicks Candle wick is woven of bleached cotton thread and graded to ½in *(1cm)* sizes to burn a specified area of wax. Thus, a 2in *(5cm)* wick is used for a 2in.

(5cm) diameter candle. It is important to use the correct size of wick or the candle will not burn satisfactorily.
Mould Seal – Plasticine or modelling clay is used to secure the wick in the mould.

DIPPED CANDLES

Dipping candles is the oldest – and simplest – method of candlemaking. No pouring of melted wax is involved and the only equipment needed is a container slightly deeper than the intended length of candle. Fill the container with paraffin wax and melt in a double boiler to a temperature of 82°C (180°F). Add dye if the candle is to be coloured throughout. It is important to maintain the wax at the correct temperature. Tie the wick to a dowel and dip the length of the wick into the wax. Repeat at 30 second intervals as it takes about 30 seconds for the candle to cool off. Continue until the candle is as thick as required. Hang up the finished candle to harden. Cut the wick from the dowel and trim to $\frac{1}{4}$in *(6mm)*.

A variety of hand-moulded candle shapes can be made from dipped candles. While the candle wax is still malleable, the candles can be rolled in the hands to make apple and pear shapes or pinched between the fingers to make fantasy shaped candles.

COLOUR DIPPED CANDLES

White dipped candles can be given an outer coating of colour, which gives them a lustrous finish and greater translucency. A greater intensity of colour is required in the overdipping mixture to counteract the whiteness of the candle beneath. Here is another way to give candles a colour coating. Float a 2in *(10cm)* layer of melted, coloured wax on water which has been heated to 82°C *(180°F)*. Dip the candle through the coloured wax layer into the water and then pull out slowly. The candle will pick up some of the colour. Continue the process until the desired depth of colour is achieved. This method is more economical as it is only necessary to dye a small amount of wax. It is important that the temperature of the wax be maintained. If it is too cool the colour will flake off, if too hot, very little colour will be picked up on the candle.

DIPPED PINCHED CANDLES

Put 4oz *(113g)* of paraffin wax into the double boiler and melt slowly until dissolved. Stearin is not needed for this type of candle. Cool the melted wax slowly until it forms a 'rubbery' sheet in the pan. Remove the wax and roll into a ball. Push a knitting needle through the centre. Thread the wick through and tie the wick to a small nail so that the ball is supported on its wick. Dip the ball in hot wax again and again, pinching and moulding the shape as the ball grows

in size. Finally, dip the candle in coloured wax to give a bright lustrous finish.

ONE COLOUR CANDLE

One-colour casting is the term used for the technique of making candles in a mould. Many household utensils and containers such as plastic tubs, milk cartons and soup cans, can be used for improvised moulds, but remember that the finished candle must be removable from the mould and therefore the neck cannot be narrower than the base unless you plan to break the mould to remove the candle. To judge the amount of melted wax required for the chosen mould, fill it with water and then pour the water into the saucepan in which the wax will be melted. Remember to dry both the mould and the pan before using them. When melting the wax, the level should be a little higher in the pan than that of the water because the wax contracts a little as it sets. Make a small hole in the bottom of the mould. Improvised plastic moulds, such as yoghurt or cottage cheese containers, can be pierced with a heated knitting needle or wire. Select the wick according to the diameter of the candle. Dip it into the melted wax and let it cool. Tie one end to a small stick or straw slightly longer than the diameter of the mould and lay the stick across the top. Thread the other end through the hole in the bottom of the mould. Pull it taut so that the wick is exactly in the centre of the mould. Secure the bottom end of the wick with Plasticine or modelling clay. Make sure that the sealing substance does not get onto the wick inside the mould or this may clog the wick preventing the candle from burning. Carefully pour the prepared wax into the mould. After one minute, tap the mould sharply once or twice to release any air bubbles. The finish of the candle will be improved if the mould is immersed in cold water with the water level with the level of the wax. The mould will probably have to be weighted to hold it down in the water. After about 30 minutes, a well will form around the wick. Break through the surface with a knitting needle. After one hour, remove the mould from the water bath. Fill the well with more wax, heated to 93°C *(200°F)*. It will be necessary to do this more than once. Be careful not to overfill the well as wax could run down the side of the candle which will by now have shrunk away from the sides of the mould. When the wax has set completely, slip the candle out of the mould, or break the mould to remove the candle.

FLEXIBLE MOULDS

Flexible moulds made of rubber or plastic are available in a variety of designs and enable the candlemaker to make an embossed candle very easily. The only

additional equipment required is a mould stand which can be purchased or improvised. The basic technique used for casting is the same but rubber moulds can be damaged by stearin. Therefore, if this type of mould is being used, reduce the amount of stearin in the mixture to 1:100. Flexible moulds cannot be used in a cooling bath because the pressure of the water tends to distort the mould. It is better to cool the wax with an electric fan. Thread the wick through the mould with a wicking needle and tie it to the wick rod. Pull the wick taut and seal off. Support the mould on a mould stand. The wick must be kept in a central position all the time. Gently heat the wax to 99°C *(210°F)* and then set it aside until it has cooled down to 93°C *(200°F)*. Carefully pour the melted wax into the mould. The mould must be supported because it becomes very floppy when warm. As the wax is poured, tilt the mould slightly and let some of the wax run down the outside. This lessens the turbulence and reduces the possibility of air bubbles forming. Slightly overfill the mould because this helps to prevent a ridge from forming when topping up. After the mould is filled, wait two minutes and then tap it all over to release air bubbles. Top up the well. Leave the candle to set. Remove the mould from the candle by lubricating the outside with detergent liquid and peeling the mould back on itself. Trim the wick on the base. Melt off the shoulder flange.

FINISHING EMBOSSED CANDLES

Mix poster paint with a little detergent liquid. Be sparing with the detergent or the paint will not dry. Paint all over the embossed surface. When dry, rub off the excess with a damp cloth. Buff with a dry, soft cloth.

METAL MOULDS

Metal candle moulds can be purchased from craft shops and are excellent because the metal enables the wax to cool quickly, thus producing a smooth, finished surface. Metal moulds can be stood in a cooling bath of water without danger of the mould distorting.

LAYERED CANDLES

Prepare the wax in exactly the same way as for one-colour casting. Partially fill the mould and leave it to set until the surface is 'rubbery' and yields to the touch. Pour in the next layer, tapping the sides of the mould to remove air bubbles. Continue in layers as desired until the mould is full.

An interesting effect can be achieved by tilting the mould at different angles and letting the layers set on diagonals. It is difficult to do this when cooling the mould in water and it may be better to allow the candle to cool naturally.

CHUNK CANDLES

A variety of techniques can be employed to produce chunk candles. The simplest way is to fill a mould with pieces of hardened wax in different colours and then pour white or coloured wax heated to 93°C *(200°F)* over the chunks. The mould should be immersed in a cooling bath as soon as possible so that the colours do not merge. The candle can be carved with a knife after it has set.

MARBLE FINISH

The marbled candles were made by whipping semi-set wax with a fork and then packing into a mould. Several different colours can be used. This type of candle cools quickly and does not need topping up.

APPLIQUED CANDLES

Small pieces of coloured wax can be used to decorate the surface of a finished candle by first placing a hot knife against the candle and then holding the decoration against the surface until the softened wax has set. The candle with the little circles on the surface was made by rolling balls of coloured wax and then pressing them into discs. The glossy finish was achieved by dipping the candle twice into undyed wax heated to 220°F *(104°C)* at 30 second intervals. This produces a finish and secures the discs.

BALLOON CANDLE

Balloon mould candles are fairly difficult to make but are very rewarding. Partly fill a round balloon with cold water until the diameter of the balloon is about 3in *(7.5cm)*. Heat wax to 170°F *(80°C)* and dip the balloon in the wax about ten times, allowing a 30 second interval between each dipping so that the coats harden. When the last coat has hardened, pour the water out carefully and pull the balloon itself away from the wax coating. Great care must be taken at this stage because the wax shell is very fragile. Prepare a small quantity of stearin and dye. When the stearin has melted, add about the same quantity of wax to the mixture. The colour must be of very strong intensity. Spoon a small quantity into the shell and swirl the shell around, as when swirling brandy in a wine glass. Pour out any wax that has not adhered to the inside of the shell. It is important to pour out the surplus quite quickly because if the hot wax remains inside the thin shell, it could distort the shape. The whole process must be worked rapidly because even a finger tip can distort the fragile wax shell. Several colours can be added to the design. Now fill the shell with wax. Heat wax to 180°F *(99°C)* and spoon in the wax, one teaspoon at a time, swirling the wax to coat the inside of the shell every time. Continue, working one teaspoon of wax at a time until a ½in *(1cm)*

Dipped candles made in pairs on lengths of wick and cut apart when hardened.

thick wall has been built up. Once this shell is quite hard, it can be rested on a support and small quantities of wax poured in. When the shell wall is quite thick and the candle about three-quarters finished, make a hole for the wick with a heated knitting needle. Insert the wick and top up the candle.

WICKING UP

If the candle is of the type which necessitates the wick being added after the candle is finished, there are two methods of doing this. A hole can be made in the candle, the wick inserted and then the hole filled with melted wax. Alternatively, push a hot knitting needle or skewer into the candle while it is still soft, leaving it there until the candle has

almost set. The wick is then inserted with a wicking needle and the hole topped up with melted wax.

TECHNIQUES FOR DIFFERENT EFFECTS

Make a bulls-eye candle by preparing a dipped candle with different coloured layers. Cut the candle into rounds about ½in *(1cm)* thick. Pour a little hot wax into a plastic mould and swirl the mould to coat the inside surface. Press the rounds into the wax and push a small pin through the outside wall of the mould to hold the rounds in place. Fill the mould in the usual way. When the candle is set, remove the pins and the mould and smooth over all blemishes. Polish candle finally with a little white spirit.

Macrame

Macramé – the art of creative knotting – is one of the most ancient crafts known to man. It was used by the ancient Egyptians, Chinese, Maoris and Peruvians, and the tradition of magical, supernatural potency in particular knots has been handed down by sailors through the ages. The origin of the word is a mystery: the Arabic 'migramah' means 'protection or headcovering', while the Turkish 'makrama' is a decoratively fringed napkin. Whatever its origin, macramé lacework was extremely delicate in material

and effect and was well established in 13th-century Arabia, from where it was carried by the Moors to Italy. Here the craft flourished during the Middle Ages. Interest in macramé waned but revived in a more robust but equally attractive form in the late 19th and early 20th century in and around Turin and Genoa. It is now one of Italy's most popular traditional crafts, and seems to be enjoying a new popularity around the world and is used to make a variety of home and fashion accessories.

MATERIALS AND EQUIPMENT

Any string can be used to work macramé, depending on the article being made and the finished result required. The most successful are the smooth, firm twines which knot easily, do not fray and do not slip. Ordinary string is one of the best—and cheapest—materials of all. If a crisp finish is required with the knotting pattern clearly defined, then it is essential that a firm material such as string, linen thread, nylon twine or any form of cotton cord is used. On the other hand if an all-over textural effect is preferred, then any knitting or crochet yarn, fine or thick, can be used. Rug wool is excellent for it is more substantial than ordinary knitting wool and makes up quickly.

Few pieces of equipment are necessary but a convenient-sized surface to work on is essential for small items. A piece of wood can be used or a pillow pad, a sheet of cork or even several thicknesses of cardboard. If using a board, it is a good idea to "pad" it first with a sheet of foam or even with a folded-up old towel.

As well as a working surface and a suitable string, some pins, scissors and a tape measure are required.

PREPARING THE CORD

Before beginning to knot, the cord must be cut into suitable lengths, and mounted onto another length of cord, known as the holding cord. This is called "setting on" or mounting cords. The holding cord is sometimes used as part of the finished design—for instance, as a handle for a bag—or it can even be withdrawn after knotting is complete.

It is not always easy to join in new string in mid-knotting so it is important that working lengths are cut long enough for the complete design. As a very general guide, if you are setting on each cord double, then the cord should be cut to eight times the length required. For instance, if you are making a braid to measure 6in *(15cm)*, then cut each cord 48in *(1.22m)* long. If setting on cords singly, then they should be cut to four times the finished length required.

HOW TO SET ON CORDS

Cut a holding cord of about 12in *(30cm)* and 10 lengths of string each 1yd *(90cm)* long. Tie a knot near one end of the holding cord by taking the end over and around itself and through the loop formed. This is known as an overhand knot. Pin the cord through this knot to the working surface near the top left-hand corner. Stretch the cord horizontally across the working surface, tie a similar overhand knot near the other end of the cord and pin it to the working surface (Fig 1).

Now take the first working cord, double it and insert the looped end under the holding cord from top to bottom. Bring the loose ends down over the holding

Fig 1

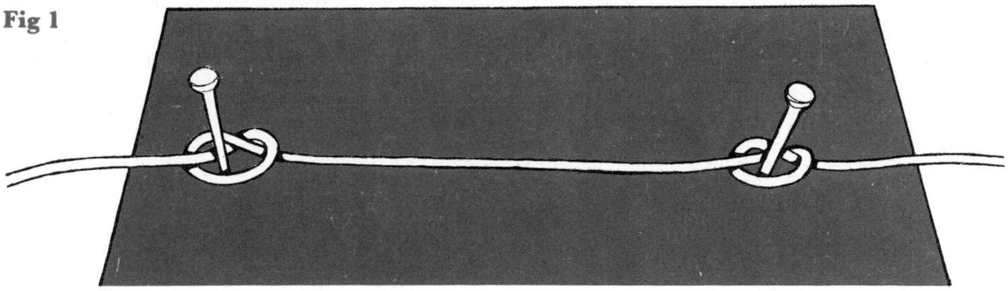

Fig 2

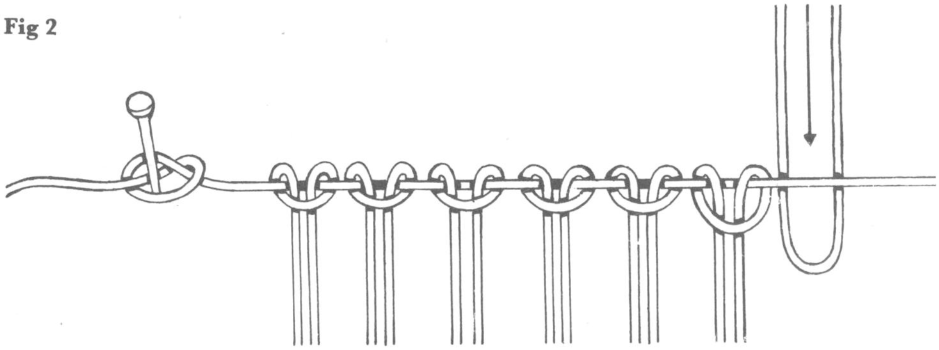

Fig 3 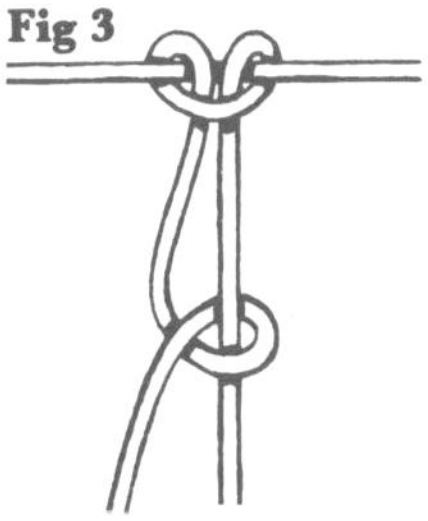 **Fig 4** 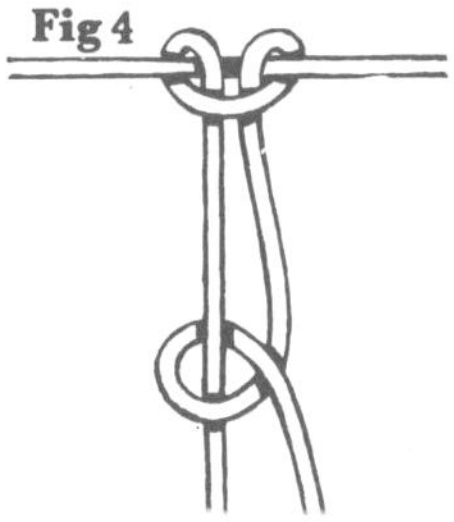 **Fig 5**  **Fig 6**

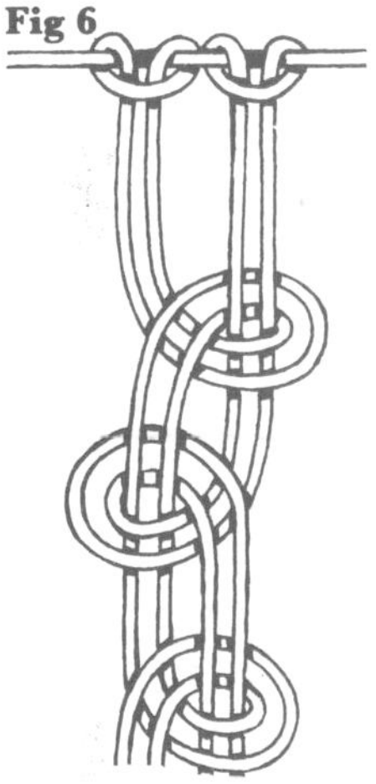

Fig 1 Holding cord pinned down.
Fig 2 Lark's Head knots mounted on holding cord.
Fig 3 Half hitch knots tied from left.
Fig 4 Half hitch knots tied from right.
Fig 5 Single alternate half hitch chain.
Fig 6 Double alternate half hitch chain.

cord and through the loop. Draw tight. This is sometimes called a Lark's Head Knot. Repeat with each length of cord, positioning each doubled set-on cord close to the previous one. When the mounting is complete there will be 20 lengths of string hanging vertically from the holding cord, each measuring a little under 18in *(46cm)* (Fig 2).

THE BASIC KNOTS

Half hitch Work on the first two cords. To tie a half hitch from the left, hold right-hand cord taut, bring cord 1 in front of it then up and behind it from right to left. Bring through the loop formed. Draw tight (Fig 3). To tie a half hitch from the right, reverse the knotting procedure: hold left-hand cord taut, and bring right-hand cord in front of it, then up and under it from left to right, and down through loop formed. Draw tight (Fig 4). This uses cords 3 and 4.

Work on cords 5 and 6: tie a half hitch from the left, then tie a half hitch from the right. Continue in this way, alternating the direction of the knot each time, and drawing each knot close to the previous one. This forms a chain of knots

known as the single alternate half hitch chain (Fig 5).

Work on cords 7, 8, 9 and 10. Tie half hitches alternately from the left and right, as for the single alternate half hitch chain, but this time use cords double, so first knot is tied with cords 7 and 8 over 9 and 10; the second knot is tied with cords 9 and 10 over 7 and 8. Continue in this way to form a chain of knots. This is known as the double alternate half hitch chain (Fig 6).

The flat or square knot The flat or square knot which is the second basic knot is tied in two parts as follows: work on cords 11, 12, 13 and 14. Hold cords 12 and 13 taut, take cord 11 under them and over 14. Take cord 14 over 12 and 13 and under 11. (Fig. 7) Draw tight. This is the first half of the knot and is known as the half knot. If the half knot is tied continuously this produces an attractive twisted spiral of knots sometimes called a sinnet (Fig 15). To complete the knot, still keeping 12 and 13 taut, bring cord 11 back under 12 and 13 and over 14. Take cord 14 over 12 and 13 and under 11. Draw tight (Fig 8). Continue in this way to tie flat knots one below the other to form a chain. This is

93

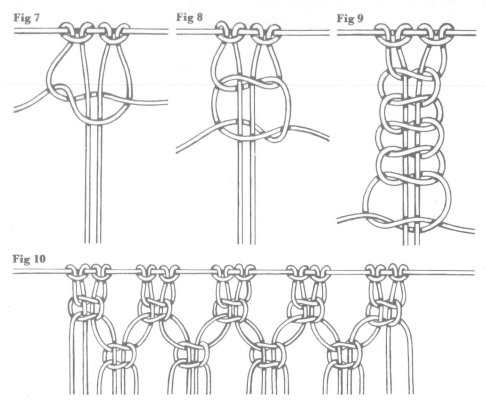

Fig 7   Fig 8   Fig 9

Fig 10

Fig 7 The half knot. **Fig 8** The flat knot completed. **Fig 9** Chain of flat knots. **Fig 10** Alternate flat knot pattern. **Fig 11** Leader cord in position. **Fig 12** Double half hitch cording. **Fig 13** Horizontal cording. **Fig 14** Diagonal cording.

Fig 15 Sinnet formed by continuous half knots. **Fig 16** Double half hitch knot. **Fig 17** Overhand knot. **Figs 18, 19** Centre cords pulled over three knots and through knot to make button.

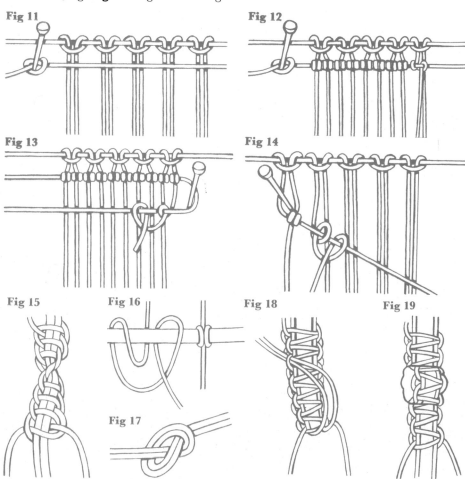

Fig 11   Fig 12

Fig 13   Fig 14

Fig 15   Fig 16   Fig 18   Fig 19

Fig 17

often known as a Solomon's bar (Fig 9).

The alternate flat knot pattern This pattern occurs frequently in all forms of macramé work, and is the one most often used to form a fabric. It is worked on any number of knotting cords, provided the total number is a multiple of 4. Begin by tying knots with each group of four cords to the end of the row. In the second row, leave the first two cords unworked, then tie flat knots with each group of four cords, to the final two cords in the row, leave these two cords unworked. The third row is the same as the first, and the fourth row is the same as the second. Continue in this way to build up a fabric. By tying knots and rows close together a denser fabric is created; space out knots and rows and it will result in an open-work lacy fabric (Fig 10).

Cording This is a useful macramé technique and can be used to create solid fabrics, to "draw" outlines and figures, and to shape edges of work. It is based on the half hitch knot.

To practise cording on mounted cords, cut a new length of cord, approximately 1yd (*90cm*) long. Tie an overhand knot near one end of it, and pin it to the working surface just to the left of working cords, lying horizontally across working cords. This is known as a leader or anchor cord as the knots are all tied onto it. Therefore it is essential that it is always kept taut. If necessary pin it to the working surface at the opposite side to keep it taut while working (Fig 11).

Now beginning with cord 1, take it up and over leader, and then down behind it, bringing end out of the left of the loop formed. Repeat sequence exactly with the same cord—this means two half hitches have been tied, or—as is more usually known—a double half hitch. Repeat with every cord along the row, pushing each half hitch as it is tied close to the previous one. At the end of the row there should be a row of tiny loops along the leader cord lying neatly and closely against each other (Fig 12).

To work the next row, place a pin in working surface close to the end of the first row, take leader around the pin and

place it horizontally across working cords, this time from right to left. Now tie double half hitches with each cord in turn, but this time, because of working from right to left, as each half hitch is tied the cord end is brought down to the right of the loop formed. This is known as horizontal cording (Fig 13).

Diagonal cording is worked in a similar way, except leader cord is placed at an angle across working cords. The leader for horizontal or diagonal cording may be a separate cord, as shown, or it can be one of the mounted cords (Fig 14).

Dog Lead

Macramé is an ideal medium for making dog collars and leads as it produces a strong fabric which cannot snap and wears well. The quantity of twine given will make a lead approximately 15in (38cm) long.

Materials required:
13½yd (12.30m) red macramé twine
1 clip for dog lead.

To make the lead

Cut two threads 16ft (4.88m) long. Cut two threads 4ft (1.22m) long. Set these cords onto the clip as shown in Fig 2, setting on first one long thread, then two short. Now work four flat knots (Figs 8 and 9) using the two long threads on either side over the central four short threads.

*Leave an unworked portion of 1in (2.5cm) and then work one flat knot. Push this knot up to lie against previous knots. This will form a picot.

Make three more flat knots. **

Repeat from * to ** three times to make four picots in all.

Leave an unworked portion of 2in (5cm) and work 14 more flat knots. This should bring the work to within 3in (8cm) of the end of the short threads. Fold the lead so that these short ends lie over the 2in (5cm) gap. With the outside threads, work four flat knots over all the cords. This makes the hand loop. Trim short ends close to the last knot and secure with a dab of clear adhesive. Glue down the last four ends behind the flat knots.

Hanging Pot Holder

Macramé plant holders look fresh and summery whether used indoors, on a patio or in the garden. This one hangs to a depth of 54in (37cm).

Materials required:
59yd (54m) cotton string, macramé twine or piping cord
1 2in (5cm) wooden or brass ring
Bowl or flowerpot 9in (23cm) diameter

To make the plant holder

Cut four cords 8yd (7.32m) long. Fold in half and bind together 2in (5cm) from the loop end for 1½in (4cm).

Starting 2in (5cm) down, work 12 half knots (Fig 7) treating each pair of cords as one cord. This will form a spiral as in Fig 15 which will measure approximately 2½in (6cm).

Cut four new lengths of cord 20ft (6.10m) long. Fold in half and set onto the ring with Lark's Head Knots (Fig 2).

Between each Lark's Head, attach two cords of the original work to the ring leaving 2in (5cm) unworked below the spiral. Attach these with a double half hitch (Fig 16).

Then with each pair of cords, make an overhand knot close underneath the ring to hold the cords in place (Fig 17).

Using two cords from Lark's Head's and two from the double half hitches, work one flat knot 1in (2.5cm) down from the ring. Repeat on all four sets to make four flat knots in all. (See illustration this page).

*Leave unworked portion ½in (1cm) Taking two cords from each flat knot, work another flat knot. Repeat all around to make four knots in all. **

Repeat from * to ** once again.

Leave unworked portion 2in *(5cm)* and make another 2½in *(6cm)* spiral.

Leave unworked portion of 2in *(5cm)*. Work five flat knots. Take centre two cords back over last three knots and take through the knot itself (Fig 18). Pull threads down to make a "button". Make two flat knots underneath to hold "button" in place (Fig 19).

Leave unworked portion of 1in *(2.5cm)*. Take centre threads of each set to outside and work one flat knot. Repeat until five flat knots have been worked on each sinnet.

From this point the net which will hold the pot is worked. Leave an unworked portion of 3in *(8cm)*. Take two cords from two adjacent sinnets and on these four work two flat knots. Repeat all around to make four flat knots in all.

*Leave unworked portion of 2½in *(6.5cm)*. With two cords from each group, work two more flat knots all around.**

Repeat from * to **.

Leave unworked portion of 1½in *(4cm)*. Work two flat knots all around.

*Leave unworked portion of 1in *(2.5cm)*. Work one flat knot all around.**

Repeat from * to **

A gradually narrowing net has been formed which will hold the pot firmly in position. Leave unworked portion of 1in *(2.5cm)*. Take one cord as a leader. Hold this horizontally and work a new row of cording all around (Figs 11, 12, 13). Take the third thread from the leader and work a second row of cording. Take any thread as leader and work a row of diagonal cording, from left to right (Fig 14).

With the next thread as leader, work diagonal cording. Again take any thread, work horizontal cording. Repeat.

Cut all cords to about 8in *(20cm)* and knot the end. Fray the cut ends.

Fig 21

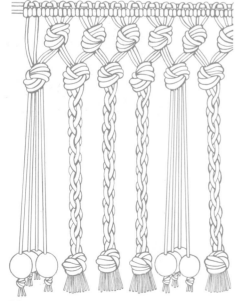

Fig 20 Working a braid with four threads. **Fig 21** Detail of bag fringe.

Fig 20

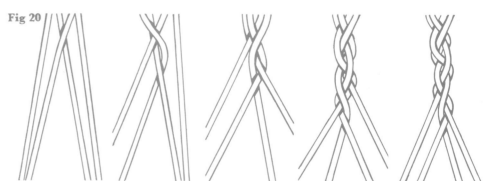

Fringed Bag

The beautiful fringed bag is made of a textured furnishing fabric. Choose the nylon twine in a colour to match the fabric. The quantities given will make a fringe 18in (46cm) wide and 7in (18cm) deep.

Materials required:
70yd (64m) spun nylon twine
Large wooden or glass beads

To make the fringe
The fringe can be made to any width as long as the numbers of ends on the foundation cord is divisible by 4. The number of ends in each repeat is 16.
Cut each cord 32in (80cm) long. Set the cords onto a holding cord (Figs 1 and 2), with reversed Lark's Head Knots so that the bar of the knot is on the wrong side of the work. Using an extra cord as leader, make a row of double half hitch knots (Fig 16).
Leave the two cords on the left free. Work the next four cords into an overhand knot, pulling the knot to lie evenly. Continue knotting each group of four. There will be two free cords at the end. Take four cords on the left and make overhand knot. Continue to the right.
Leave first group of four cords free. Make a braid with the next group of four cords (Fig 20). Finish braid with knot. Repeat on next two groups of four threads. Knot a bead onto each of the unbraided cords, making sure that they lie level with the knotted ends of the cords. (See Fig 21).
Repeat on all groups so that the fringe consists of one group of beaded threads followed by three braids then a group of beaded threads again and so on.

Finishing
Weave the ends of the foundation cord back into the work. Stitch the fringe to the bag with small hemming stitches.

Wall Sampler

Work this attractive wall hanging as a sampler to practise macramé knots and techniques. It measures approximately 22in (56cm) long, excluding the fringe, and 10in (25cm) wide.

Materials required:
Sturdy parcel string
Assorted glass and china beads

To make the wall hanging
Cut 22 cords, each 16ft (4.88m) plus length of fringe required. Set these onto a holding cord of about 24in (.60cm).
With cord on far left as leader, work a row of horizontal cording across all cords.

1st pattern panel With first four cords, work a chain of four flat knots. Work on next group of eight cords: with cord 1 as leader slanting down to the right, work diagonal cording over it with cords 2, 3 and 4. Similarly slant cord 8 down to the left and work diagonal cording over it with cords 7, 6 and 5. Link the two leaders at this central point by looping one around the other. Cord 1 now continues as leader and is slanted down to the left. Work diagonal cording slanting down to the right with cords 5, 6 and 7 over cord 8.
With next four cords, work a chain of four flat knots. Work on next group of six cords: work three rows of diagonal cording slanting down the left, each row just below the previous one. First row will have cord 4 as leader, and cords 3, 2 and 1 will be knotted over it. In the second row, cord 5 is leader, and cords 3, 2, 1 and 4 are knotting cords. In the third row, cord 6 is leader, and cords 3, 2, 1, 4 and 5 are knotting cords.
Now complete remainder of pattern panel to correspond with section already worked, reversing direction of triple row cording motif.
Divider row: With cord on far left as leader, work a row of horizontal cording across all cords.
2nd pattern panel Work in alternate flat knot pattern for seven rows. After the first row, drop two cords on each row at outside edges. After the third row, leave centre four cords unworked, then drop four further cords in the centre with each subsequent row, so that a 'W' shape of alternate flat knot pattern is created. Final row should have only two flat knots in it – one knot in each tip of the 'W'.
With cord on far left as leader and slanting down to the right, work diagonal cording over it with all cords coming from left-hand side of the 'W'.
Similarly work a row of diagonal cording down the right-hand side of the 'W', using cord on far right of work as leader. Work rows of diagonal cording in a similar way down each of the inside edges of the 'W', using left-hand central cord as leader for left-hand row; right-hand central cord as leader for right-hand row. Take four cords now lying in centre of work (two from left-hand cording row just worked, two from right-hand row). Work a sinnet of 16 half knots. With four cords on left of this spiral, work a spiral of eight half knots. With four cords on right of centre sinnet, work another spiral of eight half knots. Now with same leaders as before, work diagonal cording beneath spirals just worked to complete central diamond motif. Now complete pattern panel to match section already worked, working a row of diagonal cording at each side of panel first, with same leaders as before, then filling in remaining area with the alternate flat knot pattern.

Divider row: As previous divider row.
3rd pattern panel With centre four cords work a half knot sinnet of 24 knots. Now go back to top left-hand corner of work. With cord second from the left as leader slanting down to the right, work a row of diagonal cording with all cords on left-hand side of work. Stop cording row at midway point of central spiral already worked so that the two left-hand cords of

spiral will be used as knotting cords for the diagonal cording.

Work a second row of cording just below this first one, using cord on far left of work as leader. Use same knotting cords as in previous row.

In a similar way work a double row of diagonal cording down right-hand side of work.

Link the four cords which are leaders from cording rows now lying in centre of work by tying them in a single flat knot. Return to cords on left-hand side of work.

Work on first six cords: work a four-row zig-zag of diagonal cording, using cord 6 as leader throughout. End of fourth row of the zig-zag should line up with linked point of central 'V' of cording.

Work on next four cords. With central two cords as the knot-bearing core, work a chain of reversed double half hitches from right and left alternately.

To work a reversed double half hitch: keep central knotbearing core cords taut, as for a flat knot, then tie a half hitch from the left across the knot-bearing cords with cord 1.

Complete the knot by taking cord 1 under the knot-bearing cords, then up and across them from right to left, then down through the loop formed. Draw tight. This completes one reversed double half hitch worked from the left.

To work the knot from the right, use cord 4 as knotting cord, and work sequence as given above, but working half hitch from the right across knot-bearing cords then taking knotting cord under, up and across them from left to right.

A chain of reversed double half hitches tied alternately from the left and right is sometimes known as a "tatted bar". Work nine reversed double half hitches altogether, which should bring chain level with zigzag of cording already worked.

Now work on next group of eight cords: With first four cords tie a chain of two flat knots; with second group of four cords tie one flat knot. Now link these two sets of cords by tying a multi-end flat knot, one with double knotting cords, and a central knot-bearing core of four cords.

Divide into two groups of four cords each again, and work a single flat knot with each group. Link groups as before in one multi-end flat knot. Complete right-hand side of work to correspond with left-hand pattern.

Divider row: As first divider row.

4th pattern panel On first four cords, work a tatted bar, with a total of 12 reversed double half hitches.

Work a similar tatted bar with four final cords in row.

Now work on central cords: Work one row of flat knots across all cords. Now divide into two equal groups and continue in the alternate flat knot pattern on

each group, dropping two cords at each end of every row to form a 'V' of pattern. Work diagonal cording down each side of the 'V' shapes, using cord on far left as leader for left-hand row; cord on far right as leader for right-hand row.

Complete second 'V' in a similar way.

Work on cords in centre of work (coming from two centre rows of diagonal cording just worked). Weave these cords over and under each other to form a criss-cross lattice pattern, as shown in illustration on page 97. With same leaders as before, reverse their directions around pins and work a row of diagonal cording below lattice pattern to form a central diamond motif.

Work two final rows of diagonal cording to complete pattern panel, using same leaders as before to the left and right of central diamond motif, and reversing their directions around pins.

Divider row: As first divider row.

5th pattern panel Divide cords into groups of four cords each. On each group work a half knot sinnet with 20 half knots in each spiral.

Divider row: As first divider row.

To finish

Thread a bead onto each cord end, positioning bead where desired on the cord, then tying an overhand knot below to secure. Trim cord ends to required length and fray out ends below beads.

Untie overhand knots in holding cord, and tie ends of holding cord together so that the completed hanging may be hung on the wall.

Note: If wished, cords for this design may be set on directly to a length of wooden dowel, to give more substantial support to the work.

Shoulder Bag

Each side of this attractive bag is made in the same way and the length, excluding fringe and handle is 9¾in *(25cm)*. The width is approximately 8½in *(21.5cm)*.

Materials required:
Heavyweight parcel string
Lining if required

To make each side of the bag
Cut 26 cords each 88in *(2.24m)*. Set these onto a holding cord of about 14in *(36cm)*. With cord on far left as leader, work a row of horizontal cording across all cords.

First pattern panel With first six cords, work a chain of six flat knots. Work on next eight cords: slant first of the eight cords down to the right and work a row of diagonal cording with remaining seven cords over the first cord as leader. Arrange slant of leader so cording row lines up with base of flat knot chain already worked. With next four cords

work a sinnet of half knots. Stop spiral at same depth as flat knot chain and diagonal cording row already worked.

With each of next two groups of four cords, work a chain of seven flat knots. With next four cords, work a spiral of half knots to same depth as previous spiral of half knots. With each of next two groups of four cords, work a chain of seven flat knots. With next four cords, work a spiral of half knots.

Work on next eight cords: slant last of the eight cords down to the left and use as leader for a row of diagonal cording, knotting other seven cords over this leader cord.

With last few cords, work a chain of six flat knots. Now cross each pair of adjoining flat knot chains over each other. Pin to hold in place.

Divider rows: With cord on far left as leader work a row of horizontal cording across all cords. Reverse direction of leader around a pin, and work a second row of horizontal cording immediately below.

Second pattern panel Work on first group of eight cords: Work a chain of three flat knots with each group of four cords. Link the two chains by knotting right-hand two cords of left-hand chain with left-hand two cords of right-hand chain in a single flat knot. Work a further three flat knots with first four cords, and with second four cords. Work on next group of 16 cords: work in alternate flat knot pattern, keeping left-hand edge straight, and dropping two cords from right-hand edge on each row until row with only one flat knot in it is worked. Now work on right-hand cords to correspond with left-hand side already worked, working from right-hand side in – two chains of linked flat knots, followed by alternate flat knot pattern over 16 cords, right-hand edge kept straight, with a slanting left-hand edge.

Central panel With cord 17 as leader slanting to the left, work a row of diagonal cording across all cords from alternate flat knot pattern section. With cord 18 as leader, work a second row of diagonal cording immediately below. In a similar way work a double row of diagonal cording slanting down to the right with cords 19 and 20.

Fill in central diamond width half knot spirals. Divide cords coming from diagonal cording rows into groups of four, so central spiral will be tied with two cords from the left, two from the right. Three spirals are now on either side of this central spiral, with an odd unworked cord at either end.

Central spiral will have 32 half knots tied in it. Allow spiral to twist around itself after every fourth knot. The first spiral on either side of central spiral will each have 28 knots; spirals either side of this will have 24 knots; and final two spirals at either end will have 16 knots.

Cord 18 continues as leader. Reverse its direction around a pin, and let it slant down to the right. Work diagonal cording over it with all cords on left-hand side of diamond.

Work a second row of diagonal cording immediately below.

In a similar way work a double row of diagonal cording down right-hand side of diamond with cords 19 and 20 as leaders. Complete lower part of pattern panel to correspond with upper part so that there are linked chains of flat knots, and diamonds of alternate flat knot patterns. Link the single knot of the alternate flat knot triangle to the flat knot chains next to it by tying a single flat knot with two cords of each.

Divider rows: As previous divider rows.

Third pattern panel On first four cords, work a chain of six flat knots. Work on next eight cords: work a crossover of diagonal cording thus – with cord 1 as leader slanting down to the right, work diagonal cording over it with cords 2, 3 and 4. Similarly with cord 8 as leader slanting down to the left, work diagonal cording over it with cords 7, 6 and 5. Now link the central point of the crossover by tying a flat knot with the four central cords. Renumber cords in the position in which they now lie from one to eight. With cord 4 as leader slanting down to the left work diagonal cording over it with cords 3, 2 and 1. With cord 5 as leader slanting down to the right, work diagonal cording over it with cords 6, 7 and 8. With each of next two groups of four cords, work chains of two flat knots. Link the chains by tying two right-hand cords of chain 1 with two left-hand cords of chain 2 in a single flat knot. Then continue with chains as before, two flat knots in each chain.

Work on next six cords: with cord 6 as leader slanting down to the left, work diagonal cording over it with cords 5, 4, 3, 2 and 1.

With cord 5 as leader slanting down to the left, work a second row of diagonal cording slanting down to the left immediately below the first, knotting over it cords 4, 3, 2 and 1.

Now reverse direction of cord 5 around a pin and work diagonal cording slanting down to the right knotting over it cords 1, 2, 3 and 4. Similarly, reverse direction of cord 6 around a pin and knot over it cords 1, 2, 3, 4 and 5. Complete rest of pattern panel to correspond with first part, reversing direction of patterns as required.

Divider rows: As first divider rows.

To make handle
Cut two cords, each 5½yd *(5m)* plus eight times the length of finished handle required.

Double these cords and pin them to the working surface. Begin knotting about

9in *(23cm)* below top loops of cords. Work a flat knot chain to a depth of about 9¾in *(25cm)*. Work in half knot spirals until handle is length required. Finish with a chain of flat knots to 9¾in *(25cm)*.

Finishing the bag
Trim leader cords to about 1in of knotting. Press to back of work, and secure with a few neat stitches. Place both sides of bag together, wrong sides facing.

Position handle so flat knot chains form sides of bag, and spirals form handle. Stitch firmly in position.

Divide cords along lower edge of bag into groups of eight (four cords from back with four cords from front). Tie these groups into tassels: Take one of the cords, and form a loop in front of other cords in group. Take it around the group from left to right and then down through loop. Draw tight. Repeat four more times. Trim cord ends evenly.

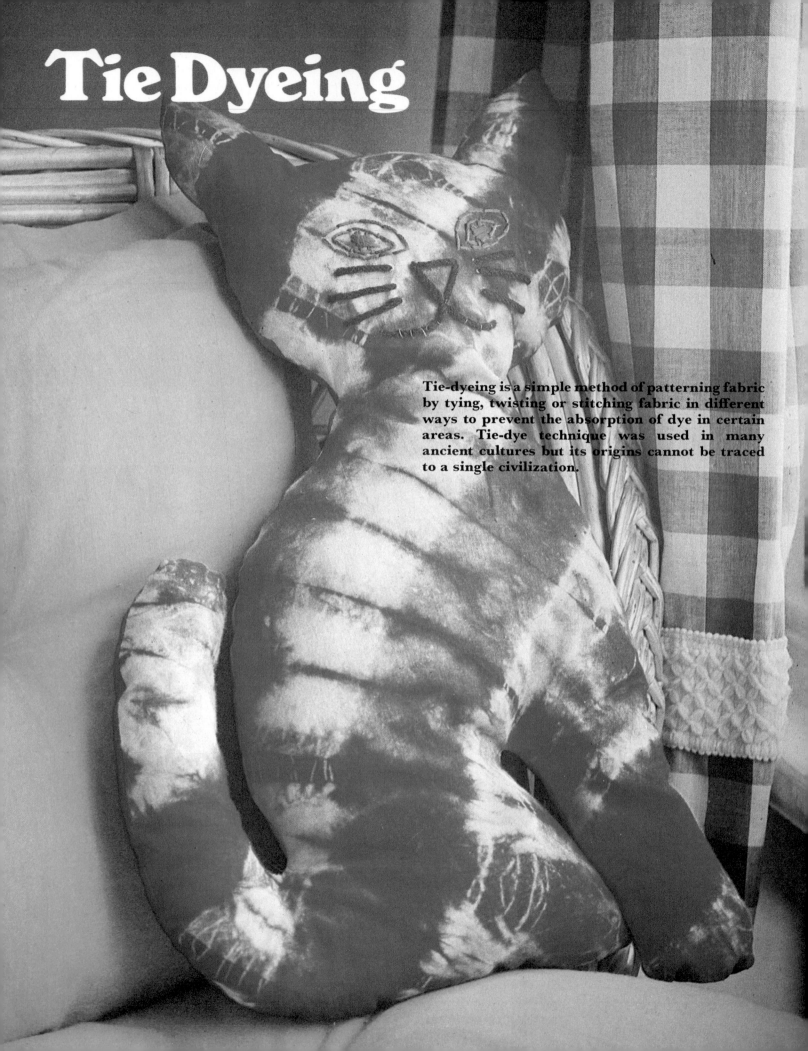

Tie Dyeing

Tie-dyeing is a simple method of patterning fabric by tying, twisting or stitching fabric in different ways to prevent the absorption of dye in certain areas. Tie-dye technique was used in many ancient cultures but its origins cannot be traced to a single civilization.

TYPES OF DYE

The examples of tie-dye in this chapter were made using cold water dyes. Any brand of dye can be used, providing that the recommendations for dyeing different types of fabric are followed.

Cold water dyes These are very easy to use and give fast colour. To estimate the amount of dye needed – as a general rule – one tin of dye is sufficient for approximately ½lb *(250g)* of dry fabric. To give an example, a dress that weighs 1lb *(500g)* and is to be tie-dyed in red and blue would need two tins of blue dye and two tins of red dye.

Multi-purpose dyes These are hot water dyes and simmering gives a greater density of colour.

Liquid dyes These are a convenient form of multi-purpose dyes.

FABRICS FOR TIE-DYEING

Choose the type of dye which is suitable for the fabric to be tie-dyed.

Cotton or linen Cold water dye is better for any item which is likely to be laundered often such as towels, sheets, pillow cases, table cloths and children's clothes. For other items, a cold or multi-purpose dye is suitable. Cotton fabrics with special finishes are inclined to dye patchily and it is better therefore to avoid these fabrics.

Silk Cold water dyes are suitable but multi-purpose hot-water dyes will give richer shades.

Rayon Use cold water dyes for viscose rayons. Use multi-purpose for acetate rayons.

Polyester fabrics Use multi-purpose or liquid dye in triple strength.

Polyester/Cotton mixtures Cold water dye, multi-purpose or liquid dye. Cold water dye should be used for items which will be laundered often.

COLOURS

If more than two colours are being used in one tie-dye project, they are likely to merge, often creating a new third colour. Successive dyeings result in a steady build-up of colour on the areas left exposed.

The basic rules of colour mixes are:

Red + Yellow = Orange
Red + Blue = Purple
Yellow + Blue = Green
Purple + Green = Grey
Purple + Orange = Brown
Violet + Blue = Indigo

Experiment first on scraps of cloth even if you have experience in colour blending with dyes.

BASIC EQUIPMENT

Large enamel or stainless steel container
Wooden spoon for stirring fabrics
Rubber gloves
Heavy cotton thread and needle
String
Pencil for marking designs onto fabric
Salt
Cold fix or washing soda

PREPARING THE FABRIC

The basic technique consists of taking a piece of fabric and tying, folding, binding, knotting, twisting or stitching it so that when the fabric is immersed in the prepared dye-bath, the colour penetrates only the untied areas of the cloth. Patterns appear on those areas which have been partially protected from the dye and complex patterns can be achieved by tying an area, then untying and retying and dyeing again in a different colour. Various ties are illustrated on page 104 and it is a good idea to practise some of these before actually starting to tie-dye a garment or a piece of household linen. Fabric can be tied around objects such as pieces of stone, corks, butter beans and clothes pegs to create new patterns. It is possible to invent new and original ties experimenting with different ties.

COLD WATER METHOD
(Colour fast cold dyes)

1 Wash, rinse and iron material to be dyed. Usually new cotton has some finish on it, so wash in hot water and detergent. Dry thoroughly, unless the colours are to deliberately merge. Then leave slightly damp.

2 Choose a large container for submerging the item – a bowl, basin, pail, sink, bathtub, or the washing machine.

3 Bind the fabric. Thread is run on from one solid band of binding to the next before being knotted off. If the bound areas are wet before dyeing, the inner areas of the material will remain white and give sharper definition to pattern.

4 Prepare the dye, wearing rubber gloves. Generally, use lightest colour first. Dissolve the dye as directed on the package and dilute with cold water. Stir well and pour into dyeing container. For each packet of dye, dissolve four heaped tablespoons of salt in the dye solution.

Dissolve one packet of commercial cold fix or one heaped tablespoon of washing soda in one pint hot water. Stir well and add to dye. Immerse sample for about one hour, stirring occasionally. Remove.

5 Wash in hot water and detergent, then rinse well until water is clear and dry out on folded newspaper. (Thorough washing and rinsing removes all loose dye particles).

6 When dry, untie. Second colour may now be dyed over the first, once the fabric has been re-tied.

7 Re-tie if required. Prepare the next dye and dye as before.

8 When sample is dry, untie, wash and iron.

HOT WATER METHOD
(Multi-purpose or liquid dyes)

1 Same as cold water dye.

2 If a greater density of colour is required, simmer in a heat-resistant container.

3 Same as cold water dye.

4 Dissolve the dye as directed on the package, stirring well. Stir in one heaped tablespoon of salt for each packet of dye. Add this dye to the minimum amount of very hot water needed to cover article. Immerse for 15–20 minutes, stirring occasionally, or, simmer over heat for 20 minutes.

5 Rinse until water is clear.

6 Same as cold water dye.

7 Same as cold water dye.

8 Same as cold water dye.

Towels

Here are three towels tie-dyed in a variety of ways and colours in cold water dye. After the final dyeing, rinse the towel thoroughly, untie and wash in a hot detergent solution rinsing until the water runs clear.

Reading from right to left:

TOWEL 1
Pleat towel lengthways into four and then fold in accordion pleats back along the length. Bind tightly at intervals. The first dye is sky blue. Move the bindings and dye leaf green.

TOWEL 2
Tie in large stones to make circles and pleat the ends and middle for stripes. Dye bright pink. Rinse thoroughly. Cover the stone-bound areas and the centre of the towel with strips of plastic and secure with string. Bind each end with more string and dye light navy blue.

TOWEL 3
Lightly pencil a wavy line across the towel, gather into small curved pleats working from the centre out to the ends. Bind tightly at intervals with string. Dye pale yellow. Rinse to remove excess dye. Bind the spaces between the string with strips of plastic, secure with string and remove original bindings. Dye dark red.

Cotton Sun-set

Use a commercial paper pattern for this design. Cut out the top and skirt. For the sun-top, back and front: Draw two wavy lines across the fabric. Tie in stones at random and pleat following the pencilled lines. Bind tightly at intervals with string. For the skirt, draw two vertical wavy lines and gather into pleats following the curves then bind at intervals with string. Dye top and skirt in light pink, rinse, move bindings and dye magenta. Rinse, move bindings and dye violet. Rinse, untie and wash in a hot detergent solution. Make up the garments.

Cat and Pony Toys

Toy making is another way of using tie-dye techniques. Draw paper patterns from the graph patterns (Fig 1 and 2), and cut out the toy after the fabric has been tie-dyed.

Pleat a piece of cotton fabric diagonally and bind with string at 2in *(5cm)* intervals. Dye bright yellow, rinse, move bindings and dye red. Rinse, untie and wash in a hot detergent solution; rinse until the water is clear, dry and iron. Draw cat outline on the folded fabric, allowing $\frac{1}{4}$in *(6mm)* for seams. Cut out two pieces. Place together wrong sides facing and stitch, leaving 2in *(5cm)* open for turning. Turn, press and stuff with kapok or other suitable filling. Embroider features.

Draw the pony outline on cotton fabric, allowing a $\frac{1}{4}$in *(6mm)* for seams. Mark out a pattern of circles and tie in small stones at these points. Dye dark orange. Rinse, untie and wash in a hot detergent solution, rinse thoroughly, dry and iron. Cut out the pony shape twice and stitch the pieces together, incorporating strands of yarn for tail and mane. Stuff with kapok or other suitable filling and embroider features.

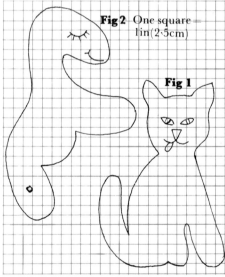

Fig 2 One square = 1in (2·5cm)

Fig 1

Two Carry-alls

Fabric paints made of cold water dyes and a chemical thickening agent are comparatively new but are fascinating to use. These two bright carry-alls can be made from heavy cotton fabric and paint-on dyes.

Materials required for cat bag

½yd *(46cm)* 36in *(90cm)* wide sturdy white cotton fabric
Fabric paint in bright green, dark green and dark blue

For the red bag

½yd *(46cm)* 36in *(90cm)* wide sturdy orange cotton fabric
Fabric paint in dark blue and dark red.

To make either bag

Cut two pieces of fabric 18in x 14in *(46cm x 36cm)*. Draw a pattern onto squared paper from the graph pattern (Fig 3) where one square equals ½in *(1cm)*, and trace the pattern down onto one piece of fabric. Mix the dye-paints following the manufacturer's instructions. Paint in the design and leave to dry for six hours.

Paint the spare fabric for the handles. When the fabric paint is dry, wash the fabric in hot water and detergent and rinse until the water runs clear.

Cut two pieces of fabric for the handles, each 12in x 4in *(30cm x 10cm)*. Fold each piece twice along the length and machine stitch. Place the two bag pieces together and machine stitch on the wrong side on three sides, leaving the top edge open. Turn a hem on the top edge and machine stitch. Pin and baste the handles to the centre of the top edges. Machine stitch to secure.

Fig 3

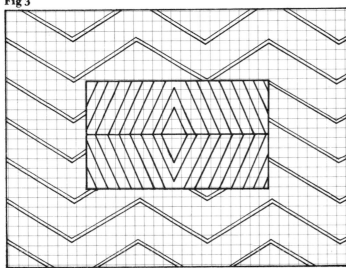

Tie-dye Effects

Knotting A Tie a length of fabric with equally spaced knots.

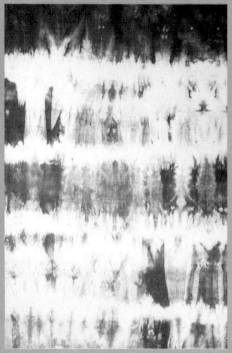

Twisting and coiling Twist the fabric tightly so that it coils back on itself. Bind at ends and at intervals along the skein.

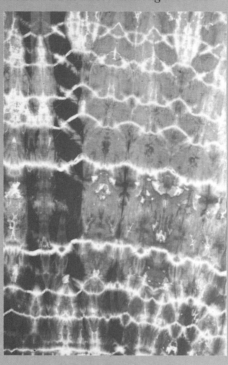

Pleating Gather the fabric in regular folds like an accordion and bind tightly at close regular intervals.

Clump tying A Tie in a stone and criss cross with thread. Bind along the loose fabric at intervals for a rippling circular effect.

Marbling Crumple the fabric in the hand. Bind into a tight hard ball. For each colour, crumple in different places for a random effect. For a large garment, bunch along length section by section for a long, firm roll.

Sewing This technique can be used for many effects. Fold fabric in half and draw (in this case) diamonds with a pencil or chalk. Stitch around the shapes and then pull the threads up tightly before fastening off.

Knotting B Mark random points on the fabric with a pencil or chalk. Pick up these marked points and knot firmly.

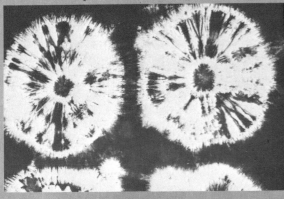

Clump tying B Tie a stone or butter-beans into the fabric for circles. Alternatively, for large or smaller effects, try coins, corks, peas, rice and shells.

Pebble Polishing

Wet pebbles glistening on the beach are an attractive sight. Their shine and lustre, their smooth and satisfying feel, give one tremendous pleasure, but within minutes of being lifted from the water the moisture dries and they lose their attraction; they even become rough to touch. How can that initial lustre and smoothness be retained? By polishing the pebbles to reveal their natural beauty.

Pebble polishing by simple tumbling machines is one of the easiest and most satisfying indoor hobbies. The initial financial outlay for the tumbler, grits and polishes is not high. Installation is no problem because domestic tumblers run from an ordinary electric socket. No great expertise is required to produce a large collection of beautifully polished and rounded pebbles of many shapes and colours.

Choosing Pebbles

All that is required for a pebble hunt on the shore are a steel pen-knife, a small, good quality steel file and bags for carrying the pebbles.

From the start, be selective in the size and hardness of the stones you collect. For tumbling purposes pebbles the size of large hens' eggs are ideal, about 1½in *(4cm)* diameter. Always include some smaller, irregular pebbles too. Their tumbling action aids the smoothing and polishing effect, taking the hard grit into the hollows of the larger stones.

Hardness is the second consideration. Discard any that are fractured with cracks running through from side to side, since these will never tumble to a smooth shape. The pretty pebbles banded with layers of brown, yellow, white and black are also not suitable.

Those bands usually indicate that one of the colours will be of a softer stone than the others, and the pebble will not tumble to an even shape as a result.

There is a third category of unsuitable pebble that is harder to pick out. A number of apparently good pebbles of green, blue, white or yellow have an attractive frosted appearance suggesting a crystalline, semi-precious stone. Use a pen-knife to try to chip a piece away. The chip will probably reveal an inner, clear material for the pebble is almost certain to be glass in one form or another. If you collect enough, it is worth remembering that beach glass will polish nicely if the whole batch is glass, but do not mix glass with stones of harder or softer substance.

Finally, sandstone pebbles are unsuitable as they will wear away to nothing in the tumbler. Sandstone is composed of tiny pieces of rock that have been welded together under pressure.

Test all the pebbles you pick up first with a pen-knife and then with a file. If neither mark the surface then the stone is good, hard and perfect for the tumbler. Those that the pen-knife cannot scratch, but which are marked by the file are of medium hardness.

DIFFERENT TYPES OF ROCK
Basically there are three rock families. *Igneous* rocks were formed from material that forced its way up from the hot, volcanic interior of the earth and solidified. These rocks are always very hard, but many do not take an attractive polish. *Sedimentary* rocks were formed by the gradual depositing of matter in salt or fresh water, or more rarely, on land. Very slowly, over millions of years, the layers of material became bonded to-

106

gether by pressure to form strata. Sandstone, limestone, slate and coal are all sedimentary rocks. Finally there are the *Metamorphic* rocks. These rocks, originally igneous or sedimentary, have been subject to enormous pressure or heat deep down in the earth. The result has been to change their nature and often the rock has been crushed and then mixed with igneous matter until it bears little or no resemblance to the original stone. The transformation – or metamorphosis – of limestone into marble is an example of metamorphic rock.

Sea shores contain a high proportion of pebbles of some form of quartz. One of these is the familiar flint, found in large, irregular lumps in chalk cliffs. Flint was formed from silica in solution filling holes in the chalk, or forming round the fossils of animals that existed a hundred million years ago. Many of the flint pebbles that have been rolling around in the shingle for centuries have developed a covering of white, yellow or brown material, which will scrape away fairly easily to reveal the true, glassy flint beneath. Other types of quartz are agate, which comes in blue, pink or red. Onyx and sardonyx are varieties of agate. Other quartz types are the rock-crystals such as amethyst, citrine, smoky quartz, chalcedony, cornelian and jasper. This last is fairly common on some beaches and tumbles to a fine, smooth red stone ideal for mounting on pendants. Many beaches consist of granite pebbles mixed with quartz. There are many forms of granite, but the main constituents are always mica, feldspar and quartz. The glitter in granite is due to the tiny flat-sided flakes of mica embedded in it.

Limestone pebbles are fairly soft and can only be polished with other limestone pebbles. When limestone has been metamorphosed into harder marble, it polishes beautifully, but it is still not quartz-hard and must be kept with pebbles of equal hardness.

Tumbling Pebbles

Wave action on the beach is the ideal tumbling motion. The pebbles are rolled one over the other continuously, and rock particles as well as sand roll with them. In time, rough-edged pebbles become round and smooth-surfaced. The major difference between nature's tumbling and machine tumbling is that in the latter a polishing stage is added so that the wet lustre is retained when the pebble has dried. The pebble will retain this silky, gleaming appearance until its surface is scratched by a substance harder than itself.

A tumbling machine consists of an electric motor, rollers and a barrel. The tumbling outfit can vary from a single barrel holding 1½lb *(0.68kg)* of pebbles,

Left Polished pebbles hold their sheen indefinitely and make an attractive picture. Jars filled with them add interest to coffee tables. **Above** Set against rough, unpolished stones, the enhanced colours of the tumbled pebbles come into their own.

to a twin 3lb *(1.36kg)* barrel set. One small barrel can only carry out one tumbling operation at a time but this size needs less grit than a twin-barrel tumbler. A dual-barrel machine can do a first-stage tumble in one barrel and a second-stage in the other; or third and polishing stages, which means the process can be finished in half the time. Barrels can be bought in 1½–3lb *(0.68–1.36kg)* sizes, with caps at one or both ends.

Some machines hold the barrels at an angle while others keep them horizontal on the rollers. The rollers are of great importance as when properly placed they offer the least resistance to the barrel-weights. This is vital, as hard pebbles may take up to a week in the tumbler and the reliability of the rollers and motor is all-important. The type of equipment required will depend on cost as well as the sort of use it will have. A simple machine backed by duplicate barrels makes the job simpler for the amateur. Each operation has its own barrel clearly labelled 'First Stage', 'Second Stage', 'Third Stage' and 'Polish'. This avoids the failure of a tumbling by a hard, coarse speck of grit finding its way into the polish and ruining weeks of work. Without separate barrels, each stage must be followed by a stringent cleaning of the barrel, washers and screw-caps. The stones must always have a really thorough washing of

A tumbler with a 3 lb *(1.36kg)* barrel.

course, but this will be done during the checking process.

THE GRITS

Tumbling grit is a man-made substance called silicon carbide, manufactured from silicon, carbon, salt and sawdust. This mixture is baked and crushed to varying sizes; the coarse grit, or number 80, means that this can be sieved through an 80-mesh-per-inch *(2.5cm)* screen.

THE STAGES OF TUMBLING

The first stage should take five days' continual grinding, using 80 grit. Fill the barrel two-thirds full of hard pebbles, add one tablespoonful of 80 grit (for the 1½lb *(0.68kg)* barrel or two tablespoonfuls for a 3lb *(1.36kg)* barrel), and enough water to cover the stones. Check that the caps with their washers are water-tight by holding the barrel horizontal for a minute or two, then place on the rollers, without forgetting to oil the bearings, and switch on. Watch for a few more minutes to check the action of the tumbling stones. If the machine is not level, the barrel can work its way along the rollers and if it comes too close to the frame, the friction can affect the tumbling and in time erode the barrel. Also watch for leaks, as water and electricity can have a lethal effect in combination.

If all is well, a steady, muted rumble will be heard. If the sound is a distinct rattle of stone upon stone, the speed of the barrel or the amount of pebbles or water may be wrong. Do not hesitate to make adjustments, for attention to detail early on will pay off later. The action inside the tumbler as it steadily rotates is a steady rolling over and over of the pebbles, grit and water. A thick, greyish liquid containing grit and stone particles in suspension will develop. This tends quickly to reduce the sound of the tumbling pebbles. Even so, it is wise to make a cover for the machine. Sturdy cardboard boxes are ideal. However, do not make the cover too air-tight in the interests of sound-proofing, for all electric installations create heat and, as the tumbler will be in continuous action for periods of up to a week, air should be able to circulate freely around the motor. Stop the machine at least once a day, remove the lid and take a few pebbles from the barrel. Wash them thoroughly and check the effect of the tumbling.

There should be a noticeable smoothing of corners, an erosion of patina to show the stone beneath. At this stage throw out any pebbles that show flaws running through them.

Top Beautiful pendants can be made from polished amethyst pebbles attached to a claw mount. **Bottom** An example of a pebble that can never take a perfect polish. The white band is softer than the hard, darker mineral and wears away.

During the tumbling process, tiny pockets of natural gases are released from the stones. This is not harmful, but if the barrels are not opened once a day, the pressure could build up enough to distort a washer so that a leak occurs. The danger is remote, for the gases are minute in quantity, but it is always worth taking precautions. After five days of tumbling with the coarse grit, stop the machine. Remove the pebbles and have a close and last check for flawed stones. Then wash out the barrel (or use the one marked 'Second Stage') and repeat the process with 320 grit for four days. During this stop it is important to check the motor and rollers. After this stage the stones will begin to look smooth but the third stage, four more days with 600 grit, is necessary to give the well-tumbled, smoothed stones their permanent polish. The pebbles should now have gone through the three grinding stages, in 80, 320 and 600 grits. At each stage flawed pebbles have been thrown out. The remainder are all smooth pebbles, with no edges, flaws, or angular surfaces.

Final Polish

This stage requires no grit but a polishing agent such as cerium oxide or tin oxide. Even if only one barrel is available for the grinding stages, there must be a separate one for the polish. The smallest speck of grit in the polish can ruin weeks of tumbling by scoring the patiently smoothed pebbles. The same procedure must be observed as before. Place the pebbles carefully in the tumbler, add the proper amount of polish depending on the size of barrel, fill up with water and tumble for four days. Listen carefully at this stage for 'pebble-clatter'. This indicates insufficient pebbles or water or a wrong tumble speed. Take great care to get it right, for falling pebbles can chip and spoil the work, even at this late stage.

There are several things that can be done to improve a 'noisy' polishing stage. Small pieces of chamois or felt placed in the barrel can sometimes help. Another remedy is to add a little detergent, just enough to create a bed of bubbles. However, do be very careful, as too many suds will force open the lid and disaster will result.

If at the end of the four days the pebbles do not seem quite right, perhaps lacking that fine sheen which remains when the pebbles have dried after their final wash, do not be discouraged. Put them through the polishing stage again. If the grinding stages have been carried out properly, if the pebble surfaces are really smooth, and if there is not the slightest speck of grit in the polish, the tumbled pebbles will look perfect. When experi-

ence has been gained with local pebbles, it is time to try more exotic stones. These are readily obtainable from craft shops or geology suppliers to be found in most major cities and larger towns. Semi-precious stones such as tiger-eye, moss and banded agate, malachite, snowflake obsidian, rose quartz, lapis lazuli and aventurine can all be bought in quantities suitable for tumbling. Hardness varies, but the retailer will always help and advise if any questions or problems arise. Many suppliers sell mixtures of stones of equal hardness for home tumbling. Many of these brilliant polished stones are perfect for setting in the many forms of jewelry mounts available. Pebble polishing not only provides a very basic pleasure but can stimulate a lasting interest and enthusiasm in geology and the wealth of precious and semi-precious stones to be found in the earth below our feet.

Above A section cut through an agate geode and polished makes a beautiful paperweight. **Below** A rough, un-polished pebble of Torrin marble. Mineral seepage and igneous activity have metamorphosed the limestone.

Tatting

The charm of tatting lies in the fact that delicate lace-like work can be produced with nothing more than thread, a small shuttle and two hands. Tatting is generally worked in white or natural coloured cotton thread and can be used for edging household linens and home accessories as well as to decorate delicate clothing.

THREADS

Crochet cotton is available in several gauges, the thickness of the thread used being determined by the delicacy of the work desired. Tatting can also be done with ordinary string.

SHUTTLES

Shuttles are made in various materials such as bone, tortoiseshell, steel and plastic. Choose one that is not more than $2\frac{3}{4}$in *(7cm)* long. A longer shuttle is more clumsy and slows down the speed of work. Shuttles are usually sold with a separate hook for joinings.

WINDING THE SHUTTLES

Wind the thread around the centre of the shuttle. If there is a hole in the centre of the bobbin, insert the thread through the hole and tie a knot. Do not wind the thread beyond the edge of the shuttle. When making motifs, it is advisable to count the number of turns of thread around the shuttle so that the amount of thread used to make one motif can be assessed. This will prevent unnecessary joining of thread.

THE BASIC TECHNIQUES OF TATTING

The directions for each stitch apply to both the right and left-handed. The left-handed work from right to left. Place a pocket mirror to the left of each illustration and the exact working position will be reflected.

HOLDING SHUTTLE AND THREAD

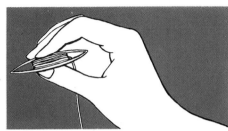

1 Hold the flat side of the shuttle in a horizontal position, between the thumb and the forefinger of the right hand. Allow approximately 15in *(38cm)* of the shuttle thread to hang free from the back of the shuttle.

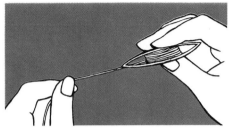

2 Grasp the free end of the shuttle thread between the thumb and the forefinger of the left hand. The diagrams to 8 show how thread and shuttle are held before commencing tatting.

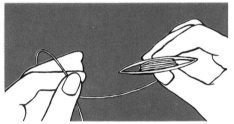

3 Spread out the middle, ring and little finger of the left hand and pass the thread over them.

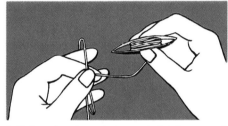

4 Bring the thread around the fingers of the left hand to form a circle and hold it between thumb and forefinger.

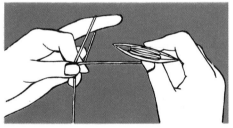

5 Raise the middle finger of the left hand to 'open' the circle.

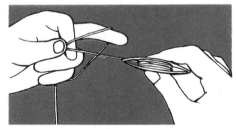

6 Bend the ring and the little finger of the left hand to catch the thread against the palm.

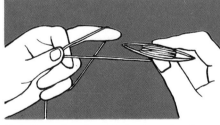

7 Adjust the thread so that the fingers do not feel strained and draw the shuttle thread out to its full length keeping the right and left hands at the same level.

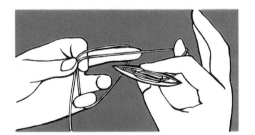

8 Pass the shuttle thread around the back of the little finger of the right hand. Both hands are now in position for the basic stitch known as the Double Stitch.

DOUBLE STITCH

9 With the thread in position, move the shuttle forward passing it under the shuttle thread and through the circle.

10 Bring the shuttle back over the circle of thread and under the shuttle thread.

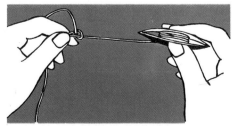

11 Relaxing the fingers of the left hand, drop the thread from the little finger of the right hand and draw the shuttle thread taut with a sharp jerk.

111

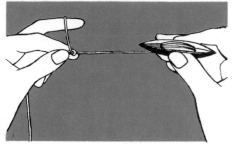

12 Slowly raise the middle finger of the left hand, slide the loop into position between the thumb and forefinger. This completes the first half of the double stitch.

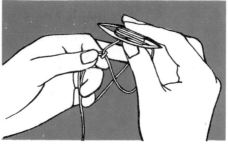

13 Move the shuttle forward, dropping the shuttle thread and passing the shuttle over the circle . . .

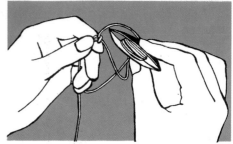

14 . . . and back through between the circle and the shuttle thread.

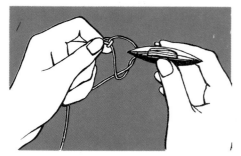

15 Drop the middle finger of the left hand.

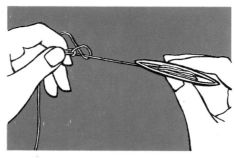

16 Relaxing the fingers of the left hand, draw the shuttle thread taut with a sharp jerk.

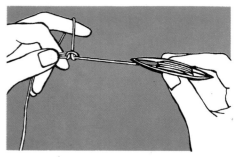

17 Slowly raise the middle finger of the left hand to slide the loop into position next to the first half of the stitch. This completes the second half of the double stitch.

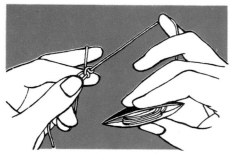

18 Hands and shuttle are shown in position to commence next double stitch. Once this stitch has been properly mastered it should be possible to work any of the designs in this chapter.

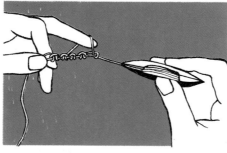

RINGS, PICOTS AND JOININGS
19 FIRST RING As each double stitch is formed, slide it along the circle of thread to meet the preceding double stitch. Hold them securely between the thumb

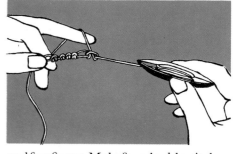

and forefinger. Make four double stitches. Then make the first half of a double stitch sliding it to within ¼in *(0.5cm)* of the preceding stitch.
20 Now complete the double stitch.

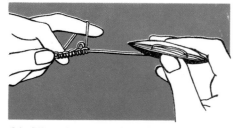

21 Slide the stitch along the ring to meet the first four double stitches. The small loop formed between the last two double stitches is a picot. The size of this may be altered as desired by adjusting the space left by the preceding stitch. Make three more double stitches. Make a second picot and four double stitches. Make a third picot and four double stitches.

22 Holding the stitches securely between the thumb and forefinger of the left hand, draw the shuttle thread tight so that the first and last stitches meet forming a ring. In general instructions the ring just completed would be written as: R of 4ds, 3ps sep by 4ds, 4ds, cl.

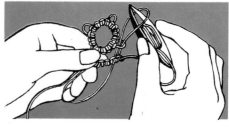

SECOND RING
23 *(i)* Wind the thread around the left hand in position for another ring. Leaving a space of ¼in *(0.5cm)* from base of previous ring, make four double stitches. *(ii)* Insert a hook through the last picot of the previous ring and pull the circle thread through, being careful not to twist it in doing so. *(iii)* Pass the shuttle through the loop. Slowly raise

the middle finger of the left hand to draw up the loop. This stands as the first half of the next double stitch. *(iv)* Now work the *second* half of a double stitch. (One joining and one double stitch have now been completed). Work 3ds, 2ps sep by 4ds, 4ds, cl. (Second ring completed).

USING BALL AND SHUTTLE

Although some designs are made up of rings and others only contain chains, most designs consist of a combination of these two. For these it is necessary to use the shuttle thread and the ball thread. Commence by tying the ends of the two threads together. Make a ring as before.

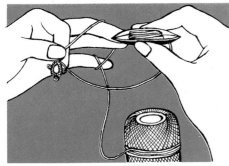

24 Unlike rings, chains are made with the thread held across the back of the fingers of the left hand, winding it around the little finger to control the tension.

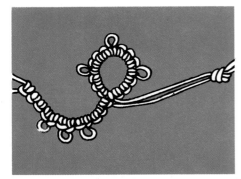

25 A chain consists of a given number of double stitches worked over the ball thread with the shuttle.
A chain may also include picots.

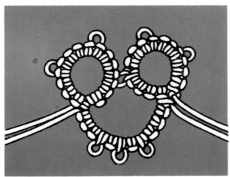

REVERSING

26 In tatting it will be noticed that the rounded end of the working ring or chain faces upwards. When working a design of rings and chains it is sometimes necessary to reverse the work.

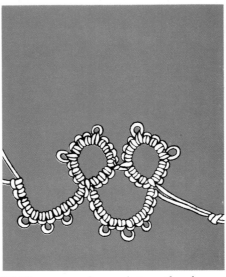

27 To reverse the work turn the ring or chain just completed face downwards, i.e. in the reverse position. The *next* ring or chain is then worked in the usual way having the rounded end facing upwards.

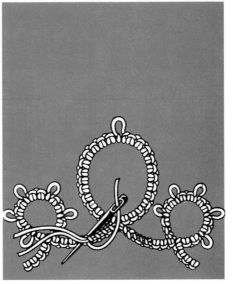

TO FINISH OFF ENDS

28 Make flat or square knot, e.g. a Reef Knot or a Weaver's Knot close to the base of the last ring or chain. Do not off off ends as the strain during working may loosen the knot. With a single strand of cotton, oversew the ends neatly to the wrong side of the work.

TWO SHUTTLES

When rings are to be worked in two colours, two shuttles are used. The two colours – one in each shuttle – may be alternated. When this takes place the shuttle which made the preceding ring is dropped and the second shuttle is picked up, making a ring as before. When the rings are separated by a chain, the thread of the second shuttle is held similarly to the ball thread in Fig 24.

TO JOIN THREADS

(a) When ball and shuttle threads are used, a knot can be avoided at the beginning of the work by filling the shuttle and commencing the ring without cutting the thread.
(b) Make a flat or square knot, e.g. a Reef Knot or a Weaver's Knot close to the base of the last ring or chain. Do not cut off the ends, as the strain during working may loosen the knot.

TATTING ABBREVIATIONS

r(s)	**ring(s)**
sr	**small ring**
lr	**large ring**
ds	**double stitch**
p(s)	**picot(s)**
smp	**small picot**
lp	**long picot**
sep	**separated**
cl	**close**
rw	**reverse work**
sp	**space**
ch(s)	**chain(s)**
tog	**together**
rep	**repeat**

Handkerchief Edging

Add a simple edging to a ready-made handkerchief for a very personal gift. (Illustrated on page 110).

Materials required:
Coats Mercer Crochet Cotton No. 40, or Clark's Big Ball Mercerised Crochet No. 40, 1 ball
Tatting shuttle

To work edging
*R of 2ds, 7p sep by 2ds, 7ds, cl. Join shuttle thread to last p, making sure that thread lies at back of work. (To do this, insert hook into p, catch shuttle thread and draw out into a loop, pass shuttle through loop and adjust knot.)**
Do not leave a space but start next r immediately. Repeat from * to ** for length required.

To work corner
Lr of 2ds, join to last free p of previous r, 2ds, 12p, sep by 2ds, 2ds, cl. R of 2ds, join to last p of previous lr, 2ds, 6p sep by 2ds, 7ds, cl. Join shuttle thread to last p. Cont edging from * to ** as required.

To make up
Press with a damp cloth and a warm iron and overcast (sew) to handkerchief.

String Belt

This is an attractive belt in natural twine and will be a useful addition to your wardrobe.

Materials required:
Large ball fine parcel twine or string
1 pair of toggles
1 large tatting or netting shuttle

To make belt
Use shuttle and ball thread. R of 9ds, p, 3ds, cl. RW. Ch of 5ds. R of 9ds, p, 3ds, cl. RW. *Ch of 3ds. RW. R of 3ds, join to p of last r, 6ds, p, 3ds, cl. RW. Ch of 5ds. R of 3ds, join to p of facing r, 6ds, p, 3ds, cl. RW. Ch of 3ds. RW. R of 3ds, join to p of last r, 6ds, p, 3ds, cl. RW. Ch of 5ds. R of 3ds, join to p of facing r, 6ds, p, 3ds, cl. RW**. Repeat from * to ** for length required.

Fastening for the toggles
Work a r of 12ds and enclose a toggle while closing r. Ch of 6ds. R of 12ds and enclose second toggle while closing r.

To finish
Divide the strands of the yarn and weave in the separated ends. Press with a damp cloth and a hot iron to set the waxy surface of the string.

Pillowcase Edging

Decorate a plain pillowcase with this attractive edging and matching panel insertion. The width of the panel is $1\frac{7}{8}$in *(5cm)*, and the depth of the edging is $\frac{7}{8}$in *(2.5cm)*.

Materials required:
Coats Mercer-Crochet No. 20 *(20g)* or J&P Coats 'Knit-Cro-Sheen' No.20, 2 balls
A plain pillowcase. Tatting shuttle.

To work panel
1st row: Tie ball and shuttle threads together. *R of 8ds, 2ps sep by 4ds, 8ds, cl. Ch of 8ds; rep from * for length required, having an even number of chs between rs and joining last ch to base of first r, without twisting work, rw.
**R of 8ds, 2ps sep by 4ds, 8ds, cl. Ch of 8ds, join by shuttle thread to base of next r; rep from **, joining last ch to base of first r. Tie ends, cut and oversew neatly on wrong side.
2nd row: Tie ball and shuttle threads tog. R of 5ds, join to p at right of any r on lower edge of previous row, 5ds, join to next p of next r, 5ds, cl., rw. * Ch of 3ds, 4ps sep by 3ds, 6ds, join by shuttle thread to next p. Ch of 3ds, join by shuttle thread to next p. Ch of 6ds, join to last p of adjacent ch, 3ds, 3ps sep by 3ds, 3ds, rw. R of 5ds, join to next p, 5ds, join to next p, 5ds, cl, rw; rep from * skipping r at end of last rep and joining last ch to base of first r. Tie ends, cut and

Above detail of pillowcase insertion.
Below detail of the pillowcase edging.

oversew neatly on wrong side.
Work other side to correspond.

To work edging
1st row: Work as for first side of first row for length required. Tie ends, cut and oversew neatly on wrong side.
2nd row: Work as for first side of second row. Tie ends, cut and oversew neatly on wrong side.

To make up
Pin panel in place 3½in *(9cm)* from edge of pillowcase. Cut away surplus material at back of panel, leaving ¼in *(0.5cm)* for hem on each side. Sew hems and panel neatly in place, attaching 2ps of each ch, as in illustration. Sew on edging, attaching at base of each r. Press with a damp cloth and a warm iron.

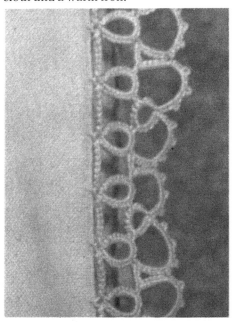

Traycloth

The edging on this pretty traycloth is approximately ¾in *(2cm)* wide with the motif/panel approximately 1½in *(3.5cm)* square. About ⅛in *(6mm)* should be left between each ring throughout the pattern.

Materials required:
14in x 18in *(36cm x 46cm)* linen
Coats Mercer-Crochet No. 20 or J&P Coats 'Knit-Cro-Sheen' No. 20, 1 ball
Tatting shuttle.

To work the edging
R of 4ds, p, 4ds, p, 4ds, p, 4ds, cl. RW. * Sr of 5ds, p, 5ds, cl, RW. R of 4ds, join to last p of first r, 4ds, p, 4ds, p, 4ds, cl. RW. Lr of 4ds, join to p of sr, 10ds, p, 4ds, cl. RW. R of 4ds, join to last p of facing r, 4ds, p, 4ds, p, 4ds, cl. RW. Sr of 5ds, join to last p of 1r, 5ds, cl. RW. R of 4ds, join to last p of facing r, 4ds, p, 4ds, p, 4ds, cl. RW. ** Rep from * to ** for 16in *(41cm)* or length required.

Working the corner
Sr of 5ds, p, 5ds, cl. RW. R of 4ds, join to last p of facing r, 4ds, p, 4ds, p, 4ds, cl. RW. Lr of 4ds, join to p of sr, 10ds, p, 4ds, cl. RW. R of 4ds, join to last p of facing r, 4ds, p, 4ds, p, 4ds, cl. Join shuttle thread to last p of r just made. (To do this, insert hook into p, catch shuttle thread and draw out into a loop, pass shuttle through loop and adjust knot). Sr of 5ds, join to p of facing 1r, 5ds, cl. Work a second sr of 5ds, p, 5ds, cl. Join shuttle thread to next p on r to which shuttle thread was previously joined.
Lr of 4ds, join to p of sr just made, 10ds, p, 4ds, cl. RW. R of 4ds, join to p already connecting the two facing rs, 4ds, join to remaining p of facing r, 4ds, p, 4ds, cl. RW. Sr of 5ds, join to last p of 1r, 5ds, cl. RW. R of 4ds, join to last p on facing r, 4ds, p, 4ds, p, 4ds, cl. RW. Repeat edging from * to ** for 12in *(30cm)* or length required, work another corner, then complete the remaining trimming similarly.

Working the motif panel
Sr of 5ds, p, 5ds, cl. RW. R of 4ds, p, 4ds, p, 4ds, p, 4ds, cl. RW. Lr of 4ds, join to p of sr, 5ds, p, 5ds, p, 4ds, cl. RW. R of 4ds, join to last p of facing r, 4ds, p, 4ds, p, 4ds, cl. RW. *Sr of 5ds, join to last p of 1r, 5ds, cl. RW. R of 4ds, p, 4ds, p, 4ds, p, 4ds, cl. RW. Lr of 4ds, join to junction of sr and 1rs, 5ds, join to centre p of 1r, 5ds, p, 4ds, cl. RW. R of 4ds, join to last p of facing r, 4ds, p, 4ds, p. 4ds, cl. RW. **
Repeat from * to ** twice more to complete the square. Tie first and last rs tog to finish off. Work six squares altogether.

To make up
Baste the edging into position and buttonhole-stitch along the inner edge, catching the picots. Cut away raw edges of linen afterwards. Baste the motif panels into position so that they are aligned and attach so that the lines of buttonholing continue from square to square. Then cut away linen behind each motif. Press with a damp cloth and a warm iron on the wrong side.

Basketwork

Making baskets is probably one of the earliest crafts known to man. From archeological research, it is known that the early North American Indians used baskets as moulds for clay cooking pots, the imprint of the basketweave showing clearly on the clay. Specimens of coiled and plaited basketwork have been found in the Nile Delta, some dating from 8000 B.C. Many museums throughout the world have a collection of basketwork, and the common factor seems to be that the design of individual baskets has always been influenced by the ready availability of local materials.

Baskets and woven containers have a wide variety of use in the modern world. Different types are used in the building industry; lobster fishermen still use a traditional lobster-basket design for their catch and laundries, potteries, glass foundries, chemical companies and farmers all use baskets in many different ways.

There are decorative baskets too, for cradling wine bottles, holding flowers and fruit, bringing bread rolls to the table, hanging up house plants, and of course, there are wickerwork lampshades, wastepaper baskets, work baskets, cribs for small babies, pet baskets, picnic hampers and cane carpet beaters, all of which are decorative as well as being functional.

BASIC MATERIALS

There are many different materials which can be used for basketmaking including willow or osier, cane, seagrass, raffia and rush. Most of these materials can be purchased in various thicknesses, lengths and textures and are sometimes available dyed in different colours. However, basketwork looks at its most natural in its un-dyed state, the colours ranging from cream to soft brown. Some people like to mix the dyed and the natural material together in one piece of basketwork.

Cane, or as it is commonly called, wicker or rattan, is the most popular basketry material and this has been used for all the projects featured in this chapter.

CANE

There are two principal types of cane:

Centre cane is a round cane varying in thickness from $\frac{1}{4}$in–2in *(1mm–10mm)*. It is easy to use, and suitable for beginners. The higher the size number, the thicker the cane.

Lapping cane is flat on one side and slightly rounded on the other. It is available in various widths and adds an attractive variation to the work. It is also used for wrapping around basket handles, as being flat, it gives a smooth and comfortable grip.

Cane is usually sold by the pound in coils, and is available from handicraft shops, crafts suppliers and those department stores with crafts counters.

Both natural-colour and bleached cane are available. Bleached cane is very white and can look very attractive used in combination with the natural colour. Finished basketwork can be dyed any colour or it can be spray painted. A dyed basket should be varnished afterwards to retain the colour and protect the dye.

BASES

Ready-made bases are recommended for the beginner and these are available in many different shapes and sizes. They are supplied with an odd number of holes drilled all around the circumference. If preferred, make bases from $\frac{1}{4}$in *(6mm)* plywood, using a $\frac{3}{32}$in *(0.5cm)* bit to drill the holes, which should be about

¾in (2cm) apart and about ¼in (6mm) from the edge. Whether a basket base is made or bought, it is a good idea to protect the surface. It can be covered with self-adhesive plastic vinyl, or painted or varnished. Never allow wooden bases to become damp or they will warp. Although cane bases are a little more complicated to work than wooden ones, they do look very professional and are much more attractive. Instructions for two such bases are included in this chapter.

TOOLS AND EQUIPMENT

Only a few basic tools are needed, and these can be obtained from most handicraft shops or hardware stores.

Side cutters 5in (13cm) for trimming ends of cane close to the weaving, and for cutting the cane

Round-nosed pliers for squeezing the cane stakes before bending at acute angles when working borders

Cane needle or a household skewer, for easing spaces in the weaving for the insertion of byestakes or handles

Long ruler for measuring

Small knife with a sharp point for splitting cane when necessary for woven bases

Clothes peg to hold down weaving canes if the work has to be left

Bowl or bucket of water and a cloth.

TERMS AND TECHNIQUES

There are a few technical terms in basketry which are useful to know, and some basic techniques. Read these through carefully before attempting any of the projects.

WORKING WITH CANE

Cane is a very brittle material which cracks and splinters when worked dry, so it is essential to use it damp. To make it pliable, soak it for about five minutes in a bucket of warm water before using. Prevent it from drying out during working by an occasional dampening with a wet cloth.

Stakes These are the upright canes which form the foundation for the weaving and should be cut from thicker cane than the weaving cane. When cutting stakes, allow for the height of the basket plus allowances for foot and top borders (Fig 1).

Bye stakes These are additional stakes to give extra strength to the weaving. They are inserted into the weaving close beside the original, after the 'upsetting' stage and must touch the base. They should be even with the original stakes all around the top of the work. In simple basketry, these pairs of stakes are treated as single stakes throughout the work. Bye stakes are not always necessary with small baskets.

Upsetting This is the term used for the initial weaving of the sides of a basket. It is the stage which sets the shape and

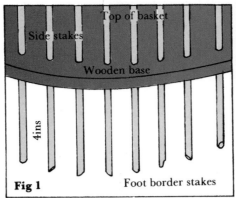

Fig 1

Side stakes · Top of basket · Wooden base · 4ins · Foot border stakes

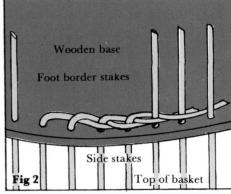

Fig 2

Wooden base · Foot border stakes · Side stakes · Top of basket

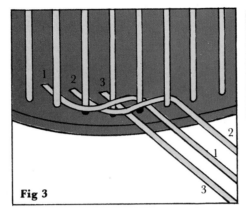

Fig 3

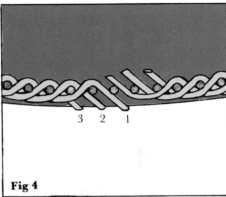

Fig 4

firmness of the basket. Waling is the weave generally used. It is when upsetting is worked that the bye stakes, if used, are inserted.

Weavers These are the finer weaving or working canes. Do not pull them too tight, just let them lie naturally. Press the weaving down firmly at intervals to keep the work the same height all around. Always work from left to right and keep the weaver less than 3yd (2.75cm) long to prevent tangling.

Foot border This is the border worked on the underside of a ready-made base to secure the ends of the stakes. Dampen the required number of stakes, and insert them through the base holes, leaving about 4in (10cm) projecting on the underside. Hold the work upside down and, with the round-nosed pliers, squeeze each stake level with the base. Take one stake, bend it over to the right behind the second stake, in front of the third stake, and leave the end to rest against the back of the fourth stake (see Fig 2). Continue all around in this manner, taking each stake in its turn. When the beginning is reached ease the first stakes up with the needle and the last stakes through in their turn to complete the border. Turn the base right side uppermost, press it down onto the foot border just completed pulling the side stakes gently to ensure that the foot border is really close to the underside of the base. Work around the stakes, easing each one outwards, before commencing weaving, to start shaping the work for the sides of the basket.

Waling (3 rod) This is a very strong and firm method of weaving, which is generally worked with three weavers. Place the ends of three weavers in three adjacent spaces between the stakes, leaving the ends on the inside. Take the left-hand weaver, pass it in front of the second and third stakes, behind the fourth, and out to the front. In doing this, it will also pass over the two right-hand weavers (see Fig 3). Work all around, always using the left-hand weaver, until the right-hand weaver falls in the space to the left of the space holding the first weaver (see Fig 4). For the next row, take the right-hand weaver and pass it in front of the next two stakes, behind the next one, and out at the front. Next, work the middle weaver, and lastly the left-hand weaver in the same manner. This 'reversal' of weaving must be done on each row at exactly the same point and ensures that each row of waling is complete and level.

When the required number of rows have been worked, finish off the waling with the same method as used to finish each row, but this time the woven work will have to be eased up with a needle for easy passage of the final weaving ends.

Randing This is the simplest form of weaving. One weaver only is used, being passed in front of one stake and behind the next, alternately (see Fig 5). Randing, worked with two canes at once looks even more attractive. They should be kept flat, with one above the other, as with one weaver.

Pairing This is worked by weaving two

117

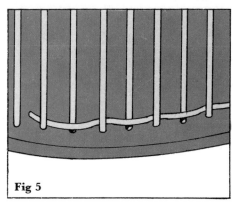

Fig 5

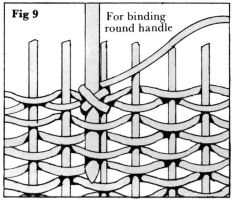

Fig 9 | For binding round handle

weavers alternately. It is a fairly strong weave, and may be used for upsetting on small baskets. Forming a firm weave makes it suitable for a trivet or platter (Fig 6).

Joining weavers To join in a new weaver, always leave the old weaver behind a stake on the inside of the basket. Insert the end of the new weaver above it, behind the same stake, also on the inside. Continue weaving as before. The join will not show on the right side (Fig 7).

Trimming ends Make sure that all ends are on the inside of the work. Clip off, leaving enough for the end to rest on its correct stake. Always cut off at a slant.

Singeing Cane gets 'hairy' when being worked and can be singed off if a flame is moved very quickly over the work. However, be careful to avoid blackening the finished article.

Maintenance of finished articles Brush gently to remove dust. The basketwork, but not wooden bases, may be swished in warm, soapy water, rinsed well, and left to dry.

Plant Pot Holder

The finished plantholder is approximately 7in *(18cm)* high, with a top diameter of approximately 7in *(18cm)*. To make a hanging pot tie on handles made of string or macramé chains.

Materials required:
Approx. 4oz *(113g)* No. 6 natural cane for:
23 stakes 20in *(51cm)* long

118

23 bye stakes 13in *(33cm)* long
Approx. 3oz *(85g)* No. 3 natural cane for upsetting and pairing
Approx. 12yd *(11m)* lapping cane for randing
Round base 6in *(15cm)* in diameter with 23 holes.

To make the plant holder
Paint, varnish or cover one surface of the base as required. Cut and prepare the required number of stakes. Then work the foot border, following Fig 2, and place the basket right side up. For upsetting, weave five rows of pairing, using No. 3 natural cane (Fig 6). Point off one end of each bye stake and insert in the weaving beside each original stake. Weave twenty-one rows of randing with the lapping cane. Tuck ends down into weaving, each beside a stake, to fasten off neatly and securely.

Trim off each pair of stakes to a point and about 5in *(13cm)* above the last row of weaving. Place basket upside down in warm water for a few minutes to dampen the stakes only. With the round-nosed pliers, squeeze each pair of stakes level with last row of weaving.

To start the scallop border, take one pair of stakes, arch it gently over to the right and in front of the next two pairs. Insert the ends down into the weaving, close beside the fourth pair of stakes, leaving a scallop about 1¼in *(3cm)* high (see Fig 8). Continue making scallops all around the top. Ease basket into shape and leave to dry out thoroughly. Trim off all spare ends at a slant on the inside of the basket. Add handles if required.

Picnic Basket

The finished picnic basket is approximately 11½in *(29cm)* high x 16in *(41cm)* long. This size is big enough to hold a thermos bottle at each end, with a standard-sized container and cups between them.

Materials required:
Approx. 8oz *(227g)* No. 6 natural cane for:
47 stakes 26in *(66cm)* long
47 bye stakes 20in *(51cm)* long
Approx. 10oz *(283g)* No. 3 natural cane for weavers
2 lengths No. 25 handle cane, each approximately 22in *(56cm)*
Approx. 4yd *(3.5m)* lapping cane for binding handles.
Base 4½in x 16in *(11cm x 41cm)* with 47 holes.

To make the picnic basket
Paint, varnish or cover one surface of the base as required. Cut and prepare the required number of stakes. Then work the foot border, following Fig 2, and place the basket right side up.
For upsetting, weave two rows of 3-rod waling, using No. 3 cane (Figs 3 and 4).
Point off one end of each bye stake and insert in the weaving beside each original stake. Weave 84 rows of randing, using No. 3 cane (Fig 5). Weave 2 rows of 3-rod waling using No. 3 cane. Weave 8 rows of randing using two weavers together. Weave two rows of 3-rod waling. Trim off the stakes to a point and about 6in *(15cm)* above the last row

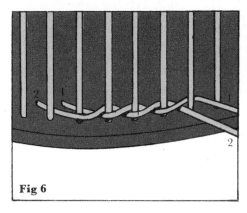

Fig 6

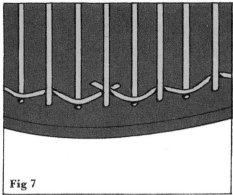

Fig 7

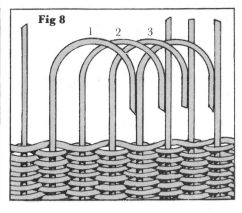

Fig 8

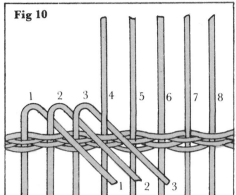

Fig 10

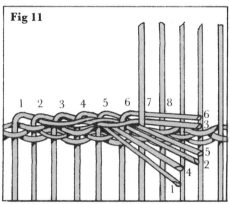

Fig 11

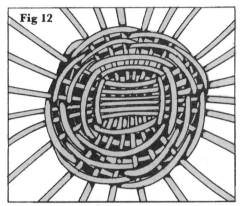

Fig 12

of weaving. Place basket upside down in warm water for a few minutes to dampen the stakes only.

Handles Take one piece of handle cane and point it at both ends for about 2in *(5cm)*. Soak to make it pliable. Push one end firmly down into the weaving about 6in *(15cm)* from the end of the basket. Make a hole in the handle cane approximately 2in *(5cm)* from point, from front to back and just under the top waling. Repeat for other end of handle. Point one end of lapping cane and push end through the hole. Tuck this end into the weaving. Bring the other end to the front under the waling and to left of handle cane. Cross over to right, around top of waling, down the back, out at front right through waling, over top of waling at left down the back. This forms a neat cross, and may be worked over a second time. Do not cut off the long end.

Wind this long end closely and firmly around the handle cane until other end is reached. Point end of lapping cane and thread it through hole at end of handle cane. Work another cross to match the first one. Repeat for other basket handle and avoid a join in the lapping cane (Fig 9).

Top border With the round-nosed pliers, squeeze each pair of stakes level with the last row of weaving (Fig 10). Bend over stake 1 behind 2. Bend 2 behind 3. Bend 3 behind 4.

Following Fig 11 carefully, pass stake 1 in front of 3 and 4, behind 5, and then out to the front. Bend 4 down alongside

1. Repeat for stakes 2 and 3. Pass 4 in front of 7, behind 8 and out to the front. Bend 7 down alongside it as before. There must always be three pairs of ends coming out at the front. The fifth from the right in this set is the one which is taken in front of the next upright stake, behind the next one, and out at the front. The left-hand·cane of each pair is the one left pointing outwards.

Continue working all around top of basket, working neatly around handles as they are reached, until only one stake remains upright.

Ease up the beginning stakes with the needle, making room for the final canes to pass through. Finish off the pattern in sequence and passing under beginning stakes as necessary.

Clip off all ends close to the border.

Waste Basket

This simply designed waste paper basket is a useful item to learn to make. Vary the size according to your requirements, this basket is approximately 10¼in *(26cm)* high, with a top diameter of 10¼in *(26cm)*.

Materials required:

Approx. 8oz *(227g)* No. 8 natural cane for:

29 stakes, 26in *(66cm)* long

29 bye stakes, 14in *(36cm)* long

Approx. 8oz *(227g)* No. 6 natural cane for weavers

Approx. 5oz *(142g)* No. 6 bleached cane for weavers

Round base, 8in *(20cm)* in diameter with 29 holes.

To make the basket

Paint, varnish or cover one surface of the base as desired. Cut and prepare the required number of stakes. Then work a foot border, following Fig 2, and place basket right side up.

For upsetting, weave three rows of 3-rod waling, using No. 6 bleached cane (Figs 3 and 4). Point off one end of each bye stake and insert in the weaving beside each original stake.

Weave 27 rows of randing, using No. 6 natural cane (Fig 5). Weave one row of 3-rod waling, using No. 6 bleached cane. Weave another 27 rows of randing using No. 6 natural cane. Weave one row of 3-rod waling using No. 6 bleached cane. Weave a third band of 27 rows of randing, using No. 6 natural cane. Finish with one row of 3-rod waling using No. 6 bleached cane. Trim off each pair of stakes to a point and about 5½in *(14cm)* above the last row of weaving.

Place basket upside down in water for a few minutes to dampen the stakes only. Work scallop border exactly as for house-plant holder. Ease basket into shape and leave to dry out thoroughly. Trim off all spare ends at a slant as necessary, on the inside of the basket.

Trivet

This trivet is a good project for beginners. Made to a larger diameter it could be used as the top for a cane table. The finished trivet measures 8in *(20cm)* in diameter.

Materials required:

Approx. 1½oz *(42.5g)* No. 6 natural cane for 12 stakes, each 16in *(41cm)* long

Approx. 1½oz *(42.5g)* No. 3 natural cane for weavers.

To make

Cane bases are a little more difficult to make, but once the basic process has been learned it will be possible to make

basketwork articles in any size or shape desired, and choice need not be restricted by the sizes of ready-made bases available. A cane base is also much lighter than a wooden one. Cut and prepare the required number of stakes. Make a slit about 1in *(2.5cm)* long through the centre of six stakes. Thread the other six stakes through these slits, sliding them close together to form a cross (Fig 12). Bend a long length of No. 3 weaver cane in half and slip the loop over one group of six stakes (Fig 14). Work two rows of pairing, treating each group of six stakes as one. Divide stakes into eight groups of three. Work two rows of pairing, treating each group of three stakes as one. Fasten off weavers by tucking ends into the weaving.

Start the next round of weaving 1in *(2.5cm)* from the last, to form the open work. Bend a length of No. 3 weaver in half and slip the loop round a stake. Work 12 rounds of pairing over single stakes. Leave ends at back. Place in warm water to dampen stakes. With the round-nosed pliers, squeeze each stake close to the last row of pairing. To start the edging, take one stake, bend it down to the right, behind the next stake, in front of the third and fourth stakes, and pass it to the back behind the fifth stake. Continue all around until the starting stakes are reached. Ease these first stakes upwards with the bodkin to enable the last working stakes to be woven through, completing the edging pattern (Fig 13). Ease trivet into shape and leave to dry out thoroughly. Cut off spare ends at a slant at the back of the trivet.

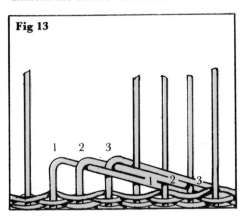

Fig 13

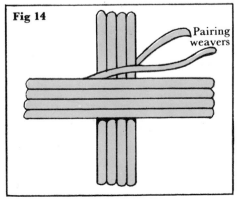

Fig 14

Pairing weavers

Fruit Basket

This elegant basket is useful for holding fruit, bread or eggs or even balls of coloured yarn to bring order to your work corner. The finished basket is about 3in *(8cm)* high with a top diameter of 9in *(23cm)*.

Materials required:

Approx. 8oz *(227g)* No. 8 bleached cane for:

8 stakes 56in *(142cm)* long
32 bye stakes, 28in *(71cm)* long
Approx. 4oz *(113g)* No. 4 natural cane for centre weaving.

To make the basket

Cut and prepare the required number of stakes. Make a slit about ¾in *(2cm)* long through the centre of four stakes. Thread the other four stakes through these slits, sliding them close together to form a cross (same method as shown in Fig 12 but fewer stakes). Bend a long length of No. 4 natural cane in half, and slip the loop over one group of four stakes (Fig 14). Weave four rows of pairing, treating each group of four stakes as one. Divide stakes into eight groups of two stakes. Weave four rows of pairing, treating each group of two stakes as one. Divide into single stakes (16). Weave four rounds of pairing. Trim one end of each bye stake to a point. Insert each bye stake into the weaving, placing one each side of each original stake. Weave six more rounds of pairing, at the same time easing stakes upwards to make slighly concave. By this time the basket should measure about 5½in *(14cm)* across.

Place work in warm water to damp the stakes. With the round-nosed pliers, squeeze each stake level with last row of pairing. Work sides by interweaving the actual stakes and finishing with a plait around the outer edge of the base. Work around the outside of the basket from left to right with a group of three stakes. From now on, each group of three stakes will be considered as one stake. Bend it up and over towards the right to form an arch 3in *(8cm)* above the last row of pairing. Pass this stake (1) in front of next stake (2) behind the third, in front of the fourth, behind the fifth and in front of the sixth to face outwards at the top edge of the base pairing. Work all around bringing in each stake (group of three) in its turn, and weaving the last stakes into the first stakes to complete the pattern. All free ends are now used for working the base plait. Place basket in warm water to dampen the ends of stakes again if they have dried out.

Working from left to right, take one stake (one group of three) and ease over to the right. Pass it under the next stake (2); over the following stake (3); and inside against the fourth stake. Take the next stake and repeat the same interweaving. Continue all around, until the starting ends are reached. Ease the last few canes under the first ones, using a needle if necessary. Ends should be slanting towards the centre of the underneath surface of the base.

Leave basket to dry out thoroughly. Trim all ends off at a slant.

Note: When base braid is being worked, make sure that arched sides are not pulled out of place. They must maintain their height of 3in *(8cm)*.

Fabric Craft

Fabric craft is not strictly a craft – the term covers a group of needlework techniques. However, the special creativity in fabric craft comes from choosing exactly the right fabric for the project – and using the colour and the design to develop the basic idea. Often the inspiration for a toy or an accessory is stimulated by the fabric itself.

To enjoy fabric craft fully, it is essential to have a rich collection or rag bag of fabric scraps. Buy end-of-season remnants, choosing them for pattern, colour and washability. Collect dressmaking remnants from friends and hoard scraps of trimmings and ribbons.

Tie and Cravat Set

Any man would appreciate this elegant matching set of accessories, made of crease-resistant fabric. The tie is made from a commercial paper pattern. The cravat is given as a graph (below) from which you can cut your own paper pattern.

Materials required:

Cravat: 28in *(71cm)* x 14in *(36cm)* patterned fabric
28in *(71cm)* x 14in *(36cm)* lining fabric
Matching thread
Necktie: $\frac{7}{8}$yd *(82cm)* 36in *(92cm)* wide fabric
$\frac{5}{8}$yd *(58cm)* interfacing
Matching thread.

Make up tie according to pattern instructions.

To make the cravat

Draw a paper pattern from the graph. Pin the paper pattern to the doubled fabric and cut out two pieces. Pin the pattern to the lining fabric and cut out two pieces. Mark the pleat lines on the patterned fabric with basting stitches.
Pin, baste and seam together two patterned pieces at AB. Press seam open. Seam two lining pieces together in the same way. Place the patterned fabric on the lining, right sides facing. Machine stitch all around, leaving 2in *(5cm)* at the neck to turn to the right side. Trim seam allowance and clip corners diagonally. Turn, close the open seam with oversewing and press, making sure that the lining cannot be seen from the right side.
Fold broken lines to solid lines to pleat the neckline. Baste pleats. Machine stitch from C–D to hold pleats. Press.

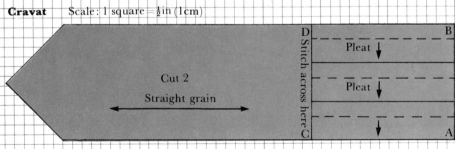

Hot Pot Holders

Scraps of gaily printed fabrics make attractive kitchen accessories. Here are two to make, an oven glove and a mitt.

Oven glove, materials required:

$\frac{1}{4}$yd *(23cm)* 36in *(90cm)* wide gaily printed fabric
Stranded embroidery cotton in black
$\frac{1}{4}$yd *(23cm)* 36in *(90cm)* wide plain fabric
Matching sewing thread
Synthetic wadding
Bias binding to tone

To make the oven glove (see page 124)
Draw a paper pattern from Fig 1. Cut out shape. Pin pattern to the fabric and cut out. Embroider around the central motif in black if required.
Using paper pattern, cut another piece of fabric to back the embroidered side of

the glove, and another two pieces for the palm in a toning or contrasting fabric. Cut two thicknesses of wadding. Place these between two palm pieces of fabric with wrong sides together and baste around the edge. Baste the embroidered

and backing pieces ws together without padding. Bind the cuff edge on both halves of the glove. Baste the two pieces together, right side out, then join all around outer edge with zigzag stitch. Trim raw edges. Bind all around.

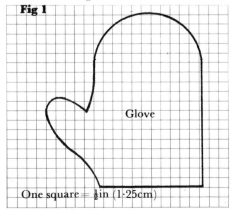

Fig 1 Glove
One square = $\frac{1}{2}$in (1·25cm)

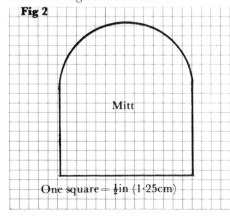

Fig 2 Mitt
One square = $\frac{1}{2}$in (1·25cm)

Oven mitt, materials required:
½yd *(46cm)* 36in *(90cm)* wide gaily printed cotton fabric
½yd *(46cm)* plain fabric
Matching sewing thread
Stranded embroidery cotton in black
Black ric-rac
8 white lace daisies
Synthetic wadding
Bias binding.

To make the mitt
Trace a pattern from the graph (Fig 2). Pin the pattern to the fabric and cut out. Cut the second mitt end in a similar way. The two ends need not be in identical fabric, in fact it is more fun if they are

not. Outline fabric design in ric-rac and embroider with black thread. Stitch on the daisy motifs.
Cut a backing piece for each embroidered mitt and with the wrong sides together, baste around the edge of each mitt. Then bind the straight edge on each as shown.
Cut two lengths of plain fabric 27in *(68.5cm)* long by 8in *(23cm)* wide, and one or two thicknesses of wadding. Baste the wadding between the two pieces of fabric, right sides outside. Place the mitts, right side up, on top of the strip, one at each end, and baste in place. Join all the way around, following rounded edge of mitts with zigzag stitch. Trim raw edges and corners. Bind all around.

Sunshine Breakfast Set

Choose a cheery cotton fabric in sunshine yellows and golds for this breakfast set. It will make all the difference in the world to your early morning mood!

Materials required:
½yd *(46cm)* 48in *(1.22m)* wide printed cotton
½yd *(46cm)* ¾in *(2cm)* wide double-edged broderie Anglaise [eyelet embroidery]
½yd *(46cm)* ¾in *(2cm)* wide frilled broderie Anglaise [eyelet embroidery]
1½yd *(1.32m)* narrow broderie Anglaise [eyelet embroidery] or guipure lace
½yd *(46cm)* ½in *(1cm)* wide bias binding in white
Synthetic wadding
Narrow elastic
Threads to match fabric and edgings.

Preparing the patterns
Draw up the pattern for the teapot cosy as follows:
Draw a 9in *(23cm)* diameter circle and mark the centre, point A. Mark a straight line from the top edge of the circle to the bottom, through A (see Fig 3). Then mark point B 2½in *(6cm)* below A, and draw line C–D at right-angles to A–B. Mark point E ¾in *(2cm)* from the edge of the circle (point F), and draw line G–H parallel to C–D. Now extend line E–F ¼in *(6mm)* to point J (1in *(2.5cm)* above point E), and draw line K–L, 6in *(15cm)* long, centre J and parallel to G–H. Then join K–G and L–H. Finally, draw an arc between points K and L with the point of the compass at A. Cut out, omitting the shaded section at the base, so that it looks like the smaller drawing in Fig 3.
Draw a 5in *(12.5cm)* diameter circle for the base. Allow ½in *(1cm)* turnings all around, cut out the pattern four times and the base circle twice from the printed cotton.
Cut the pattern twice more, and the base circle once, in doubled wadding.

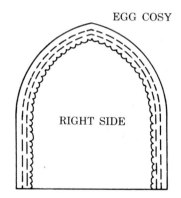

EGG COSY

RIGHT SIDE

Fig 4a

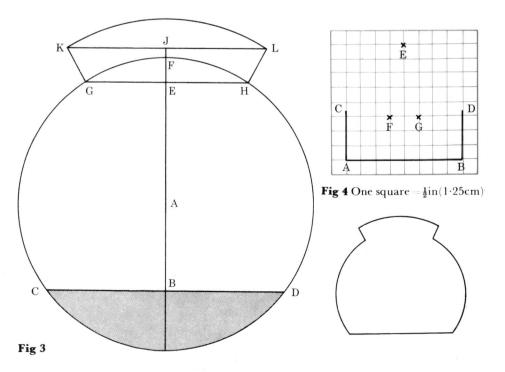

Fig 3

Fig 4 One square = ½in(1·25cm)

This time cut same size as the pattern, without allowing turnings.

To make the teapot cosy

Baste a layer of double wadding to the wrong side of each lining piece for the cosy and to the base circle lining. Mark the edge of the pattern shape on the wrong side of the two outer pieces, then place each piece onto the linings, with right sides together. Stitch all around, leaving the straight lower edges open. Trim seams, clip curves and corners and turn right side out. Turn in raw edges and baste.

Pad and stitch base pieces in the same way remembering to leave a section unstitched to turn to right side. Use slip stitch to close the section. Oversew to join straight lower edges of each half of the cosy to the base, corners meeting. Stitch the binding to the wrong side of the double-edged broderie Anglaise [eyelet embroidery], forming a channel. Thread elastic through and join the short ends to make a circle. Draw up the circle and slip over the top of the cosy to hold the two sides together.

To make the egg cosy

Rule a sheet of paper into $\frac{1}{2}$in (1cm) squares or use suitable graph paper (See Fig 4). Draw line A B (4in (10cm) long), then A–C and B–D (each $1\frac{3}{4}$in (4.5cm)). Mark point E (4in (10cm) above A–B) and, with the point of a pair of compasses at F, draw an arc to join E–D, and with the point at G, join E–C. This makes the egg cosy pattern. Allowing $\frac{1}{2}$in (1cm) turnings all around, cut out the pattern in fabric four times. Cut the pattern out twice more in single wadding without turnings. Baste the single layer of wadding to the wrong side of each lining piece. With right sides facing, join all around the top edge, leaving the lower edge open. Trim and clip seam.

Mark the edge of the pattern shape on the right side of one outer cosy piece, stitch frilled broderie Anglaise [eyelet embroidery] along this line, with the scalloped edge toward the centre (See Fig 4a). Allow a little extra at the top of the cosy. Place the second outer cosy piece on top of this trimmed piece, right sides facing and, following the previous stitching line, stitch all around, but leaving lower edge open. Trim and clip seam and turn the cosy to right side. Fit the padded lining inside the outer case. Turn in the edges of the outer cosy and lining neatly and slip stitch to close.

To make the napkin

Cut a 12in (30cm) square of printed cotton. Make the edges neat with zigzag stitch, or by turning a narrow hem. Trim with narrow broderie Anglaise [eyelet embroidery].

Striped Bath Mat

The bathmat illustrated is of soft terry cloth towelling with a close pile. The underside is the same dark blue as used for the striped top side. Unless you are using the fabric for making colour matched accessories for the bathroom, this design is rather extravagant in its use of material. For instance, a large piece of the dark blue towelling will be left over—enough for a pair of guest hand towels. For economy, you could dye partially-worn white bath towels instead of buying new fabric.

Materials required:

36in (92cm) wide terry cloth towelling: $1\frac{1}{4}$yd (1.15m) dark blue; $\frac{1}{4}$yd (23cm) pink; $\frac{1}{4}$yd (23cm) turquoise; $\frac{1}{8}$yd (12cm) orange.

50g ball thick crochet cotton in orange.

To make the bathmat

Cut a piece of the dark blue for the underside of the mat 20in x 28in (50cm x 70cm). Cut the dark blue piece for the top side to the measurements on the diagram (Fig 5).

Cut the strips to the measurements given. Each strip is 4in (10cm) deep and all

125

Fig 5

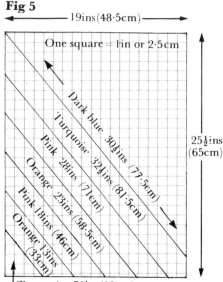

One square = 1in or 2.5cm

19ins (48·5cm)

25½ins (65cm)

Dark blue 30½ins (77.5cm)
Turquoise 32½ins (81.5cm)
Pink 28ins (71cm)
Orange 23ins (58.5cm)
Pink 18ins (46cm)
Orange 13ins (33cm)
Turquoise 7½ins (19cm)

the measurements include ½in *(1cm)* seam allowances. Join the strips on the long sides in the colour sequence shown. Seam the long side of the turquoise strip to the dark blue piece. Press all seams open. Place the top and under-side together, right sides facing and baste all around. Machine stitch all around twice but leaving approximately 6in *(15cm)* of the seam open for turning. Trim seam allowance closely and turn to right side. Close the opening with oversewing.

To finish
Cut the orange crochet cotton into 9in *(23cm)* lengths. Tie 10 strands together tightly at the middle of the bunch, to make tassels. Sew the bunches to both ends of the bathmat as shown.

Emmeline

Emmeline is a traditional rag doll with a lot of charm, and any little girl would treasure her. Emmeline is quite sophisticated enough to be an adult mascot too.

Materials required:
¼yd *(23cm)* 36in *(92cm)* wide light weight muslin for the body
⅜yd *(34cm)* 36in *(92cm)* wide printed cotton for the dress
¼yd *(23cm)* 36in *(92cm)* wide white cotton for pantalettes
9in *(23cm)* square black felt
¼yd *(23cm)* 1in *(2.5cm)* wide broderie Anglaise [eyelet embroidery]
¼yd *(23cm)* narrow satin ribbon
¼yd *(23cm)* narrow elastic
1yd *(92cm)* white ric rac
1yd *(92cm)* 1in *(2.5cm)* wide velvet ribbon
Gold bead
25g ball double knitting yarn in black
¼yd *(23cm)* narrow black braid
2 buttons with four holes in each
Buttonhole twist
Stranded cotton in black and pink
Carpet thread
Kapok or other suitable stuffing
Thin cardboard.

To make the doll
Draw all pattern pieces onto ½in *(1cm)* squared paper and cut out. Mark but do not cut across dotted lines on body, leg and arm.

Pin one long edge of muslin and printed cotton materials together, right sides facing, and sew along with ½in *(1cm)* seam. Press seam open. Spread out joined pieces. Pin patterns for arm and body with dotted lines at seam of two materials and cut out. (Remember to reverse patterns to give two pairs of each). Cut out with ½in *(1cm)* seam allowance all around (See Fig 1). Mark X for button on wrong side of arms. Join a 9in *(23cm)* square of felt to the other

side of the body material and cut out legs and feet in the same way.

Cut four head pieces from body material, reversing two, and two soles from black felt. Glue these onto thin cardboard.

Body With right sides facing, join head and body pieces at centre front and back, carefully matching joins on material. Snip into seam allowance at $\frac{1}{2}$in *(1cm)* intervals. Again with right sides facing, join each pair of head pieces to a pair of body pieces. Pin and baste together the two resulting shapes all around the sides and join, leaving straight bases A–B open for stuffing.

Legs With right sides together sew around legs leaving tops and sole edges open. Snip into seam and turn right side out. Turn seam allowance at top of legs to inside and fold so that front and back seams are together. Oversew along straight tops. (See Fig 2).

Arms Using buttonhole twist, sew a button to two arm pieces at X on the wrong side of the material, making sure there is a pair. The thread should form a clear cross on right side of material. (Fig 3). With right sides together, sew all around arms, leaving about 1$\frac{1}{2}$in *(3.5cm)* open on the backs of the sleeves. Snip into seam allowance and trim all around hand. Snip into join of thumb. Turn work to right side.

Stuffing Fill body very firmly with stuffing. Turn in seam allowance and oversew matching centre front and back seams.

Fill hands and lower arms very firmly using a little stuffing at a time and paying particular attention to thumb and finger parts of hands. Stuff sleeve part of arms a little less firmly. Turn seam allowance to inside and close gaps. Stuff legs firmly. Before completing, oversew soles to feet, matching C and D, finishing stuffing at same time.

To assemble the doll
Using carpet thread and an extra long darning needle, fasten arms to body as follows: Push needle under cross made by sewing on button. Do not stitch through fabric. Mark points on seam sides of body 1$\frac{5}{8}$in *(4cm)* down from neck join and push needle right through body from point to point. Pass needle under cross made on the other arm and push it through again to emerge at the point it entered originally. Repeat the whole operation once more, then pull thread tight. Knot ends firmly and cut off excess. The thread must be pulled tight to pivot the arms successfully. (Fig 4).

Place doll upside down between the knees and oversew legs to body at the backs, holding them in a sitting position while sewing.

To sew the dress
From dress material cut a piece 4$\frac{1}{2}$in x 21in *(11cm x 54cm)* for skirt. Cut a skirt frill 34in x 2in *(87cm x 5cm)* and two sleeve frills each 9in x 2in *(23cm x 5cm)*. Press in $\frac{1}{4}$in *(6mm)* on one long edge of frills and

oversew to make neat or machine stitch with zigzag. Join short edges of each frill and skirt.

Press in $\frac{1}{2}$in *(1cm)* on other side of frills and one edge of skirt and gather, stitching $\frac{1}{8}$in *(3mm)* in from edge through double material. Draw up frills to fit skirt and sleeves. Do not draw up skirt gathering yet. With right sides facing, pin skirt frill to ungathered edge of skirt, overlapping each by $\frac{1}{2}$in *(1cm)*. Top stitch frill to skirt. Top stitch one row of ric-rac just above frill. Draw up skirt gathering to fit lower edge of bodice and oversew in place. Oversew sleeve frills to sleeves and stitch one row of ric-rac around each sleeve. Cut 6in *(15cm)* from 1in *(2.5cm)* velvet ribbon and tie the rest around the waist, with a bow at the back. Catch stitch in place. Sew narrow black braid around the neck with a bead in the centre front.

To sew the pantalettes
Draw and cut out pattern from squared paper. Cut pieces with $\frac{1}{2}$in *(1cm)* seam allowance. Join centre front seam from E–F. Thread the narrow satin ribbon through broderie Anglaise [eyelet embroidery]. With right side facing join broderie Anglaise [eyelet embroidery] to straight bases G–H–G, then join inner leg seams F–G including frilled edges. Try on, adjusting length at waist if necessary. Stitch $\frac{1}{2}$in *(1cm)* seam to inside at top of pantalettes and run elastic through. The pantalettes may be stitched to the body at the top of waist.

Hair
Cut 55 strands of black yarn each 20in *(51cm)* long. Lay across head starting and finishing 1$\frac{1}{2}$in *(3.5cm)* away from seam running from side to side. Back stitch along centre part. Arrange evenly around head and back stitch down all around at eye level. (See Fig 5).

For front, cut the remainder of the wool in 28in *(71cm)* strands. Lay across head along part, at right angles to first strands of hair. Centre of strands should be at lowest point of fringe. Back stitch across strands at centre. Fold back strands at stitching and tie the yarn together about 3in *(7.5cm)* back from fold. Stitch to head. Arrange remainder of velvet ribbon over stitching and sew in place.

Features
Measure along centre seam of face 1in *(2.5cm)* up from neck join and embroider a mouth about $\frac{3}{4}$in *(2cm)* wide in rows of pink stem stitch. For eyes, measure 1$\frac{3}{4}$in *(4.5cm)* up from neck join for inner eye level. Embroider in black stem stitch 1in *(2.5cm)* long pointed ovals, each inner point $\frac{3}{8}$in *(1cm)* away from centre seam, as shown in the illustration. Pupil of eye is stem stitch with a single stem stitch line of white down centre for highlight and to give expression.

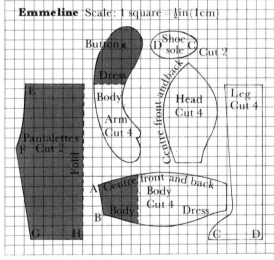

Emmeline Scale: 1 square = $\frac{1}{2}$in(1cm)

Button x

D Shoe sole C Cut 2

Dress

Body

Head Cut 4

Leg Cut 4

E

Arm Cut 4

Centre front and back

Pantalettes Cut 2

Fold

F

A Centre front and back

Body Cut 4

B Body

Dress

G H

C D

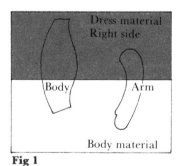

Dress material Right side

Body

Arm

Body material

Fig 1

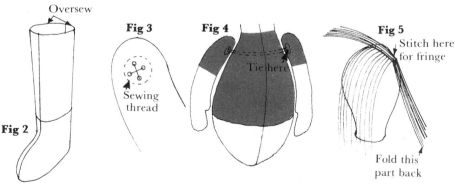

Oversew

Fig 2

Fig 3

Sewing thread

Fig 4

Tie here

Fig 5

Stitch here for fringe

Fold this part back

Lampshades

Lampshades can be expensive to buy and yet they cost comparatively little to make – especially if old frames are re-used. Basically, there are three kinds of lampshade: classic, hard and soft. These include the stretched, swathed and pleated styles and the various types of novelty shades such as the Tiffany design.

The classic balloon-lined shade is quite difficult to make and requires some expertise. Hard shades are probably the easiest to start on.

MATERIALS AND EQUIPMENT

Apart from the actual frame, very little equipment is required. A pair of sharp scissors, needles, pins and a thimble are essential however. The needles should be short so that they do not break if they strike the frame – No. 5 or 6 are recommended, and small fine pins are most suitable for this craft. The choice of materials for the shade depends on the room, the type of shade visualised and the amount of money available for the project. For a paper shade, enough suitable paper, a little adhesive or sewing thread and perhaps some fringe for trimming are all that is required. For fabric shades, binding tape and fabric lining as well as the material for the actual shade should be purchased. For a soft fabric shade the trimming is important. A fancy braid can be used to decorate the edge and a luxurious fringe to trim the bottom, or just a self fabric trim.

PREPARING THE FRAME

Check that the edges of the frame are smooth. If it is not already painted, paint it with a quick-drying enamel to prevent the metal from rusting. Alternatively, if making a fabric shade, the frame is bound on all rings and struts where fabric will be attached.

Measure each strut and allow double the length for binding material. As can be seen in Fig 1 the binding always starts and finishes at the point where a ring and strut meet. The binding must be tight and smooth (Figs 2 and 3). Bind each strut separately and then bind the top and bottom rings. The binding is knotted to secure (Fig 4). No sewing is needed except on hard lampshades where there are only top and lower rings to be bound.

HARD LAMPSHADES

These are the easiest kind of shades to make requiring only two rings and stiffened material. Handicraft shops and department stores provide a variety of suitable stiffened materials in plain colours and printed designs, or adhesive-backed or bonding parchment can be used to stiffen a fabric. This is ironed onto the fabric with a hot iron. Only fabrics which will stand a hot iron can be stiffened in this way.

Hard Shade

This hard lampshade is easy to make and would be a smart addition to both modern and traditionally-styled homes.

Materials required:
¾yd *(69cm)* 36in *(92cm)* wide non-fraying fabric
Two 8in *(21cm)* diameter lampshade rings, one with an inner lamp fitting

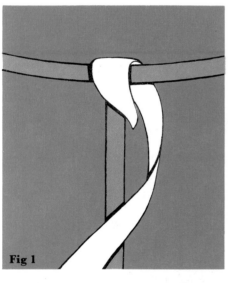

Fig 1

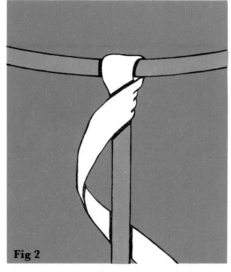

Fig 2

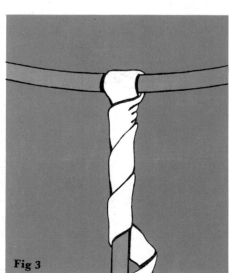

Fig 3

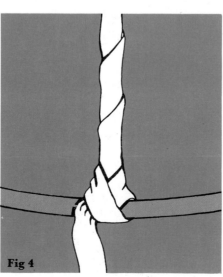

Fig 4

Adhesive or bonding parchment
1½yd (1.38m) ⅜in (1cm) wide gilt braid
Lampshade binding tape
All-purpose clear drying adhesive.

To make the lampshade
Bind the rings. Measure around the outer edge of one ring and add 1in (2.5cm). Cut a piece of parchment to this length by 7½in (19cm). If necessary, adjust the depth to suit the pattern of fabric being used. Cut a strip of fabric ½in (1cm) longer than the length of parchment and to the same depth. Iron the parchment onto the fabric, overlapping ½in (1cm) at one end, making sure that the fabric has adhered firmly all over.
Using double thread, oversew one edge of the fabric-covered parchment to one ring. Do not stitch the overlap. Oversew the bottom edge to the second ring. Glue the overlap to close. Complete the stitching at top and bottom.
Glue braid around the top and bottom edges.

Yellow Drum Shade

This shade is even simpler to make. A printed, plasticised material is used which requires no stiffening or sewing. Prepare the frame and cut the material to the depth required by the circumference of the rings, plus 1in (2.5cm). Glue the overlap to make the drum. Apply adhesive to the top ring and glue the top edge of the shade to the ring. Hold it in position with clothes pegs or paper clips until the adhesive dries. Glue the lower edge in the same way. The edges can be finished with decorative braid if desired.

Flowered Shade

An old lampshade frame can be given a quick face-lift with this simple technique. All that is required is a length of fabric and some pieces of coloured felt or scraps of plain material.

Materials required:
Half-circle lampshade frame
Covering fabric, the depth of the shade plus 1½in (3.5cm) by the circumference plus 1in (2.5cm)
Lining fabric, an equal amount
Scraps of dark green, yellow and turquoise felt
All-purpose clear drying adhesive
¼in (6m) wide tape

To make the shade
Paint the frame if required and bind with lampshade tape. Seam the two short sides of the cover fabric with a

double seam. Press. Make a narrow casing in the top edge. Cut a hole and buttonholestitch the opening, to insert ¼in *(6mm)* tape. Turn ½in *(1cm)* hem on the bottom edge of the shade and hem or machine stitch. Draw up a paper pat-

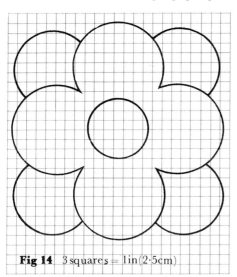

Fig 14   3 squares = 1in(2·5cm)

tern from the diagram of the flower (Fig 14). Cut templates and then cut out the shapes in felt. Glue or stitch the flowers round the shade cover, just touching the bottom edge. Insert tape into casing at the top. Do not cut off the tape ends. Knot them and tuck them into the casing with a knitting needle. Slip the cover onto the frame and secure with one or two stitches through the tape. If the shade is to be washable, make the appliqué motifs in colour-fast fabric adding ¼in *(6mm)* seam allowances.

Classic Shade

Lampshade frames with curved struts require a different covering technique because the fabric is stretched onto the frame. Once the basic method has been mastered, a variety of shaped lampshades can be made in the same way.

Materials required:

For a 10in *(25cm)* bowed empire lampshade with a balloon lining:

$\frac{3}{8}$in *(1cm)* wide lampshade binding tape
$\frac{1}{2}$yd *(45cm)* 36in *(90cm)* wide fabric for cover
$\frac{1}{2}$yd *(45cm)* 36in *(90cm)* wide lining fabric

To make the outer cover

Bind the frame. Fold the cover fabric in half with rs together, insert a pin at each corner to hold the pieces together. With the fold at the top and the grain running from top to bottom, place material onto one side of the frame. Insert pins to hold the fabric to the frame (Fig 5).

Start pinning fabric to the side struts placing pins every $\frac{1}{2}$in *(1cm)* with the heads to the centre of the shade. Do not pin to top and bottom rings. Some wrinkles may appear in the fabric at this early stage. When the side struts are pinned, pin the top and bottom rings. Pull the fabric to tighten and to remove wrinkles. Complete pinning down the side struts by inserting pins every $\frac{1}{4}$in *(6mm)* (Fig 6).

Using a soft pencil, mark down the struts between the pins extending the pencil line $\frac{1}{2}$in *(1cm)* beyond the last pin.

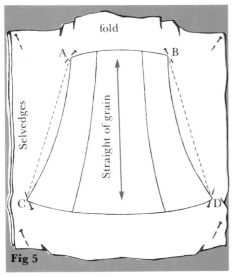

Fig 5

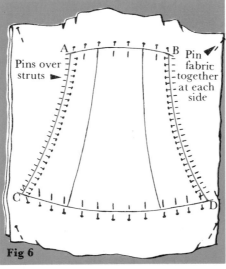

Fig 6

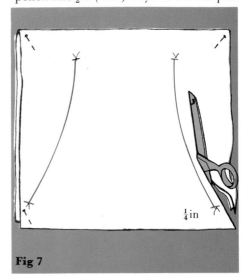

Fig 7

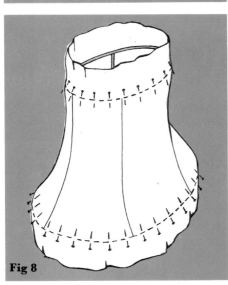

Fig 8

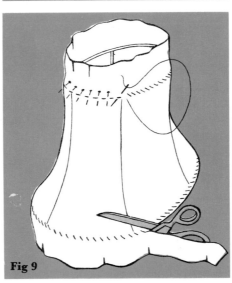

Fig 9

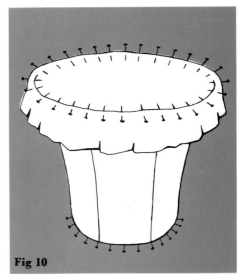

Fig 10

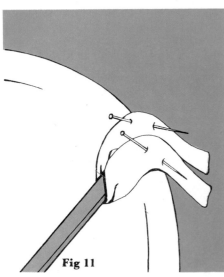

Fig 11

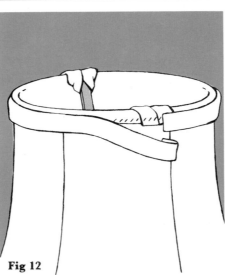

Fig 12

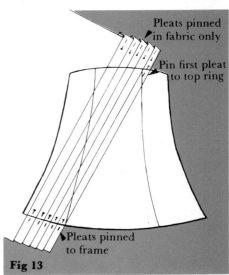

Fig 13

Mark a pencil line ½in *(1cm)* at the top and bottom ring. Remove the pins but keep the four pins holding the fabric together in position. Machine stitch down the pencil line from top to bottom, using a medium-sized stitch. Stretch the fabric while doing this so that when the shade is pulled onto the frame, the stitches will not break. Trim away the excess fabric, ¼in *(6mm)* from the stitching line at each side (Fig 7). Cut through the fold in the fabric at the top edge. Do not trim any of the fabric away at the bottom edge. Prepare the lampshade lining in exactly the same way.

Press the cover flat and then slip it onto the frame, right side out. The seams should align with the side struts. The pencil marks made on the top and bottom rings should line up with the rings. Insert a pin to secure the shade on the side seams. Insert pins every 1in *(2.5cm)* around top and bottom rings (Fig 8). Now oversew the cover to the frame. Work from right to left and place the stitches on the outside edge of the top and bottom rings. Cut away the surplus material from the top and bottom of the lampshade, trimming close to the stitches (Fig 9).

Fitting the lining

Hold the lampshade upside-down and drop in the lining. Match the seams and pencil marks on the top and bottom rings. Pin the lining to the top and bottom rings, inserting the pins on the outside edge of the lampshade (Fig 10). Adjust the pins, pulling the fabric until all the fullness has been taken up. Stitch the lining to the frame as for the cover. The stitches should be on the outside edge of the lampshade.

To fit the lining neatly around the gimble, unpick the seam down to the horizontal pencil mark. Spread the fabric. The gimble is neatened with a crossway strip 1in x 4in *(2.5cm x 10cm)*. Turn in ¼in *(6mm)* at each side to make a ½in *(1cm)* wide strip. This is positioned under the gimble as shown in Fig 11. Oversew, but keep the stitches on the outside edge of the top ring.

Trimming classic lampshades

A crossway trimming looks by far the most professional but braid can be used if preferred. To prepare the crossway trim, measure round the top and bottom of lampshade and allow 2in *(5cm)* for turnings. Cut the strip on the diagonal and 1in *(2.5cm)* in width. Turn in ¼in *(6mm)* on both long edges and press. The strip is glued to the top and bottom rings. (Use piece of the lampshade fabric.)

Apply the adhesive to the wrong side of the cross-strip, spreading it with the tip of a small knife. Take great care in applying the adhesive as it will mark the fabric if used carelessly. Start to apply

the strip ¼in *(6mm)* beyond one of the side seams. Stretch the strip slightly and press it down with the fingertips. The strip should just cover the oversewing stitches and be placed so that it does not extend over to the inside of the shade (Fig 12). Cut off any excess. Turn under ¼in *(6mm)* at the end and glue down to complete the trim, overlapping the other end. Apply the trim to the bottom edge of the lampshade in the same way aligning the join with that on the top ring.

Pleated Shade

This is a most elegant style of lampshade, which involves a little time and patience but is well worth the effort. Choose a fabric in a deep colour to emphasise the shading of the chiffon when the lamp is lit. Use a toning satin for the lining, the shiny side facing the chiffon.

Materials required:

10in *(25cm)* diameter bowed Empire lampshade frame
Lampshade binding tape
1yd *(90cm)* crêpe-backed satin
1yd *(90cm)* 36in *(90cm)* wide silk chiffon
1yd *(90cm)* toning silk fringe
1½yd *(138cm)* silk braid
Fabric adhesive.

To make the lampshade

Bind the frame. Fold the satin lining

fabric diagonally, shiny surface to the inside. Pin the edges. Pin this triangle of doubled fabric over half the frame (Fig 6 shows the basic principle). Mark the line of the two pinned side struts in pencil as for the classic shade. Pin the fabric together at each side of marked struts, and cut away excess about 2in *(5cm)* above and below top and bottom edges. Remove pins and fabric from frame, leaving pins at each side of struts holding fabric together. Stitch the fabric together neatly along the pencil lines, trim close to seam, then turn to the other side. Finish as run and fell seam. Put lining to one side.

To pleat the outer covering, divide the fabric widthways into three 12in *(31cm)* deep strips, each 36in *(90cm)* wide. Cut off the selvedges. Fold the first pleat on one short end–about ⅜in *(1cm)* in width. Pin the pleat to the top and bottom rings as shown in Fig 13. If the frame has six panels, stretch the fabric diagonally across one and a half panels. Make another pleat close to the first, and pin to the bottom ring. Folding the pleat along the line of the fabric, pin the fold in the fabric only just below the top edge; do not pin to top ring yet. Continue pleating and pinning to the bottom ring, pinning each pleat into the fabric at the top–until the next strut is reached. As the top ring is considerably smaller than the bottom, the pleats will obviously need to overlap; it can now be judged by how much the top pleats must overlap to distribute them evenly. Pull each pinned pleat taut and pin it to the top ring. Continue pleating until half the frame is covered. Join in each new strip of fabric by turning under the raw edge, as before, and pinning this first pleat over the raw edge at the end of the previous strip. Oversew the top pleat securely to the frame, removing pins but do not sew the first two pleats–just leave them pinned. Once the top pleats are firmly attached, adjust and re-pin bottom pleats if necessary, before stitching securely into place as for the top. Pleat the remaining half of the frame in the same way, lifting the first two pleats and pinning over the raw end of the very last pleat, to make a neat join. Oversew securely as before.

Cut away surplus fabric close to top and bottom rings. Place the lining inside the shade, shiny side against the chiffon, pinning seams to rings at top and bottom, and then pulling the surplus fabric over the top and bottom rings and pinning over trimmed edge of chiffon. Keep adjusting and re-pinning at top and bottom until the lining is absolutely smooth. Then oversew securely to both rings before trimming away surplus fabric close to stitches. Stitch fringe round lower edge. Then glue braid around top of shade and over the edge of fringe at the bottom.

133

Collage

There is very little to learn about collage because there are so few rules. Very few tools are needed and the basic materials can be anything which is on hand – paper, fabric, foil, pasta, seeds, grasses, feathers, eggshells, string, shells, rope, wood, glass.

In its simplest form, collage is the technique of gluing a material onto a background to make a pattern, a design or a picture. In this chapter, four different collage designs illustrate the various techniques. The flower picture is made of pasta, seeds and dried beans. The beautiful house 'portrait' is a fabric collage. The lady in Edwardian costume is made of fabric and ribbons, and the charming nursery picture is worked in felt alone.

The essential equipment for collage is a suitable adhesive, scissors, a large pair for cutting up fabrics and a small pair for cutting out details, a backing of some kind and the materials being used for the collage.

ADHESIVES

Most professional collage designers use a fabric adhesive because it is clean and convenient to use, but any all-purpose clear drying adhesive can be used. Adhesive should be used sparingly, spread either with a matchstick or with a tooth pick. Use the finger tips if preferred. Adhesive is always applied to the back of each pattern piece which is then placed on the background, rather than the other way round.

BACKGROUNDS

Choose a fabric for the background and mount it onto a piece of Vilene (Pellon) or similar non-woven interfacing. Spread the adhesive onto the fabric in broad horizontal strokes. Allow 3–4in *(8–10cm)* extra fabric all around for finally mounting the collage.

FABRICS FOR FABRIC COLLAGE

Begin by making a collection of fabric scraps in as many colours and textures as possible. No matter how small a remnant, it will be useful for some kind of effect. Generally, it is uneconomic to buy lengths of fabric especially for collage, except perhaps for a background where a large area of colour might be needed. Dressmaking friends, however, are usually delighted to contribute remnants of fabric to a ragbag. Remnant sales can be a source of pieces and sample books of furnishing fabrics are useful because they sometimes contain several pieces of one type of fabric in different shades. Household sales can also provide beautiful old fabrics.

Collect all sorts of material for different effects in collage work. Net, for instance, is a useful fabric because it can be used to reproduce smoke, sea, clouds or give the effect of shadows on buildings.

Silk and cotton nets are soft and can be pleated and bunched. Nylon nets are stiff and will lie flat on the background. Chiffon is useful for sky and sea effects. If preferred, collage can be worked on a stiffened fabric background and mounted when completed by lacing the fabric on the wrong side of the mount.

Lion Wall Hanging

This bright and amusing collage, suitable for hanging in a child's room, is great fun to work because it uses a variety of coloured felts and trimmings to achieve the effect. However, scraps of woven fabrics, both patterned and plain, can be used instead of felt if preferred.

Materials required:
16in x 12in *(41cm x 30cm)* olive green hessian (burlap)
Vilene or Pellon
Gold terry cloth towelling
Gold, pink, deep pink, cream, black, white, brown, green, red, yellow, blue, orange felt
Synthetic wadding
Scraps of brown, dark brown, gold and

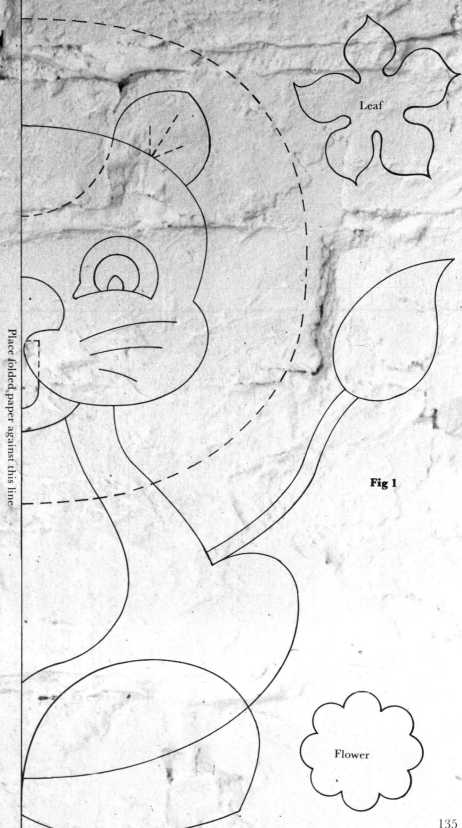

Place folded paper against this line

Leaf

Fig 1

Flower

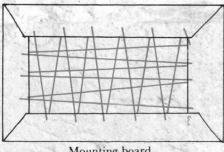

Mounting board

135

black braid
Thick embroidery thread in black
Guipure lace daisies in black
Double knitting yarn for mane in gold mixture
Light green raffia
Approx. 30in *(77cm)* bamboo cane or wooden dowel
Transparent adhesive tape
Fabric adhesive
String

Preparing the pattern

Trace the design, (Fig 1), onto a sheet of folded tracing paper, omitting the tail. Trace the design through to complete it, open the paper and use as the pattern.

Trace the body of the lion onto the Vilene or Pellon, excluding the paws, tail, and all broken lines except the forelock. Turn over and trace the eyes, nose, whiskers and forelock through to the back. Trace the paws separately.

Cut out the main lion shape and the separate paws. Cut off the head, then the lower mouth (including the tongue), and the ears (mark left and right).

Glue the head and paws to the wrong side of the terry cloth towelling. Glue the body to gold felt, the ears to pink felt and the lower mouth to cream felt and cut out.

Glue short lengths of yarn to each ear— as broken lines. Place the head, right side down, over the pattern: add the ears. Tape the ears back into position against the head. Glue narrow dark brown braid around the back of each ear, so that just the edge of the braid overlaps. Trace a paper pattern for the tongue, cut in deep pink felt. Place the tongue over the main pattern, spread adhesive on the top corners and press the head piece down on top. With the head face down add the lower mouth.

Trace the nose, and the eyes, pupils and centres separately onto Vilene or Pellon. Glue the eyes to white felt, the pupils to brown and the centres and nose to black felt. Cut out. Glue narrow black or dark brown braid to the back of each eye. Glue nose and eyes into position, then add the pupils and centres to the eyes.

To make the whiskers, push a pin through to mark the outer end. Knot and bring thick black thread up at the inner end of the whisker, then cut the thread to length and glue in a slight curve to meet the pin.

For the forelock glue short lengths of yarn closely side-by-side to form a fringe, overlapping the top edge. Trim the overlap to $\frac{1}{2}$in *(1cm)*, and glue to the back of the head.

For the mane cut and glue together a number of $1\frac{1}{2}$in *(3.5cm)* lengths of yarn around the back of the head, radiating out over the edge. Trace the tuft at the end of the tail onto Vilene or Pellon. Glue a length of yarn all around the

edge, beginning and ending at the tip, and continue until the centre is reached. Trim the ends. Trace a paper pattern for the lion's chest and cut in synthetic wadding. Glue lightly into position on the body. Place the body, right side up, on the pattern, and glue the paws into position. Glue decorative braid along the lower edge of each paw.

Place the head face down on the pattern, trim the mane and then add the body, right side down, overlapping the mane. Tape together securely.

To make the flowers and leaves, trace the shapes onto Vilene or Pellon. Glue to the felt and then cut out. Glue a small black lace daisy in the centre of each flower.

Cut a piece of hessian (burlap) 16in x 12in *(41cm x 30cm)* for the background. Turn under a narrow $\frac{1}{4}$in *(6mm)* hem at each side; press. Make a 1in *(2.5cm)* deep hem at top and bottom.

Glue the back of the lion (not the mane) and place him on the background, about $1\frac{1}{2}$in *(4cm)* above the lower edge. Position the leaves across the top and glue them down. Glue lengths of green raffia at each side of the lion for grass. Mark the position of the tail from the pattern. Glue narrow gold braid along the line of the tail and add the tuft at the end. Position and glue flowers into place. Cut two pieces of bamboo or dowel about 13–14in *(33–36cm)* long depending on width of fabric. Thread rods through channels at top and bottom and then fix string at each end of top rod to hang.

Jane Austen Style House

This Austen-period house makes a charming collage and the same technique can be used to make a 'portrait' of your own home. Whether you live in a pretty country house or in a row of town houses, or in an apartment building, your home can be translated into a very attractive collage picture.

Working the design

First make a drawing of your home, to work out the perspective, or take several photographs. If you are unable to draw very well, aim for a flat representation rather than the more difficult three-dimensional effect of the collage.

Mount the background 'sky' fabric on Vilene (Pellon) or other interfacing. The trees and the background buildings are applied next. The middle area, the building itself, trees, paths etc., are then glued down, working towards the foreground of the picture. Cut the main building out of interfacing first and use this for planning the positions of doors and windows etc.

Ideas for effects

Skies look pretty if shaded chiffon is used over cotton or satin but a flat, textured fabric will do just as well. Net or chiffon scraps make realistic clouds.

Trees, bushes and shrubs Use a variety of different fabrics for the greenery, and fray the edges. Olive green tones look better than bright greens, but sunlit areas can be worked in yellow-green fabrics. Dye or paint scraps of lace in olive green and cut into irregular shapes. Lay the pieces of lace over cords ravelled from braids for the effect of leaves over branches. Use thick strands of yarn for tree trunks.

Flowers Ribbons and scraps of braid massed together look like flower borders and it is better to aim for a massed effect rather than try to make up individual flowers. Fruit on fruit trees can be cut out of felt. Knitting yarn, especially the bouclé variety, makes good foliage and it can be dipped in paste to stiffen it.

Stone and brickwork Textured fabrics are useful for reproducing most building fabrics, but it may be better to paint brickwork using watercolours. Stonework is simulated by dipping a textured fabric such as moquette in black coffee. The perspective of buildings is achieved by placing black net over the shadowed side of the building.

Roofs Corduroy can look like slates or tiles, and rough-textured tweed also looks very effective. Fur can represent thatch and tiles should be cut out individually from felt.

Paths and paving Cut these from matt fabrics or felt. Mount stones over a dark coloured fabric for the cement between paving stones.

Windows Windows should be black unless the curtains are a feature of the house. Do not attempt to detail interiors. If the window frames and glazing bars are distinctive, outline these with a single strand unravelled from a length of braid. The outside of window frames must be carefully cut and mitred. Diamond panes can be simulated by using a black and white checked fabric glued down on the cross. If there are windows on a side wall of the house, make sure that the perspective of the window frames and the glazing bars is accurate.

Doors Glazed or satinised fabrics make effective doors, and panels can be detailed with a single strand of braid. Door hardware can be worked in metallic braids or with beads.

Words and letters

A house 'portrait' may well become a family heirloom and it is a nice idea to identify it with the date of when the collage was made. The lettering and numerals can be worked in a single strand of cord unravelled from a length of braid and glued down. Russian braid is particularly suitable for this.

138

Edwardian Lady

The emphasis in this collage is on the fabric and the clever blending of colour. This subject demonstrates the use of lace and proves the effectiveness of a subtle colour scheme. The order of working is given so it can be seen easily how the effect is achieved.

Materials required:
Tracing paper
White cartridge or construction paper
3½in (9cm) wide deep cream moiré ribbon
½yd (46cm) 2½in (6cm) wide cream and deep brown lace
½yd (46cm) 1in (2.5cm) wide coffee and deep brown lace
½yd (46cm) ½in (1cm) wide black lace
12½in x 7½in (31cm x 19cm) sage green felt glued to a piece of sturdy cardboard
Scraps of coffee, dark brown and cream satin ribbon
Fabric adhesive
Tooth pick.

To work the design
Enlarge the design (Fig 2) and transfer it to white cartridge or construction paper. Cut out the pieces. Begin by cutting off the top of the left arm along the line of the back and cover with deep cream moiré ribbon. Let the fabric overlap the edge which joins the body and cover the ribbon with a scrap of cream lace. Then use the overlap to stick behind the body, replacing the arm in its previous position. Cut a strip of ribbon for the back, down to the bow of the bustle, carefully placing the marking of the ribbon to the best effect. Cut the right arm again using moiré ribbon and cream lace with a scrap of coffee coloured satin ribbon for the glove, and coffee lace trimming the cuff and neck. The full sweep of the bustle as it forms a train is in moiré ribbon – and also the top section of the skirt, just below the band of ribbon. Cut up between the side of the train and the skirt – to the top of the highest frill. To make the frills, cut the entire frill section off along the line of the top frill. Then cut off the top frill, along its lower edge, and cover it with coffee lace, the lower edge of the lace just overlapping the top and each side by about ½in (1cm). This top surplus is glued behind the skirt, so that the frill is back in its original position. Cut off and cover the next frill in the same way – using deep brown lace – and replace it by gluing the surplus behind the top frill.
Continue with the remaining frills in the same way, alternating coffee and deep brown until the lowest is reached, which is made in black. Fold the overlapping lace at the front neatly around and glue it to the back of the figure, doing each frill separately, beginning with the low-

Fig 2

1 SQ = 1 inch

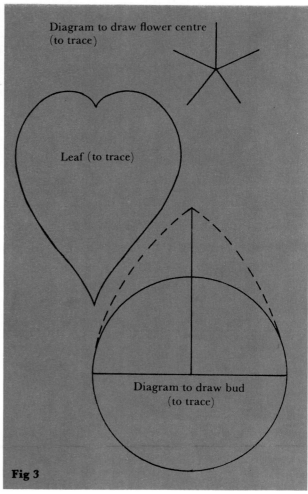

Diagram to draw flower centre
(to trace)

Leaf (to trace)

Diagram to draw bud
(to trace)

Fig 3

est. The excess on the inside is tucked smoothly behind and stuck to the back of the train.

Mask the cut edge of the train (indicated by a broken line) with a scrap of cream lace, then glue slightly gathered deep brown lace around behind the lower edge, as illustrated.

Cut the front sweep of the bow, the two ends and the bow itself, in three separate pieces of paper, covering each with dark brown satin ribbon, and gluing them into position in that order.

Following the edge and the motif, cut deep brown lace into suitable shapes to cover the hat, sticking one on top of another so that the edge of the lace just overlaps all around the edge of the hat, finishing with a single motif in the centre to hide the cut ends. For the border, cut narrow cream lace into pieces to stick behind the hat, leaving just the edge visible all around.

Mount the figure onto the prepared background. The parasol is cut in paper and covered with remaining scraps of moiré ribbon and cream lace, the top edged first with coffee and then deep brown lace, stuck behind the paper to overlap the top as illustrated. Wooden toothpicks make the handle and ferrule, and a tiny bow of narrow cream ribbon trims the base, completing the effect.

Seed Picture

Pastas, dried beans and seeds are a more unusual kind of material for collage design, yet they are colourful and are great fun to work with.

To work the design

Decide the size of the panel and background required. Coarsely woven purple dress fabric was used for the picture illustrated. Plan the flowers, and draw a circle on a piece of tracing paper the size of the finished flower. Trace the angles in Fig 3, matching the centres of angles and circles exactly. Extend each line to meet the edge of the circle. Cut out and arrange this and other flowers as required on the background. Trace leaves and draw buds from diagram, adding these to the design. Move the tracings around until satisfied with the arrangement and then plan the treatment of the different flowers.

Mark the centre and five outer points of each flower with chalk, crayon or felt tip pen. Make the marks so they will eventually be covered. Add lines of stems, indicate positions and leaves and outline the buds. Remove the tracings. Now decide the arrangement of the assorted items planned for each flower. Use clear drying adhesive for sticking down the seeds, pastas, beans and braids.

The largest flower which is 5in *(13cm)* in diameter has a $1\frac{1}{4}$in *(3cm)* diameter centre of coiled thin piping cord, and the shape of the flower is then built up with beans. A line of yellow split peas is arranged up the centre of each petal. Then spread the fabric liberally with adhesive before sprinkling pearl barley over the remainder of each petal, pressing it firmly down into the adhesive. When thoroughly dry, shake gently to remove surplus.

The centre flower is 4in *(10cm)* in diameter and has a 2in *(5cm)* diameter centre of yellow split peas. It is outlined in macaroni and the petals filled in with rice grains.

The top flower is $3\frac{1}{2}$in *(9cm)* in diameter and has a $2\frac{1}{2}$in *(6cm)* diameter centre of coiled thick piping cord with the petals outlined in thinner cord. The petals are filled in with yellow split peas around a line of green split peas. The buds are green split peas, the bud itself outlined in narrow braid filled in with pearl barley. Rough hessian (burlap) is used for the leaves.

Finally a row of green split peas is glued up the centre of each leaf.

Before fixing the leaves, glue the stem into place. Lacing cord is used for the thick stem, with matching narrow braid laid for the stalks of the leaves.

139

Batik

Batik, the technique of using hot wax to prevent dye from penetrating specific areas, is one of the most exciting and fascinating methods of creating a design on fabric or paper. Now an extremely popular craft, batik is thought to have originated on the Indonesian island of Java some two thousand years ago, though early examples have also been found in Egypt and Persia, India, China and Japan.

Over the centuries traditional designs were evolved for royalty, courtiers and servants. Batik did not reach the Western world until the 17th century, when traders from the Dutch East Indies introduced these richly designed fabrics to Holland and from there this method of decoration spread throughout Europe.

THE BASIC TECHNIQUE

Although over the centuries the techniques and dyes used for batik have become more sophisticated, the basic principle remains the same. Hot liquid wax is applied to the fabric which is subsequently dyed with a cold water dye. Whereas the unwaxed areas absorb the dye, the wax repels it, preventing its overall penetration, and thus creating a pattern. The process is repeated several times using different coloured dyes until the design is complete. The wax is then removed, leaving the fabric soft and supple. Traditionally the detailed and often intricate designs of batik are created with a tool called a tjanting. This consists of a wooden handle attached to a small copper bowl with a narrow spout through which the hot wax is poured and directed onto the fabric. Repeat patterns are produced with a tjap, or block, made usually of thin metal strips welded together in an intricate pattern or design and used to stamp the hot wax onto the fabric. A particular characteristic of batik is the 'crackle' or 'veining' which appears with each dyeing, and caused by the wax cracking, allowing the dye to seep into the tiny fissures.

USES FOR BATIK

Perhaps the loveliest aspects of batik are its translucency and richness of colour which make it ideal for dresses, skirts, shirts, scarves and ties, as well as for furnishings such as window shades or blinds, screens, lampshades and cushion covers. A batik wall-hanging makes an unusual and attractive alternative to an oil painting or print, especially if hung across an alcove and lit from behind so that the colours come alive, glowing like sunlight through stained glass.

DESIGN IDEAS

Although it helps to have some skill in drawing, it is by no means essential; an appreciation of colour and design is far more important. Geometric patterns are extremely attractive and easy to achieve. Simple abstract designs can be made up by drawing around different sized plates and saucers, and pictures and other designs can be copied or traced from books and magazines. An excellent example of this simple adaptation is to use the outlines and transfers of embroidery designs for batiks. Interesting repeat patterns can be produced by improvising on the tjap technique, for ordinary metal kitchen utensils like forks, pastry cutters, spatulas and potato mashers will all hold sufficient hot wax for transfer to the fabric. With a little ingenuity simple blocks can also be made. Try heavy gauge fuse wire twisted into shape and pushed partially into cork mounted on wood. Similarly, try varying sized pins and nails stuck into bottle corks so that all the heads are even and use them to create recurring random patterns.

FABRICS, MATERIALS AND EQUIPMENT

Despite the development of synthetic fabrics, natural fabrics like cottons, linen and silk, are still the best materials for batik. Batik wax is usually a mixture of paraffin wax and beeswax but ordinary household candles can be used. Equipment consists of a small saucepan in which to melt the wax, a wooden frame on which to stretch the fabric, tacks or staples, a soft pencil, a selection of firm bristle paint-brushes and a tjanting. As hot water would melt the wax it is advisable to use a cold water dye for dyeing the fabric, such as Dylon, Tintex or Rit dyes. Dylon's colourfast cold dye is ideal. When deciding on colours, bear in mind that where two or more colours overlap they will blend together; for instance, yellow over red becomes orange and blue over pink creates purple. Dyeing can be done in a plastic bowl, or for larger amounts of fabric, in the sink or bath tub.

Other materials are Cold Dye Fix, salt, a measuring cup, a tablespoon, newspaper and clean absorbent paper. It is advisable to wear rubber gloves when working with dyes.

METHOD OF WORKING

Wash and iron the fabric to remove any dressing or sizing which would prevent the dye taking evenly. Using the soft pencil, lightly draw the design onto the fabric, stretch it onto the frame and secure with tacks or staples. Cover the work surface and surrounding area with newspaper to protect them from the hot wax. Melt the wax in the saucepan and, if possible, work next to the stove, otherwise use a hotplate to keep the wax molten; it must be very hot but take great care if melting it over a gas flame as wax is highly inflammable. Keep the flame very low, or, better still, stand the saucepan on an asbestos mat over the flame. Depending on the area to be waxed use either a brush or tjanting. Large decorator's paintbrushes are ideal for waxing large areas, use artists brushes for smaller areas and straightforward designs, and the tjanting for fine lines and intricate detail. Use the improvised tjap, or block, for repeat patterns. Apply wax only where the subsequent dye colour is not required. As the hot liquid wax is applied the fabric will become transparent; if it looks 'milky' then the wax is not hot enough and will not permeate right through the fabric. For a good dye-resist the wax must completely penetrate the fabric.

APPLYING COLOUR

Starting with the lightest colour, mix the Cold Dye following the instructions on the pack. Thoroughly wet the fabric in cold water, crumpling it to crack the wax if the extra crackle is required and dye for up to an hour, stirring continuously for the first ten minutes and then occasionally. Small areas of colour can be painted on and will be contained by the wax. To do this, wet the fabric and lay it on polythene sheeting before painting on the dye. After dyeing rinse the fabric in cold water until it runs clear to remove any loose dye and drip-dry. When the fabric is completely dry pin it back onto the frame and apply more wax where this first colour is to be retained, wet in cold water and dye as before in another, darker colour. Rinse and drip-dry. This sequence may be repeated several times to create a more complicated design.

To remove the wax, sandwich the batik between sheets of clean absorbent paper and place them on a wad of newspaper. Iron over the top, replacing the absorbent paper when necessary, until most of the wax is absorbed. Remove the residue of wax and any excess dye by washing the batik in a solution of detergent and very hot water. Wax can be removed from brushes using the same method. Use a bowl for this stage because water containing wax should never be poured down the sink. Very large batiks are dry-cleaned after removing surplus wax.

SIMPLE BATIK TECHNIQUES

A simplified form of batik, and one that is a great favourite with children, can be achieved by dripping wax from a lighted candle onto a suitable material. Pin the washed fabric, either cotton, linen or silk, or perhaps a handkerchief, onto a wooden frame and drip the melting candlewax onto the fabric. Faint pencil outlines can be used as guidelines but random patterns are more fun. Keep the frame horizontal for neat wax polkadots. For some really exciting effects, lift the frame to an almost vertical position and vary the angle so that the drops of hot wax slide down the fabric creating attractive elongated drop shapes. Wet the fabric in cold water and, starting with the lightest colour, dye in cold water dye, rinse thoroughly and drip-dry. Repeat several times for an interesting colourful design. Remove the wax by ironing the fabric between sheets of absorbent paper and wash in hot water and detergent.

PAPER BATIK FOR PICTURES

As an alternative to fabric, batik can also be worked on paper, producing designs with the same kind of translucency and depth of colour. Paper batiks make beautiful and unusual pictures. This is a medium which can also be adopted for creating very original greetings cards and decorative gift wrap. Cartridge or construction paper is preferable for pictures and cards, although any white

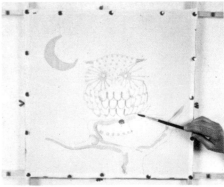

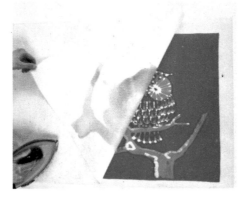

paper with a matt surface can be used. As with fabric, the hot wax can be dripped onto the paper or applied with a tjanting or tjap block. Another ideal dye craft for young children is to draw on the paper with an ordinary candle, using it as a crayon. This is also a good way of putting special messages or names on greeting cards. After waxing, cover the paper with a colour wash using ink, water colours or cold water dye. Lay the paper onto a plastic sheet and paint on the colour, or colours, as required. When dry, iron off the wax between sheets of clean absorbent paper.

Owl Wall Hanging

This delightful wall hanging is dyed using only two colours and is an ideal project for a newcomer to the craft.

Materials required:
100% cotton, linen or silk fabric
Batik or candle wax
An old saucepan
Batik or picture frame
Tacks or staples
Paint brush or tjanting
Cold water dye in bright yellow and coral
Salt and Cold Dye Fix.

Method

Wash and iron fabric to remove any dressing as this will prevent the dye from penetrating thoroughly. Using a soft pencil, trace the design down onto the fabric. Stretch fabric over frame and secure with tacks or staples. Melt wax in an old saucepan and apply to the fabric with a paintbrush or tjanting in

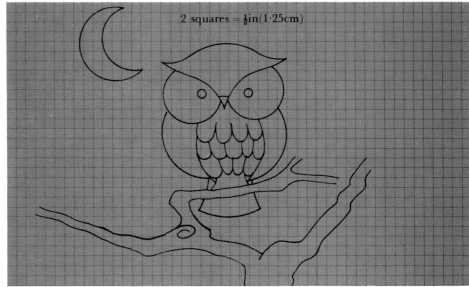

2 squares = $\frac{1}{2}$in(1·25cm)

the areas that are not to be dyed. As the wax hardens, the fabric takes on a transparent appearance.

First dye Starting with the lightest colour (bright yellow) mix the cold water dye in accordance with the instructions. Thoroughly wet the fabric in cold water and immerse it in the dye solution for up to one hour, depending on the depth of colour required. Stir constantly for the first ten minutes and then occasionally to ensure even penetration of the dye. Remove fabric from the dye, rinse in cold water until it runs clear and drip-dry away from direct heat.

Second dye When dry, pin fabric to frame and apply more hot wax where it is intended to retain the yellow and resist the next dye colour. Mix second darker colour, wet fabric in cold water

and dye as before. The coral and yellow will combine to create a rich orange over the unwaxed areas. When dyeing is complete, rinse in cold water and drip-dry. Remove the wax by ironing between wads of absorbent paper and then wash in a bowl of hot water and detergent. Never pour water containing wax down the sink.

To make the wall-hanging

Trim the finished batik panel to size and shape. Turn in 1in *(2.5cm)* on both top and bottom of the panel and stitch. Cut two pieces of $\frac{1}{4}$in *(6mm)* wood dowelling to the width of the panel plus $1\frac{1}{4}$in *(3.5cm)*. Slip the dowel through the stitched channels at the top and bottom of the panel. Suspend the top dowel from a cord or length of wire.

Evening Skirt

This beautiful long skirt is decorated with a swirling design of tropical flowers and leaves.

Materials required:
White cotton lawn
Batik or picture frame
Cold water dye in rose, nasturtium, pink, leaf green
Batik or candle wax
Tacks or staples
Paintbrush or tjanting
Salt and Cold Dye Fix.

Method
Wash and iron fabric. Mark out skirt from a commercial pattern and draw design freehand copying from the photograph onto pattern pieces with a pencil or dressmaker's chalk. Pin fabric to frame and apply hot wax to those areas which are to remain white. (The flower shapes are white out of the red). Move the fabric up on the frame and repin as necessary until the whole design has been worked out.
First dye Dye fabric in rose, rinse and drip-dry. Re-pin the fabric on the frame. Apply hot wax over the dyed areas on the areas to remain rose or white.
Second dye Nasturtium. Rinse and drip-dry. Wax again and prepare for third dyeing.
Third dye Pink. Lay the dry fabric onto plastic sheeting and paint on leaf green dye keeping well inside wax outlines. When dry, rinse in cold water until clear. Remove most of the wax by ironing the fabric between sheets of absorbent paper and then wash thoroughly in a hot detergent solution.
Buy a zipper to match fabric. Cut out the pattern pieces and make the skirt according to the pattern instructions.

Hoopoe Wall Hanging

This design (page 140) is worked in brown, orange and pink for subtle effect.

Materials required:
White cotton lawn
Cold water dye in rose, nasturtium, bronze rose
Batik or picture frame
Paint brush or tjanting
Batik or candle wax
Salt and Cold Dye Fix.

Method
Wash and iron fabric. Draw out the design in pencil freehand copying from the photograph. Pin fabric to wooden frame. Apply hot wax where fabric is not to be dyed (white areas).
First dye Rose. Rinse and drip-dry. Re-pin fabric to frame and wax to retain the rose dye.
Second dye Nasturtium. Rinse and drip-dry. Re-wax.
Third dye Bronze rose. Rinse and drip-dry. Iron fabric between sheets of absorbent paper to remove most of the wax. Do not wash as the wax that remains will give 'body' to the wall-hanging and enhance the translucent quality, typical of batik hangings.

Flying Dragon

This sophisticated panel would make an impressive wall panel or covering.

Materials required:
White cotton lawn
Cold water dye in rose, nasturtium, pink, red and charcoal
Batik or picture frame
Paintbrush or tjanting
Batik or candle wax
Paint or shoe dye in gold
Salt and Cold Dye Fix.

Method
Work batik as for the Hoopoe wall hanging. After first three dye baths in rose, nasturtium and pink, completely wax the background.
Apply more wax to the dragon between the fourth and fifth dye baths in red and charcoal. After the final dyeing, remove wax in the same way as for the Hoopoe wall hanging. Highlight the dragon with gold using a paintbrush.

Embroidery

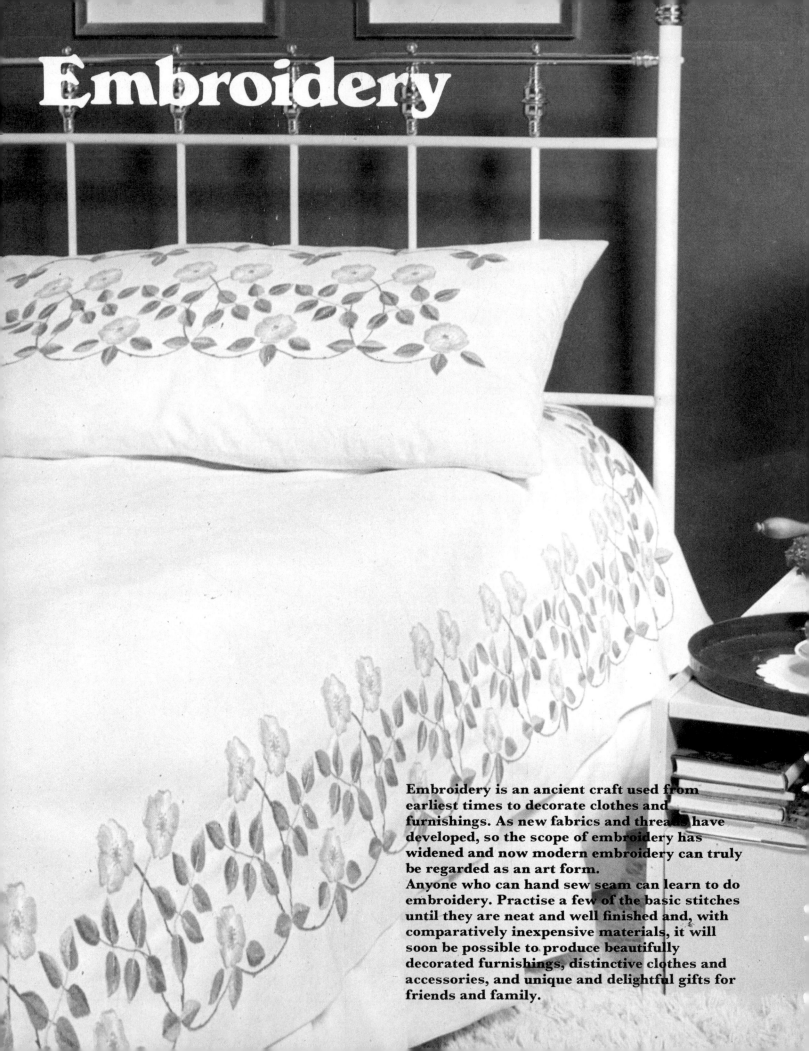

Embroidery is an ancient craft used from earliest times to decorate clothes and furnishings. As new fabrics and threads have developed, so the scope of embroidery has widened and now modern embroidery can truly be regarded as an art form.

Anyone who can hand sew seam can learn to do embroidery. Practise a few of the basic stitches until they are neat and well finished and, with comparatively inexpensive materials, it will soon be possible to produce beautifully decorated furnishings, distinctive clothes and accessories, and unique and delightful gifts for friends and family.

THREADS AND MATERIALS

Whether the finished piece of embroidery is to be delicate or deliberately coarse depends on the combination of threads, materials and stitches. The work will be fine if worked on organdie with two or three strands of stranded cotton, or coarse if worked on hessian or burlap, felt or linen with wool (yarn) and Sylko Perle cotton (perle cotton). Tapestry or crewel wool is used for working on woollen fabrics and stranded cotton or soft embroidery thread on linen or cotton fabrics.

Thimbles A thimble should be used in embroidery. When working with a coarse fabric and thread a thimble is essential.

Needles Different types of embroidery require different types of needles. Fine embroidery requires a thin needle with a small eye while a stronger needle with a larger eye is used for coarser types of embroidery such as needlepoint.

Scissors A sharp-pointed pair of scissors with narrow blades is very important, especially in cut work embroidery when the surplus fabric has to be cut away.

FRAMES

The finished work will be much neater if the fabric is held taut in a frame, because then the stitches are most likely to be neat and accurate. The beginner will find that an embroidery ring will make work easier. This consists of two wooden hoops, one fitting inside the other, with the material stretched over the inner ring and held in place by the outer ring and which can be tightened with a screw.

For more advanced work, the embroidery can be mounted on a square or rectangular frame. This type of frame usually consists of two rollers, one at the top and one at the bottom, with a wide piece of tape tacked to each roller and a lath on each side fitting into holes on each roller. The fabric is then stitched onto the tape and the side laths secured with four screws. The sides of the embroidery fabric are then firmly laced around the laths with strong thread.

TRANSFERRING THE DESIGN TO THE FABRIC

For those who feel inspired to design their own embroidery, there are several ways of transferring the design to the background fabric.

Carbon paper This is the simplest method of transferring a design. Dressmaker's carbon paper should be used because typewriter carbon paper tends to smudge. Dressmaker's carbon can be bought in dark and light colours, to suit the colour of the fabric.

Secure the fabric in an embroidery ring and place the carbon paper face down on the fabric with a tracing of the design on the top. Draw over the lines of the design with a pencil so that the design is transferred to the fabric.

Perforating or pouncing Trace the design onto a heavy piece of tracing paper and prick holes about $\frac{1}{16}$ in *(1.5mm)* apart around the design outlines with a needle. Place the design on the fabric, smooth side upwards, hold in position with weights and rub powdered charcoal or powdered chalk over it, depending on whether the material is dark or light. Remove the tracing paper and, after blowing away the excess powder, paint over the lines with water colour paint.

Direct tracing If the fabric is fine, like nylon, silk or organdie, the design may be transferred to the fabric by placing the design underneath the fabric and tracing the lines with a soft pencil or painting them with water colour.

Basting This method is used if the fabric is coarse or textured. Trace the design onto fine tracing or tissue paper, baste the paper onto the fabric and sew over the lines with small running stitches. The paper can then be torn away from the material and the basting removed when the embroidery has been completed.

ENLARGING EMBROIDERY DESIGNS

Sometimes, if the outline of a design is simple, it can be enlarged by the squared paper method. To do this, draw lines horizontally and vertically over the page, making the lines about $\frac{1}{4}$ in *(6mm)* apart. Draw a similar grid on a sheet of paper but making the lines $\frac{1}{2}$ in *(1cm)* or 1 in *(2.5cm)* apart or to whatever scale is required. Now reproduce all the design lines on this squared background thereby enlarging the design.

For more complicated designs, it is recommended that the page be photographed and reproduced to the recommended size. A company which makes blueprints and photostats can do this.

A design can be reduced in size using the same techniques as described.

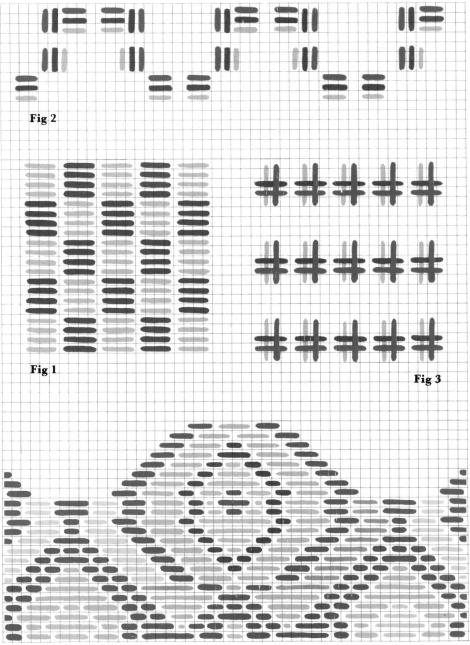

Fig 2

Fig 1

Fig 3

MOUNTING FINISHED EMBROIDERY

Work a line of basting stitches around the edge of the finished piece of work, making sure that there is at least 1in *(2.5cm)* around the edge for turning and glueing the embroidery onto the backing.

Cut a piece of strong cardboard the size of the finished piece and stretch the embroidery over it, making sure that the warp and weft threads are kept parallel and that the basting line matches the edge of the cardboard. The piece of work is then glued into place and the corners mitred. Finally, the embroidery can be backed or glued onto a piece of hardboard or very stiff cardboard and framed, with or without glass.

PATTERN DARNING

Pattern darning is the simplest form of embroidery and is a quick way of decorating household linens and clothes. It is worked on even weave fabrics such as linen, coarse cotton or wool. The only stitch used is running stitch. The stitches are worked in varying lengths, close together in rows so that patterns are made, or in open formations. Brick patterns for instance can be formed by working regularly spaced blocks of stitches (Fig 1), or a more fluid design can be obtained by working two or three rows as in Fig 2. Plaid patterns are simple to achieve and can be worked all over a background or as a border (fig 3). The bottom band shows how a richly coloured border could be worked. Similar borders in pattern darning are found in Middle-Eastern and mid-European peasant embroideries.

CIRCULAR SAMPLER

Once the beginner has become used to working with needle and thread, the next step is to practise some embroidery stitches. Having built up a repertoire of stitches, it will be a natural step to consider undertaking larger embroidery designs. A sampler is a good way of practising stitches and a circular sampler such as that illustrated is more impressive than a straightforward rectangle or square.

The sampler, approximately 4in *(10cm)* in diameter, includes a variety of stitches, among them raised chain stitch, open chain stitch, French knots, knot stitch, threaded back stitch, feather stitch, fly stitch and a spider's web. Soft embroidery thread, stranded embroidery cotton and knitting wool have been used for texture contrast but it is possible to experiment with raffia, tapestry wool or even metallic threads. A thick yarn such as rug wool can be included by couching it down with a silky thread, and beads can be threaded onto lengths of thread and worked into the design. Both results are most effective.

When the sampler is completed, mount it onto a piece of stiff cardboard for a

small wall picture, or perhaps incorporate it into a personal accessory such as a handbag or a book cover.

A selection of embroidery stitches is shown on pages 152–3.

Butterfly Accessories

Work these pretty accessories for your sewing basket or for a gift. Only four stitches are used to work the butterfly motif on both needlecase and the pincushion.

Materials required:
¼yd *(22cm)* 36in *(90cm)* wide red linen
Two 4in *(10cm)* squares red canvas
Scraps of black, blue and green felt
Stranded cotton: one skein lemon yellow; one skein white
Perle cotton No. 5: one ball each aqua, red, lemon yellow and navy blue
Sewing thread
Small amount kapok or other suitable filling.

Key to Butterfly diagram
A   navy blue French knots, perle cotton
B   white French knots, stranded cotton
C   lemon yellow, knot stitch
D   lemon yellow backstitch
E   white chain stitch, stranded cotton
F   white backstitch, stranded cotton
G   red backstitch
H   blue backstitch
I   lemon yellow backstitch

To work the design
Cut four pieces of red fabric 6½in *(16.5cm)* square. Enlarge design (Fig 4) onto tracing paper and transfer it onto the right side of the fabric on two of the squares, by putting dressmaker's carbon paper face down on the fabric underneath the tracing paper and drawing over the lines of the design with a pencil. Using the tracing as a pattern, cut three pieces of black felt for the body, two pieces of green and two pieces of blue for the wings and stitch in position. Work the lines of yellow knot stitch in six strands of stranded cotton. Then work the lines of backstitch in yellow,

blue and red perle cotton and the French knots in navy blue perle cotton and six strands of white stranded cotton.

To make up the pincushion place one plain square wrong sides facing one embroidered square, and machine stitch together around three sides ½in *(1cm)* from the edge. Use red thread to match the fabric. Stuff firmly with Kapok or other suitable stuffing and machine stitch the last side together. Withdraw threads from the edges almost to the machine stitching.

To finish the needlecase, stitch one plain and one embroidered square together along the left-hand side, ½in *(1cm)* away from the edge. Then machine stitch the two pieces of canvas to the inside of the plain piece of fabric, ½in *(1cm)* away from the machine stitched outer edge. Withdraw threads from the edges of the fabric for a fringed edging.

Cross-Stitched Mats

Cross stitch is an ideal embroidery stitch for beginners. It is quick, easy and gives a really professional result.

This versatile design, Scandinavian in feeling, can be adapted to articles of any size. It can be used in strips for a cushion, as a border for a tablecloth—or for motifs to decorate a wide variety of home accessories. In these two examples, which show contrasting colour schemes, an even weave linen-like dress fabric with 20 threads to 1in *(2.5cm)* has been used with six strands of embroidery cotton to give a bold effect. If using a more finely

woven fabric, use fewer strands—and remember that the stitches will be smaller as a result. Each cross has been embroidered over two threads. To make larger crosses on a finer fabric, embroider over three threads in each direction.

Materials required:
Even weave fabric such as linen in light and dark shades.
Stranded embroidery cotton in dark brown, mid brown, bright leaf green, lime green and olive green for the light background, and in dark brown, light corn, lime green, light blue and light olive green for the dark background.

To work the mats
Cut the fabric to the required size, then begin by embroidering the double line of single stitches at the outer edge. Count the number of crosses in this line and centre either a large or small motif, depending on the number of motifs which will fit into the complete line. Embroider this the correct distance from the outer border, then complete the remaining motifs above and below. Follow by working the decorative inner borders on each side of the motifs, and finish with another row of single crosses. To balance the design, work another double line at the opposite edge. The edge of the light, creamy-coloured mat illustrated has been hem-stitched by hand, using three strands of the brown used in the outer border.

To finish the mats, machine stitch about 1in *(2.5cm)* from the edge and fray the edges of the fabric back to the stitching by withdrawing threads to make a fringe.

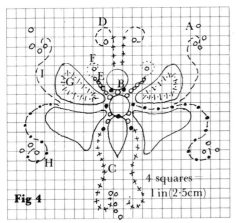

Fig 4   4 squares = 1in (2·5cm)

Aquarium

This wall panel is a challenging project because, although only a few embroidery stitches are used, subtle effects are achieved with the use of brilliant colours and the contrasting textures of three different kinds of thread. Silvery plastic domes, buttons or sequins can be stitched to the background to simulate the fish's eye and air bubbles. The finished panel will measure 16in *(40cm)* deep by 9in *(23cm)* wide before framing.

Materials required:

½yd *(45cm)* 36in *(90cm)* wide blue linen
16in x 9in *(40cm x 23cm)* strong cardboard
Stranded cotton: one skein each dark pink, medium rose, pale pink, old gold, medium orange, gold, dark emerald green, pale leaf green and apple green
Perle cotton: one ball each brown, yellow, red, pink, orange and black
Tapestry wool: one skein each dark green, medium green and mustard brown
Four silver plastic domes or sequins.

To work the panel

Have the design (Fig 5) enlarged to 9in *(23cm)* wide photographically. Follow design and the key provided for stitches, colours and threads. Stitch domes for eyes. Stretch the embroidery over the cardboard and glue the turnings to the wrong side, mitring the corners.

Key to Aquarium wall panel

Stranded embroidery cotton
1 dark pink, satin stitch
2 medium rose pink, satin stitch
3 pale pink, satin stitch
4 medium orange, satin stitch
5 gold, satin stitch
6 pale old gold, satin stitch
7 dark emerald
8 apple green
9 pale leaf green

0 apple green, satin stitch
o dark emerald green. French knots
c dark pink, feather stitch
C pale pink, feather stitch
Perle cotton
——— brown backstitch
∘∘∘— brown knot stitch
——— yellow backstitch
•••• yellow knot stitch
–·–·– red backstitch
+·—· red knot stitch
–··–·· black backstitch
⬤ black satin stitch
black French knots
••• red satin stitch
A orange feather stitch
B pink feather stitch
Tapestry wool
A dark green   **B** medium green
⊙⊙ mustard brown, French knots
++ dark green, French knots
Stitches
〉〉〉〉 feather stitch   Y Y fly stitch
– – – backstitch   ••• knot stitch

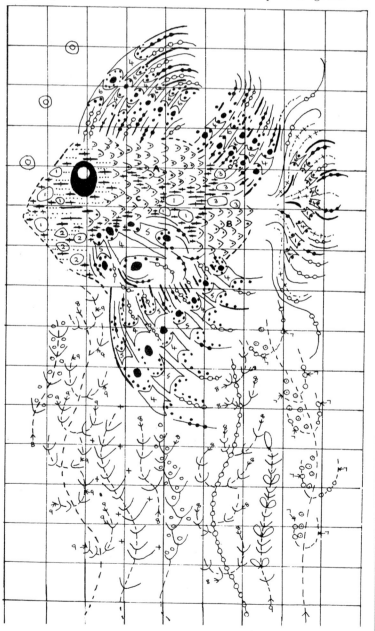

Fig 5

Rose Bedspread

A beautiful embroidered bedspread and pillow cover such as this might well become a family heirloom. The wild rose design borders all four sides of the counterpane and three motifs are used on the pillow cover. (See page 144).

Materials required:

Linen, unbleached muslin or unglazed cotton to suit size of bed, plus allowances for overhang, turnings and hems. Ready-made pillow case or fabric to size of pillow.
Stranded cotton: pale olive green, medium olive green, olive green, bright green, brown, buttercup yellow, pale pink, medium pink, pink.

Working the embroidery

Enlarge Fig 8 photographically using Fig 6 as guide to size. (Fig 6 is life size). Trace off sufficient motifs to go round the counterpane on all four sides. The motifs are positioned approximately 5in (12.5cm) from the edge. Three strands of embroidery cotton are used throughout. Work colours and stitches as follows. Flower petals are worked in long and short satin stitch, the colours shading from the deepest tones on the outside of the petal to the palest near the centre.
The leaves are also worked in long and short stitch, the three tones of green shading as shown in Fig 6. Vary the colouring as indicated. The centre of the rose is worked in satin stitch, using two strands pale olive green and one strand medium olive green. The stamens are French knots in buttercup yellow. Work the main stems in two rows of stem stitch using medium olive green and brown. Make sure that the brown row is always on the underside of the stem. The thinner leaf stems and the leaf veins are worked in stem stitch using two strands bright green and one strand pale olive green. The pillow cover (page 150) uses three main motifs and a linking border (Fig 7) to complete the design. Enlarge the border to the same scale. Press embroidery on the wrong side under a damp cloth when completed.
Note: Make sure that the background fabric is pre-shrunk before starting embroidery.

Key for leafstems

2 Medium olive greer
5 Brown
1 Pale olive green
4 Bright green

Fig 6
Key
Leaves
1 Pale olive green
2 Medium olive green
3 Olive green
Stem
2 Medium olive green
5 Brown
Flower
6 Buttercup yellow
7 Pale pink
8 Medium pink
9 Pink

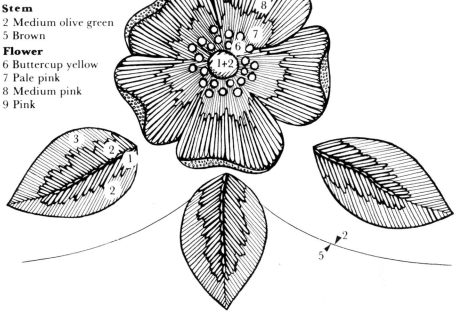

Fig 7

Fig 8

149

Fig 9 Key

1 Orange red
2 Medium blue
3 Dark blue
4 Bright orange
5 Pale canary
6 Lilac
7 Mauve
8 Chestnut brown
9 Dark gorse yellow
10 Maroon
11 Old rose
12 Pale blue
13 Olive green
14 Yellow green
15 Medium olive green
16 Pale olive green

Flower Garland

Embroider a garland of summer flowers on a white shirt and it instantly becomes luxurious and fashionable. The garland is a life-size motif which can be traced from the page and it is a simple matter to pick out one or two flower motifs to decorate the collar or cuffs. Bright, summer garden colours are used for the shirt illustrated but the design could be worked in shades of one colour, if preferred, or in an all-white scheme on a coloured background fabric.

Materials required:

Stranded cotton: orange red, medium blue, dark blue, bright orange, pale yellow, lilac, mauve, chestnut brown, dark gorse yellow, maroon, old rose, pale blue, olive green, yellow green, medium olive green, pale olive green.

To work the embroidery

Trace the design (Fig 9) and transfer to the right hand side of the shirt. Reverse the design for the left hand side. Work the embroidery following the colour key. Use two strands of cotton throughout. All the flowers and leaves are worked in satin stitch. Stems are worked in stem stitch.

Press embroidery on the wrong side under a damp cloth when completed.

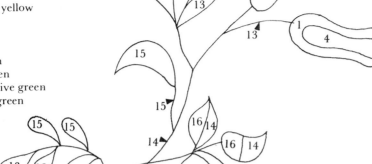

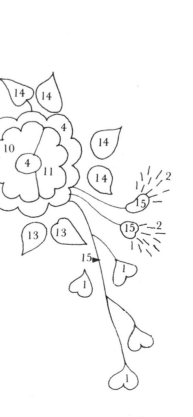

Basic Embroidery Stitches

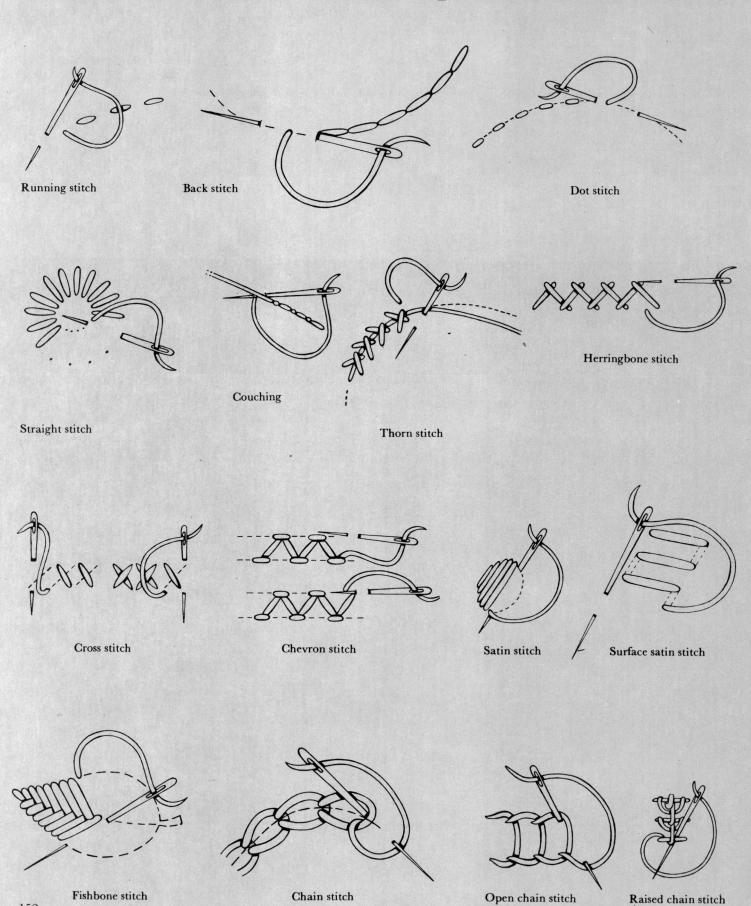

Running stitch   Back stitch   Dot stitch

Straight stitch   Couching   Thorn stitch   Herringbone stitch

Cross stitch   Chevron stitch   Satin stitch   Surface satin stitch

Fishbone stitch   Chain stitch   Open chain stitch   Raised chain stitch

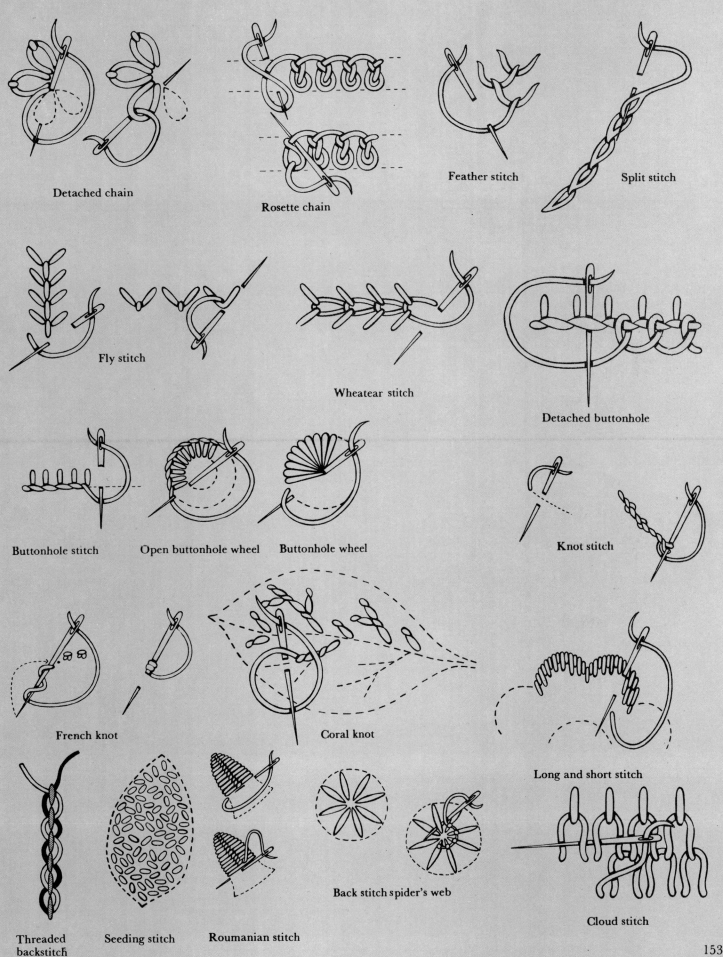

Detached chain

Rosette chain

Feather stitch

Split stitch

Fly stitch

Wheatear stitch

Detached buttonhole

Buttonhole stitch

Open buttonhole wheel

Buttonhole wheel

Knot stitch

French knot

Coral knot

Long and short stitch

Threaded backstitch

Seeding stitch

Roumanian stitch

Back stitch spider's web

Cloud stitch

153

Crewel Work

Crewel embroidery is usually worked in wool on a heavy background fabric. There were two main styles of design. The first was similar to the Elizabethan style of work and featured scrolls, leaves and flowers. The other was derived from oriental embroideries and used a shading technique.

Crewel embroidery is distinctive from other forms of embroidery with wool because it is usually worked as individual motifs and patterns on a natural coloured background, the fabric being part of the overall concept of the design. Large areas of all background are left unworked.

Evening Bolero

The pattern given below is a guide to the embroidery only. A suitable paper pattern should be used for the garment.

Materials required:
Purple felt in quantity recommended by pattern
Matching bias binding
3 ply synthetic gold knitting yarn
Crewel or tapestry wool in the following colours: moss green, dark peacock blue, purple
Lining fabric (optional).

To make the bolero
Pin pattern pieces to felt and cut out. Enlarge the flower design by the squared paper method or photographically (see Fig 1). Transfer the design to the bolero fronts, reversing the design from right to left for one side. Join shoulder seams and side seams. Work embroidery as follows. The flower and leaf outlines are worked in chain stitch using gold thread. Begin working the border $\frac{3}{8}$in *(1cm)* from the front edges. Work one row chain stitch in purple; one row chain stitch in moss green; one row herringbone stitch in gold thread; one row chain stitch in peacock blue. Finish the front edges and the armholes with bias binding.

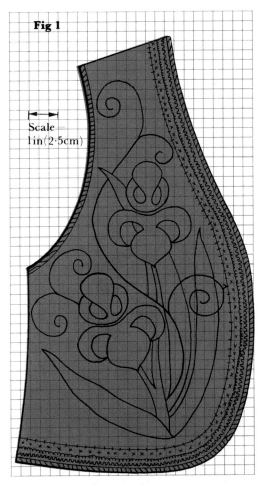

Fig 1

Scale
1in(2·5cm)

Place Mats

Linen place mats, richly bordered with wool and gold thread embroidery, make a brilliant table setting for a party.

Materials required for six mats:
1yd *(91cm)* gold linen
3 ply synthetic gold knitting yarn
Crewel or tapestry wool in the following colours:
1 skein each of dark brown, peacock blue, vermilion, sage green, mink brown (Use three strands of crewel wool together or a single strand of tapestry wool).
Gold sewing thread.

To make the mats
Cut each mat 12in x 15in *(30cm x 38cm)*. Machine stitch all around $\frac{1}{2}$in *(1cm)* from the edge. Fringe back to the machine stitched line. The borders on both short sides are worked from the outside inwards as follows:
First row: chain stitch in dark brown over-worked in herringbone stitch in peacock blue; **second row:** chain stitch in gold thread; **third row:** chain stitch in vermilion; **fourth row:** chain stitch in sage green; **fifth row:** chain stitch in mink brown, over-worked in herringbone in gold thread (see Fig 2).

Note: Since crewel or tapestry wool is used for the embroidery, the mats will have to be dry-cleaned.

Fig 2

155

Shoulder Bag

The design on this lovely bag is based on the rich colours and motifs of modern Greek peasant embroideries. Either work the design on one side only, backing the bag with a contrasting fabric – or embroider both back and front. The finished size is 13in x 11in (33cm x 28cm).

Materials required:
16in x 26in (41cm x 66cm) hessian burlap) or coarse linen
Crewel or tapestry wools in the following colours: pale yellow, chestnut brown, pale turquoise, maroon, dark beige, dark green, light brown, light green, mid-blue, medium turquoise, dark turquoise, vermilion, dark pink-beige, light pink-beige, yellow, yellow-green
36in (90cm) double knitting wool, 10 strands each colour: dark green, pale yellow, yellow-brown
Lining fabric
Zipper if required.

To embroider the bag

Cut fabric into 2 pieces 16 x 13in (41 x 33cm). Draw a pattern from the diagram (Fig 3) to approximately 11in (28cm) wide by 13in (41cm) deep, and trace it off onto tissue paper. Transfer the design to the fabric using the basting method. Place the design 1½in (3.5cm) from the top edge. Oversew the edges to prevent fraying.

The diagram is keyed for colours and stitches as follows:
A Buttonhole stitch ring in pale yellow Outline in chain stitch in chestnut brown.
B Buttonhole stitch ring in pale turquoise. Outline in chain stitch in maroon.

C Rows of chain stitch in dark beige worked across the width of the bag.
D Horizontal rows of chain stitch in dark green.
E Vertical rows of chain stitch, from outside edges: two rows dark green, one row pale turquoise, one row light brown, one row light green, one row dark green.
F Buttonhole stitch in light turquoise.
G Chain stitch in maroon, over-worked in herringbone stitch in gold thread.
H Chain stitch, one row yellow-green, one row mid-blue.
I Chain stitch in pale turquoise to fill shape, edge with one row in medium turquoise. Work crosses in straight stitches in dark turquoise (Lower row of diamonds only).
J Chain stitch filling in pale yellow. Work one row in chain stitch in maroon on the dividing line marked. Work one row of chain stitch in vermilion to divide J and K areas.
K Buttonhole stitch worked horizontally, dark pink-beige, light brown, light pink-beige.
L Buttonhole stitch rings in gold yarn.

To make up the bag

Trim the embroidered fabric to 15in x 12in (38cm x 30cm). Cut a piece of fabric for the back of the bag to the same size. Place front and back together, right sides facing, and machine stitch on three sides taking ½in (1cm) seams. Make up lining in the same way if required. Turn in the top edges to the edge of the embroidery and baste diagonally. Press lightly. Remove basting stitches. Turn the top edges of the lining to the wrong side of the fabric.

Braid the shoulder straps in 10 strands each of dark green, pale yellow and yellow-brown knitting wool. Tie a knot 4in *(10cm)* from the ends to make tassels. Stitch the knots to the sides of the bag. Insert the lining and slip stitch the lining to the bag. Insert a zipper if required.

Musical Angel Cushion

This fabulous cushion, worked in brilliant crewel wools and gold thread, has the richness of eastern embroidery. Only one side is worked, the cushion being backed in wine-coloured velvet. (The cushion is illustrated on page 154.)

Materials required:

16in *(40cm)* square linen
16in *(40cm)* square velvet
Crewel or tapestry wool in the following colours: black, navy blue, pink, pink-beige, salmon pink, deep pink-beige, emerald green, vermilion, old gold, light-beige, light brown, mid-blue, turquoise, lilac-blue, coral pink, dark brown, white, light green, mid-green, dark green, cyclamen, deep cyclamen, maroon, dark beige
3 ply synthetic gold knitting yarn.

To embroider the cushion

Reproduce the design (Fig 4) either by the squared paper method or photographically. Transfer the design to the fabric. Work the embroidery following the key for colours and stitches as follows:

Wings

A Buttonhole stitch in gold thread.
B Buttonhole stitch in pale pink.
C Buttonhole stitch with a row of chain stitch between in pink-beige.
D Buttonhole stitch in salmon pink.
E Buttonhole stitch in deep pink-beige.
F Chain stitch in emerald green, outlined in chain stitch in gold thread.

Crown

G Buttonhole stitch in vermilion.
H Chain stitch and French knots in gold yarn; Satin stitch in old gold wool.

Face and Hands

I *Face tones* Stem stitch shading in light and dark beige, outline in stem stitch in light brown. (Split wool and use one strand only).
Mouth Stem stitch coral pink.
Eyes and brows Stem stitch dark brown and white sewing thread.

Upper sleeve band and lower skirt border

J Satin stitch in old gold wool. French knots in gold yarn on sleeve.

Fig 3

Fig 4

157

Undersleeve
K Chain stitch rows in dark and light green alternately and worked vertically.

Wide sleeve
L Buttonhole stitch alternating vermilion and cyclamen pink, outlined in chain stitch using deep cyclamen pink.

Skirt hem and inside sleeve
M Chain stitch in maroon outlining in stem stitch in old gold wool.

Legs
N Chain stitch throughout; outline in maroon, then fill in this colour sequence: vermilion, gold thread, cyclamen, maroon, vermilion etc.

Chest and lower skirt
O Chain and satin stitch using cyclamen and vermilion. Outline in chain stitch in maroon.

Sleeve bobble
P French knots in gold thread.

Shoe
Q Chain stitch in medium and dark green. *Buttons:* French knots in light green.

Lute
R Rows of chain stitch to fill the shape using old gold wool and light brown. French knots in gold thread.

Background
S Buttonhole rings in black. Outline in chain stitch using navy blue (work linking lines in navy blue).
T Buttonhole rings in black with stars overworked in gold thread.

Work the curved lines as follows: two rows chain stitch in mid-blue; two rows chain stitch in turquoise. Fill between rows in chain stitch in lilac-blue.

To make up the cushion
Press embroidery on the wrong side under a damp cloth. Cut the backing fabric to the same size. Place together right sides facing inserting piping if required. Machine stitch on three sides. Turn to right side and press. Insert cushion pad and sew up fourth side.

Griffon and Birds

This beautiful wall hanging is worked on a coarse brown linen and uses a rich colour scheme of blues and tones of gold and brown. The finished panel measures approximately 25in x 15in *(64cm x 38cm)*.

Materials required:
30in x 20in *(75cm x 50cm)* brown linen. Tapestry wool in the following colours: 1 skein each of: pale yellow, pale orange, bright orange, amber, deep amber, rust, mustard, pale blue, medium blue, silver blue, pale silver blue, baby blue, sky blue, deep olive green, purple, gold, pale olive green, cinnamon.

To embroider the wall hanging
Mark the centre of the fabric by basting. Enlarge the design photographically to 11in *(27.5cm)* wide (see Fig 5). Trace

onto tissue. Transfer the design to the fabric using white dressmaker's carbon paper and a tracing wheel. Follow the chart and the colour key for stitches and colours. Use two strands of wool together to outline the star. Use two strands for the griffon's head and two strands for the wide flower petals. Vary the number of strands throughout the remainder of the design for textural interest. When complete, press the embroidery on the wrong side under a damp cloth.

To make up the wall hanging
Work a row of machine stitching down both sides ½in *(1cm)* from the edge. Fringe back to the stitching. Make a casing at the top to fit a supporting rod. Turn a narrow hem at the bottom. Cut 7in *(17.5cm)* lengths of cinnamon wool and small amounts of rust and deep amber. Take 10 threads at a time and fold in half. Pull the bunch of threads through the hem edge with a crochet hook. Knot into a tassel (Fig 6).

Fig 5

Stitch key

⋘	Buttonhole (stitches close together)
⊞	Buttonhole filling
⊗	Buttonhole wheel
⊶	Detached buttonhole
⋀⋀	Chain stitch
⧺	Couched stitch
⊶	Cretan stitch
⋙	French knot
○○○	Herringbone stitch
⋙	Laid and couched
⧺⧺	(Oriental stitch)
⫾⫾⫾	Long and short stitch
⫿⫿⫿	Rosette chain
⤳	Roumanian stitch
⫽⫽⫽	Satin stitch
▫▫▫	Square chain

Colour key

1 pale yellow
2 pale orange
3 bright orange
4 amber
5 deep amber
6 rust
7 mustard
8 pale blue
9 medium blue
10 silver blue
11 pale silver blue
12 baby blue
13 sky blue
14 deep olive green
15 purple
16 gold
17 pale olive green
18 cinnamon brown

Fig 6

159

Motifs

Here are some traditional crewel embroidery motifs which can be used on a variety of furnishings. Use them singly or in groups. Crewel or tapestry wool can be used to work the motifs but the designs look just as effective worked in soft embroidery thread or stranded embroidery cotton. Stitches suitable for crewel work are shown on pages 152–3.

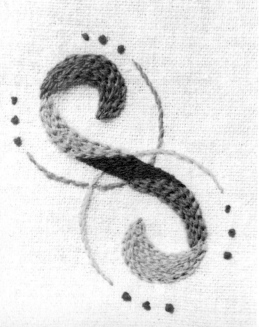

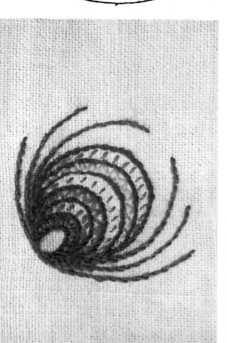

Needlepoint

At some period during the early development of the craft of embroidery it became the custom to employ as ground material a coarser type of fabric than had originally been used. This meant it was necessary to cover the whole of the coarser surface with stitchery, and there arose as a result a completely new type of embroidery, which has become known variously as canvas work, canvas embroidery, tapestry, petit point and needlepoint. Tapestry is the wrong term to use, as that is a woven fabric with a warp and weft. Petit point was once used to describe all canvas embroidery when most pieces were worked in tent stitch (petit point), and the term is still used for fine embroidery in tent stitch on single-thread canvas.

PRACTISING STITCHES

A great deal of pleasure can be obtained from working a piece of needlepoint for the home. Purchase some mono or single-thread canvas 27in *(68cm)* wide with either 14 or 16 threads to 1in *(2.5cm)* and cut off a piece approximately 9in x 12in *(23cm x 30cm)*. This is a good size to practise on. The advantage of using a small piece of canvas is that it can be held quite easily in the hand during working, thus dispensing an embroidery frame.

For a first piece try working without a formal design. Begin by working a group of several large stitches, each one over ten or more threads of the canvas, with some stitches larger than others, and place them either in the centre of the canvas or slightly off centre. Continue by working some smaller, different stitches around the first group and allow these to wander off at various angles from the centre in channels, some of which may continue to within 1in *(2.5cm)* of the edge of the canvas. These channels will help to divide up the canvas into areas which can be filled with other stitches.

This care-free method of working can be great fun and helps in memorising the stitches and learning how to get the correct tension, as well as providing an introduction to the problems of colour and textural contrast. The finished piece will also form a record of stitches to be referred to later. Some needlepoint stitches are given on pages 152 and 164.

WHAT TO MAKE

After a sampler has been completed, it is time to embark upon something more ambitious; either something practical, such as a stool top, a cushion or a chair seat, or something purely decorative, such as a picture or a wall panel. If you decide to work a practical object which is likely to encounter hard wear, then the choice of stitches becomes all-important. Only stitches which cover the canvas fully should be used for this kind of work – stitches such as tent stitch (petit point), rice, smyrna, cushion etc.

It is best to avoid most straight stitches, surface stitches and large, bumpy stitches in working furniture coverings. Straight and surface stitches are weaker than stitches which cross over the intersection of the canvas and bumpy stitches would be uncomfortable to sit on. Tent stitch is best used for outlining shapes or for working a linear design which requires intricate shading. This stitch should be avoided for working large areas of one unbroken colour. Such areas gain much in character if other stitches are used to add a textural quality to the finished effect. There are many square stitches which are durable enough for this purpose. Avoid using square stitches alone to interpret a design with curved lines, as this leads to a clumsy, badly defined shape, the design becoming indistinct.

SAMPLER

Part of the fun in needlepoint is learning how to work the different stitches because, having built up a repertoire, it is possible to create your own new and original designs. Working from top left to right, here are the stitches used on the sampler below. Panel 1: mosaic stitch, oblong cross stitch, Smyrna with large back stitch. Panel 2: rococo stitch, large cushion stitch. Panel 3: rice stitch. Panel 4 (2nd row): straight cross stitch. Panel 5: Hungarian stitch. Panel 6 (3rd row): cushion stitch, small Smyrna stitch. Panel 7: small diagonal stitch, eyelet stitch. Panel 8 (worked vertically): satin stitch, oblong cross stitch, satin stitch. Tent stitch worked across sampler. Panel 9 (4th row): oblong cross stitch. Panel 10: large Smyrna stitch. Panel 11 (5th row): rice stitch. Panel 12: long legged cross stitch. Panel 13 (divided into 3 areas): Rhodes stitch, satin stitch. Panel 14 (6th row): satin stitch, mosaic stitch, cushion stitch with tent stitch. Outline the sampler with tent stitch.

When working something purely decorative, such as a wall panel, adopt a free treatment and give the imagination free rein. There is a great assortment of stitches to choose from which can be varied with an exciting assortment of materials. The surface need not be completely covered with stitchery. It can be left bare in places, or holes can be cut out of the canvas. Areas can be padded and materials such as shells, stones, jewels, beads, pieces of metal or leather can be attached to the canvas and incorporated into the stitchery.

The choice of colour is very important but a well-balanced design is even more important. No amount of beautiful colour or textural interest will compensate for weakness in the original design.

COLOUR SCHEMES

When preparing the colour scheme, plan a definite but not abrupt break between the various shades of a single colour. By limiting the colour scheme in this way the finished work will have a bright effect. The design should be drawn on paper and outlined with a felt-tip pen so that it will show through clearly when the canvas is pinned down over it. Mark the horizontal and vertical centre

lines on both the drawing and the canvas. Then match these lines. Trace the outline of the design onto the canvas with the felt-tip pen.

MATERIALS

Canvas can be bought in either single or double thread. Single thread is more versatile because all stitches can be worked on it easily. For working chair seats, stool tops and cushion covers, canvases with 18, 16 or 14 threads to 1in *(2.5cm)* are the most suitable. Any canvas can be used for wall hangings and pictures. Wool is the principal material used for working items which will receive heavy wear, such as chair seats. Wool is strong, covers the canvas well and is easy to work with. Any kind of wool can be used, except very soft wools like mohair which stretch easily. There is a large choice of materials for working panels including linen, string, lurex, raffia, metallic threads and silk—anything, in fact, that can be passed through the holes in the canvas.

BLOCKING AND STRETCHING

A finished piece of needlepoint, whether it has been worked in the hand or on a frame, generally needs to be pulled back

into shape before mounting or making up. To do this, cover a wooden board with clean white paper. Draw the outline of the original shape and pin the needlework face downward with drawing pins (thumb tacks), pulling the edges to fit the shape. If the canvas is very misshapen, it will help if a little water is sprinkled all over it. Rub this well in and leave the canvas stretched for 24 hours until it has dried out naturally.

MOUNTING PICTURES AND WALL PANELS

When the work has been blocked, the canvas is mounted onto a piece of hardboard or plywood. To do this, turn the edges of the canvas over to the back of the board and glue them down with a strong adhesive. The edges can be finished fixing a braid or gimp all around. For the best effect canvas work panels should be suitably mounted and framed. Do not cover with glass as this detracts from the appearance of this work.

MAKING UP OTHER ITEMS

Needlepoint can easily be made up as a cushion cover or simple handbag, but it is best to have chair seats, stool tops and items such as elaborate evening bags professionally made up.

Pin Cushions

When you first begin to work the canvas, it is a good idea to start with something small which is portable and can be completed quickly. By the time you have finished one of these delightful pincushions, you are likely to have become a needlepoint enthusiast. Work on a single thread canvas, such as 14 threads to 1in *(2.5cm)* and to vary stitches, sometimes work over one thread, at others over two or more threads. (Illustrated on page 162 and page 165).

Rectangular pincushion

The border is worked in cross stitch, tent stitch and Smyrna or double cross stitch. The squares at each corner are outlined in cross stitch using medium and dark green wool. In each corner of the square are five Smyrna or double cross stitches in white on a background of tent stitch, worked diagonally across the canvas in alternating rows of red and yellow. The central motif of a carnation is worked on a background of white silk in tent stitch. Make up the cushion with black felt.

Flower pin cushion

Four rows of wheatsheaf are worked around a centre of orange tent stitch in gold-coloured wool and outlined in dark red. Two rows of stem stitch in red alternate with two rows in pink, to encircle the flower shape. Red velvet is used for making up the cushion. Sew on beads.

Turquoise pin cushion

Work large and small eyelet, oblong

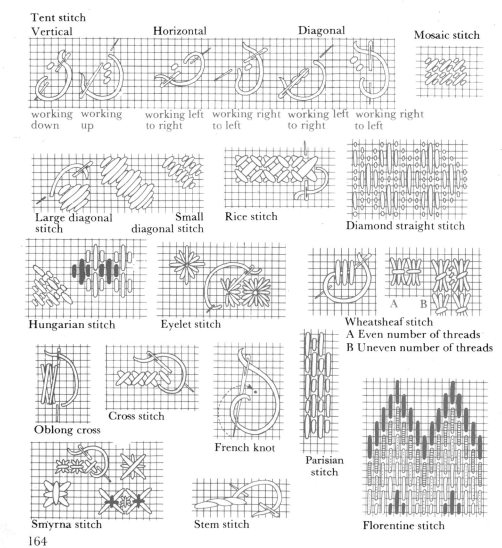

Tent stitch
Vertical   Horizontal   Diagonal   Mosaic stitch

working down   working up   working left to right   working right to left   working left to right   working right to left

Large diagonal stitch   Small diagonal stitch   Rice stitch   Diamond straight stitch

Hungarian stitch   Eyelet stitch   Wheatsheaf stitch
A Even number of threads
B Uneven number of threads

Oblong cross   Cross stitch   French knot   Parisian stitch

Smyrna stitch   Stem stitch   Florentine stitch

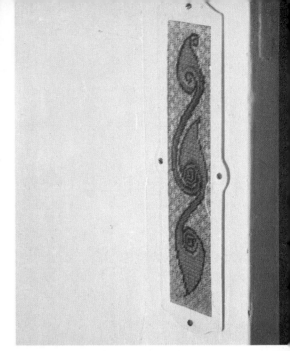

cross, satin and tent stitches at random in wool and perle cotton. Shades of canary yellow, turquoise, green and royal blue have been used for this pincushion. Use turquoise felt and braid for making up.

Heart shaped pincushion

This pincushion is designed to be worn on the wrist. Rice stitch in red wool and tent stitch in black wool are used to outline the rice stitch centre which has been worked in metallic thread.

 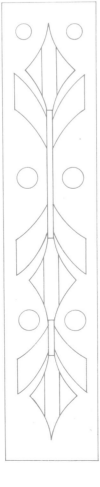

Door Finger-plates

Very attractive finger-plates for doors can be made by working pieces of embroidery on fine canvas and mounting them in plastic frames. As the work must be protected by a cover of transparent plastic, only flat stitches can be used and these are best worked in silk, stranded cotton or very fine wool. The colouring should generally be chosen so that it will not be too dominant and will thus fit easily into any furnishing scheme.

A suitable plastic cover for a finger plate can be purchased from specialist handicraft stores. If such a cover is to be used however, it should be obtained before the embroidery is worked so that the dimensions of the piece of work required can be established beforehand. The finger plates illustrated are made up in the following way.

A narrow frame, exactly fitting the worked piece of embroidery, is cut out of a sheet of plastic and painted a suitable colour to set off the work. To enable the completed finger plate to be fixed to the door, four screw-holes are provided in the frame. After the embroidery is completed, trim the canvas to within $\frac{1}{4}$in *(6mm)* of the embroidery; turn and glue down onto the wrong side of the work, so that the embroidery exactly fits the frame.

Finally, place the clear plastic cover over the embroidery carefully to cover the frame, attaching it to the frame with a strong adhesive.

The design of the black-edged finger plate illustrated is worked in eyelet, small diagonal and tent stitches upon a background of oblong cross stitch worked horizontally over four vertical threads and one horizontal thread of the canvas. The white-framed finger plate has a background of diamond straight stitch, the design worked mainly in tent stitch and filled in with mosaic stitch.

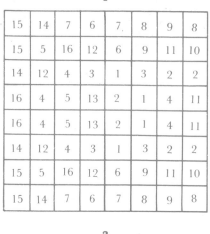

1

15	14	7	6	7	8	9	8
15	5	16	12	6	9	11	10
14	12	4	3	1	3	2	2
16	4	5	13	2	1	4	11
16	4	5	13	2	1	4	11
14	12	4	3	1	3	2	2
15	5	16	12	6	9	11	10
15	14	7	6	7	8	9	8

2

3	1	1	3	2	13	16	12
2	11	13	5	4	5	16	12
10	9	8	6	7	7	12	5
11	10	9	8	14	16	6	14
11	10	9	8	14	16	6	14
10	9	8	6	7	7	12	5
2	11	13	5	4	5	16	12
3	1	1	3	2	13	16	12

3

13	2	3	1	1	7	14	15
5	16	12	5	3	2	13	14
16	11	8	4	4	6	15	7
12	10	9	8	9	10	11	6
12	10	9	8	9	10	11	6
16	11	8	4	4	6	15	7
5	16	12	5	3	2	13	14
13	2	3	1	1	7	14	15

Key for cushion charts

1	Maroon
2	Shocking pink
3	Cherry red
4	Dusty lilac
5	Pale blue violet
6	Lilac
7	Light purple
8	Light bright orange
9	Dark bright orange
10	Orange
11	Rust
12	Violet
13	Bright pink
14	Medium purple
15	Purple
16	Dark mauve

Three Cushions

Here are three beautiful cushions in a simple geometric design, which use a selected range of colours. Smyrna or double cross stitch is used throughout.

Materials required

1½yd x 19in *(137cm x 48·2cm)* double thread canvas 10 threads to 1in *(2·5cm)*
Cushion 1 Tapestry wool: 2 skeins maroon, shocking pink, dusty lilac, pale blue violet, light bright orange, dark bright orange, violet, light purple, purple, medium purple, lilac, rust, cherry red and dark mauve; 1 skein light bright orange, bright pink, orange
Cushion 2 Tapestry wool: 2 skeins maroon, shocking pink, cherry red, dusty lilac, pale blue violet, purple, light bright orange, dark bright orange, orange, rust, violet, bright pink, medium purple, dark mauve; 1 skein lilac
Cushion 3 Tapestry wool: 2 skeins maroon, shocking pink, cherry red, dusty lilac, pale blue violet, light purple, light bright orange, dark bright orange, orange, rust, violet, bright pink, medium purple, purple, dark mauve
3 16in *(41cm)* square cushion pads
1yd *(91cm)* 48in *(121·7cm)* wide matching purple furnishing fabric
Tapestry frame with 23in *(58·3cm)* tapes

(optional) No. 18 tapestry needle

To work the cushions

Cut the canvas into three ½yd *(45·7cm)* lengths and mark the centre of each piece both ways with a line of basting stitches. The three diagrams give the complete design for each cushion, showing the colour sequence of all the squares. The cushions are worked throughout in Smyrna or double cross stitch over two double threads of canvas. Each numbered square on the layout diagram represents a square of eight double cross stitches. If a frame is being used, mount the canvas in the frame, the raw edges to tapes. Start working the design in the centre and follow the layout diagram and colour key.

Finishing

To make up, trim the canvas to within 1in *(2·5cm)* of embroidery. Cut a piece the same same size from the backing fabric. Place back and front pieces right sides together and sew close to the embroidery leaving an opening on one side so that the pad may be inserted easily. Turn to the right side. Insert pad. Turn in the same allowance on the open edges and slip stitch together. Alternatively, a zipper can be inserted on the open side.

Telephone Pad Cover

This attractive telephone pad uses only four basic stitches and the design is 'mirrored', repeating in reverse above and below the centre band. The finished size is approximately 8¼in x 6in (21cm x 15cm).

Materials required

10in x 13in (25cm x 33cm) single thread canvas, 13 threads to 1in (2·5cm)
Tapestry wool: 1 skein each of: light olive green, emerald green, forest green, white, pale yellow, beige yellow.
No. 18 tapestry needle
16½in x 6in (42cm x 30cm) thin cardboard
16½in x 6in (42cm x 30cm) stiff paper
17½in x 7in (44·5cm x 17·5cm) cotton lining fabric (optional)
9½in x 7in (24cm x 17·5cm) fine wool for back cover
Fabric adhesive

Left: Cushion 1, top left; Cushion 2, middle; Cushion 3, right.

To work embroidery

Mark the lengthwise centre of the canvas. Begin at the centre right, 2in (5cm) in from the edge. Following the chart, work the centre band. There are three groups of two diagonal blocks worked in white over four intersections of the canvas.
Slant the top three blocks from left to right, the bottom three from right to left. Work three large blocks over eight intersections of the canvas, using pale yellow. Slant alternately, right to left, left to right and right to left.
Continue with oblong cross stitches in forest green. Outline this section with green herringbone stitch over two threads. Complete the centre band, working rest of the pattern from the chart. Note that the stitches change direction. The upper section slants from left to right, the lower section from right to left. Each block is over six intersections of the canvas. The cross stitches are worked over two threads and small blocks over four intersections.

Making up the telephone pad

Press the embroidery lightly on the wrong side using a damp cloth and a warm iron. Trim the canvas to ½in (1cm) from the finished embroidery. Cut the cardboard into two pieces 8¼in x 6in (21cm x 15cm). Cover one piece with the embroidery and one with the fabric backing, as follows:
Lay back cover fabric and embroidery face down onto tissue paper. Centre the cardboard on the fabric. Spread adhesive along the four sides of the cardboard a little way in from the edge. Fold the fabric onto the adhesive, mitring the corners. Press the fabric firmly in position. Glue the two long sides and then the short sides. Make the inside of the two covers neat with either the stiff paper or with lining fabric. If intending to use lining fabric, mount this first on thin cardboard as for the cover boards. Glue the fabric-covered linings to the wrong side of the telephone pad covers.
Join the back and front covers with Cretan stitch or with two buttonholed ties, worked 1in (2·5cm) in from edges.
Make a cord by twisting three 80in (204cm) lengths of pale yellow. Fix the cord at one end and turn clockwise until tightly twisted. Fold in half and turn counter-clockwise. Pull firmly to lock the cord.
Oversew to the edges of the front cover. Glue a band of stiff paper inside the back cover to hold a tear-off note pad.

Florentine patterns

Bargello or Florentine work is a very exciting form of needlepoint embroidery because it is quick to do, easy enough for a complete beginner to undertake and produces a brilliant colourful effect.
Traditionally, several shades of one colour are used for a soft, glowing effect, but modern Bargello often uses brilliant and striking colour contrasts. Basically, Bargello consists of straight stitches worked over single thread canvas. The stitches can be all of the same length or a combination of short and long depending on the pattern. The colour and stitch arrangements produce the unique patterns, the best known of these being the zigzag or flame pattern which itself has several variations.

Chart labels

Centre band

Herringbone 2
Herringbone 2
Oblong cross 3
Herringbone 2
Oblong cross 3
Herringbone 2
Diagonal satin stitch 5
Diagonal satin stitch 4
Herringbone 2

Cross stitch
Cross stitch

Mirror repeat for final section

Centre line

Key

1 Light olive green	4 White
2 Emerald green	5 Pale yellow
3 Forest green	6 Yellow
	7 Beige

Crochet

Crochet never seems to be out of fashion! It is quick and easy to do and is an extraordinarily versatile technique. Worked in thin threads and yarns, crochet is delicate and lovely, producing exquisite lace fabrics. In heavier weight yarns and threads, crochet can be used to make a wide range of garments – bright sportswear, smart suits and coats, novelty clothes, hats, scarves and bags, baby wear and children's clothes, and jackets and sweaters for men. In the home too, modern crochet is used to make exciting furnishings from bulky yarns.

The crochet patterns in this chapter use only the simple, basic stitches, the effect being achieved with novelty yarns and use of color.

Knitting and Crochet abbreviations

alt	alternate
beg	beginning
ch	chain
cl	cluster
cont	continue
dc	double crochet
dec	decrease
dtr	double treble
g	garter stitch
gr(s)	group(s)
hdc	half double crochet
in(s)	inch(es)
inc	increase
K	knit
KB	knit into back of stitch
lp	loop
M1K	make 1 knitwise by picking up loop between st just worked and following st and knit into the back of it
M1P	make 1 purlwise by picking up loop between st just worked and following st and purl into the back of it
p	purl
patt	pattern
PB	purl into back of stitch
psso	pass slipped stitch over
rem	remaining
rep	repeat
RS	right side
sc	single crochet
sl 1	slip 1 knitwise
sl 1P	slip 1 purlwise
sp	space
ss	slip stitch
st(s)	stitch(es)
st st	stockinette stitch
tbl	through back loop(s)
tog	together
tr	treble
WS	wrong side
yo	yarn over
ytb	yarn to back
ytf	yarn to front
foll	following
str	straight or work even
WS	wrong side

Crochet hooks are available in steel for working with fine cotton yarns, and in aluminum or plastic for coarser cottons, wools and synthetic yarns. The size of hook you use depends on the weight and type of yarn you are working with, and crochet patterns usually recommend which size this should be. The important thing however, is not necessarily to use the precise hook size quoted but to check your gauge first by working a small sample in the stitch pattern. Provided you achieve the correct gauge as given in the instructions it does not matter what size hook you use. The sizings of crochet hooks have been standardized. The chart below compares the size of hooks in the International Standard Sizes range with American sizes. Australian, Canadian and South African sizes are in ISS measure.

New Milward international range	ISS Old English range	American range
	8 (steel)	
	7	
	6.50	
0.60 (steel)	6	14
	5.50	
0.75	5	12
	4.50	
1	4	10
	3.50	
1.25	3	8
1.50	2.50	7
1.75	2	4
	1.50	
2 (aluminum)	14 (aluminum)	1 (steel)
2.50	12	0 (steel)
	11	C/2 (aluminum)
3.50	10	D/3
	9	E/4
4	8	F/5
4.50	7	G/6
5	6	H/8
5.50	5	H/8
6	4	I/9
	3	J/10
7	2	K/10¼

YARNS AND GAUGE

The pattern instructions in this chapter recommend specific yarns and to achieve the best results, these yarns should be used. However, if a type of yarn or a color is difficult to obtain, an alternative yarn can be used but only that which, when worked, gives the same number of stitches and rows to the inch. The suitability of the yarn can be checked by making a gauge swatch. Work a 4in x 4in (10cm x 10cm) square of the pattern in the selected yarn and check the number of stitches and rows against the gauge specified in the pattern. If the gauge is different, the finished garment will not be the correct size! If there are fewer stitches than the number given use a hook one size smaller. If the swatch has too many stitches or rows, use a larger hook.

Peasant Maxi Skirt

Sizes
Skirt: Directions are to fit 24in (61cm) waist. Changes for 26 and 28in (66: 71)cm waist are in brackets [ ]
Shawl: One size, about 34in x 70in (178cm x 86cm)

Gauge
4 sts = 1in (2.5cm) with size G hook

Materials required:
Spinnerin Wintuk Sport Yarn, 2oz skeins
Skirt: 3 [3:4] skeins each green (color A) and yellow (B), 4 [5:5] skeins red (C) and 3 [3:4] skeins blue (D).
Shawl: 3 [3:3] skeins each green (A) and yellow (B), 2 [2:2] skeins red (C) and 3 [3:3] skeins blue (D)
Crochet hooks size F and G
7in (17.5cm) skirt zipper
1yd (1m) 1in (2.5cm) wide grosgrain ribbon
2 hooks and eyes
Note: Turning chain counts as one stitch.
Changing color: Just before drawing yarn through the last loop of the last stitch in row, drop old yarn, pick up new yarn and draw through to complete stitch, turn and cut old yarn.

Shawl
With size G hook and A make 242 ch.
Pattern Stripe 1 (PS1) Row 1: (RS) 1 sc in 2nd ch from hook, 1 sc in each ch to end, turn—241 sts. Row 2: 1 ch as first sc 1 sc in next and each st to end, change to B, turn. Row 3: 3 ch as first dc, working into back loop only work 1 dc in next and each st to end, change to C, turn. Row 4: 1 ch as first sc, * 1 dc in next st, ss in next st, rep from * to last 2 sts, ending 1 dc in next st, 1 sc in turning, chain to B, turn. Row 5: 3 ch as first dc, 1 dc in next and each st to end. Fasten off and do not turn. Row 6: (RS) With RS still facing attach A at beg of row, ** 1 ch, 1 sc in next and each st to end, turn. Row 7: Rep last row from **, turn. Row 8: Working into back loop only skip 5 sts, attach D into 6th st, 4 ch, 1 tr in next and each to last 5 sts, turn—231 sts. Row 9: Working into top 2 loops normally (ss into next st) twice, 4 ch, 1 tr in next and each to last 2 sts, turn—227 sts. Row 10: (Ss into next st) 3 times, 4 ch, 1 tr in next and each to last 3 sts, turn—221 sts. Rows 11–15: Rep rows 9 and 10 twice and row 9 again. Fasten off, turn—197 sts.

PS 2 *Row 1:* Skip 3 sts, attach B in 4th st, 1 ch, 1 sc in next and each to last 3 sts, turn—191 sts. Cont as for PS 1 with the following colors: *Row 2:* B. *Row 3:* C. *Row 4:* D. *Row 5:* C. *Rows 6 and 7:* B. *Rows 8–15:* A.—147 sts.
PS 3: As PS 2 with the foll colors: *Rows 1 and 2:* C. *Row 3:* D. *Row 4:* A. *Row 5:* D. *Rows 6 and 7:* C. *Rows 8–15:* B.—97 sts.
PS 4: As PS 2 with the foll colors: *Rows 1 and 2:* D. *Row 3:* A. *Row 4:* B. *Row 5:* A. *Rows 6 and 7:* D. *Rows 8–15:* C. —47 sts.
PS 5: Work rows 1–7 as PS 2 with the same colors as for PS 1. Fasten off = 41 sts.

Fringe
Wind yarn around 6in *(15cm)* wide cardboard and cut through one edge to make strands. Take 3 strands tog folded double and knot through both edges and narrow end of shawl as follows:

Patt. Rows 1–7: 1 tassel into edges of rows 2, 4 and 7—use 1 strand of each of the 3 colors involved in the 7 rows per tassel.
Patt. Rows 8–15: 1 tassel into corner of each row end—all 3 strands of each tassel same color as fabric.
Narrow end: 1 tassel into approx. every 4th st, using A for all strands.
Trim fringe evenly.

Skirt
Follow the same col sequence as for shawl. With size F hook and A make 114 [123:132] ch.
Pattern Strip 1—PS1 *Rows 1–7:* As for shawl, changing to next color yarn before turning = 114 [123:132] sts. Change to size G hook for the rest of skirt. *Row 8:* 4 ch, working into *back loop only* 2 tr in next st, * (1 tr in next st) twice, 2 tr in next st, rep from * 37 [40:43] times ending 1 tr in last st, turn—152 [164:176] sts. *Row 9:* 4 ch, working into top 2 loops normally, 1 tr in next and each st to end, turn. *Rows 10–17:* Rep row 9 eight more times, changing to next yarn before turning. Always starting patt row 1 with 1 ch as first sc, work PS 2, 3 and 4 as for PS 1, inc at each patt row 8 as follows:
PS 2 *Row 8:* Work 2 tr into 3rd st, then into every 4th st 37 [40:43] times—190 [205:220] sts.
PS 3 *Row 8:* Work 2 tr into 3rd st, then into every 5th st 37 [40: 43] times—228 [246:264] sts.
PS 4 *Row 8:* Work 2 tr into 4th st, then into every 6th st 37 [40:43] times = 266 [287:308] sts. Cont with C in tr patt straight as necessary until work measures 40in *(102cm)* or desired length. Fasten off.

Finishing
Press. With RS together, join seam and insert zipper at top. Sew grosgrain and hooks and eyes into waistband.

Baby's Shawl

Size
Approx. 40in *(102cm)* square.

Gauge
3 patterns (sc and 2dc) = 2in *(5cm)*.

Materials shown here
16 1oz *(28g)* skeins Coats & Clark's Red Heart Baby Wintuk
Crochet hook size G.

To make the Shawl
Make 149 ch.
Row 1: 2 dc in 2nd ch from hook, skip 2ch, * 1 sc, 2 dc in next ch, skip 2 ch; rep from * to last ch; 1 sc in last ch—49 pattern. *Row 2:* 2 ch, 2 dc in first sc, * 1 sc, 2 dc in next sc, rep from * across ending with 1 sc in top of 2 ch. Rep Row 2 until work measures 32in *(80cm)*.
Do not fasten off.

Ruffle edging Work evenly around shawl starting with 4 ch, 1 dc in edge * 1 ch, 1 dc in edge, rep from * to corner, work 1 ch, 1 dc, 1 ch and 1 dc in corner, rep from * around, ending with 1 ch, 1 dc in same stitch as beginning, ss to 3rd of 4 ch.
Round 1: Ss to first 1 ch lp, 3 ch, 1 dc in 1 ch lp, * 3 ch, skip 2 lps, 9 dc in next lp, 3ch, skip 2 lps, 2 dc, 1 ch and 2 dc in next lp; rep from * around, ending with 9 dc, 3 ch.
Round 2: Ss to 3 ch, ss between 3 ch and first dc, 4 ch, 1 dc between 3 ch and first dc, 1 ch, 1 dc in 1 ch lp, 1 ch, 1 dc, 1 ch and 1 dc between next 2 dc, 3 ch, * 1 sc in each of 9 dc, 3 ch, 1 dc, 1 ch and 1 dc between next 2 dc, 1 ch, 1 dc in 1 ch lp, 1 ch, 1 dc, 1 ch and 1 dc between next 2 dc, 3 ch; rep from * around, ending with 9 sc, 3 ch.
Round 3: Ss to 3rd of 4 ch, ss to 1 ch lp, 4 ch, 1 dc in first lp (1 ch, 1 dc in next lp) twice, 1 ch, 1 dc, 1 ch and 1 dc in next lp, * 3 ch, skip 1 sc, 1 sc in each of next 7 sc, 3 ch, 1 dc, 1 ch and 1 dc in first of 1 ch lp, (1 ch, 1 dc in next lp) twice, 1 ch, 1 dc, 1 ch and 1 dc in next lp; rep from * round, ending with 7 sc, 3 ch.
Round 4: Ss to 3rd of 4 ch and into first 1 ch lp, 4 ch, 1 dc in first lp, (1 ch, 1 dc in next lp) 3 times, 1 ch, 1 dc, 1 ch and 1 dc in last lp, * 3 ch, skip 1 sc, 1 sc in each of next 5 sc, 3 ch, 1 dc, 1 ch and 1 dc in first 1 ch lp. (1 ch, 1 dc in next lp) 3 times, 1 ch, 1 dc, 1 ch and 1 dc in last lp, rep from * around, ending with 5 sc, 3 ch.
Round 5: Ss to 3rd of 4 ch and into first 1 ch lp, 4 ch, 1 dc in first lp, (1 ch, 1 dc in next lp) 4 times, 1 ch, 1 dc, 1 ch and 1 dc in last lp, * 3 ch, skip 1 sc, 1 sc in each of next 4 sc, 3 ch, 1 dc, 1 ch and 1 dc in next 1 ch lp, (1 ch, 1 dc in next lp), 4 times, 1 ch, 1 dc, 1 ch and 1 dc in last lp, rep from * around, ending with 4 sc, 3 ch.
Round 6: Ss to 3rd of 4 ch and into first ch lp, 4 ch, 1 dc into first lp, (1 ch, 1 dc in next lp) 5 times, 1 ch 1 dc, 1 ch and 1 dc in last lp, * 3 ch, skip 1 sc, 1 sc in each of next 3 sc, 3 ch, 1 dc, 1 ch and 1 dc in first lp, (1 ch, 1 dc in next lp) 5 times, 1 ch, 1 dc, 1 ch and 1 dc in last lp, rep from * around, ending with 3 sc, 3 ch.
Round 7: Ss to 3rd of 4 ch and into first lp, 4 ch, 1 dc into first lp, (1 ch, 1 dc in next lp) 6 times, 1 ch, 1 dc, 1 ch and 1 dc in last lp, * 3 ch, skip 1 sc, 1 sc in each of next 2 sc, 3 ch, 1 dc, 1 ch and 1 dc in first lp, (1 ch, 1 dc in next lp) 6 times, 1 ch, 1 dc, 1 ch and 1 dc in last lp, rep from * around, ending with 2 sc, 3 ch.
Round 8: Ss to 3rd of 4 ch, * (sc in next ch 1 lp, ch 4, sc in 4th ch from hook for picot) 9 times, 3 ch, 1 sc in between next 2 sc, 3 ch, rep from * around, ss to first sc. Fasten off.

Indian Boy Nightdress Case

Size
About 25in high *(63cm)*

Gauge
5c = 1in *(2.5cm)* with size E hook

Materials required:
Sport yarn: 6oz *(168g)* red, 2oz *(56g)* purple, 1oz *(28g)* each light brown, green and yellow
Small amount white, blue and black yarn
Crochet Hook size E
9in *(23cm)* red zipper
Piece of lining material 18in x 30in *(46cm x 76cm)*
Kapok or other suitable filling
2 curtain rings approx. 1in *(2.5cm)* in diameter
Spool of gold thread

Body
Front Begin at lower edge of pants as follows:
Using size E hook and red, work a ch of 14 sts. Skip 2 ch, work 1 sc into each of the foll 12 ch. Work throughout in sc. Turn each row with 1 ch. Inc 1 sc at the beg and end of next row and each alt row until 40 sc are across row. Fasten off. Work another piece the same. Work across the two pieces (80 sc across row). Work 6 rows across these 80 sc. Dec 1 sc at the beg and end of the next row and each foll 5th row until 20 sc are across row. Work 2 further rows. Fasten off red; attach purple. Work 4 rows. Inc 1 sc at beg and end of next row and work on these 22 sc for a further 20 rows. Ss across 7 sc, 1 ch, work 1 sc into each of the next 8 sc. Turn. Work 8 rows on these 8 sc. Fasten off.
Back Work as for the Front until 80 sc are across the row and work 6 rows on these 80 sc. Divide for the zipper as follows:

Dec 1 sc at beg of next row. Work 38 sc. Turn and work on these sc only. Dec at the outside edge only each 5th row and keep inside edge str until 27 sc are across row. Fasten off. Attach red to rem sc, work to correspond, reversing the shapings accordingly. Fasten off. Work across the two pieces and dec as before at the beg and end of each 5th row until 20 sc are across the row. Fasten off. Attach purple and work as for the front to complete.

Head
Using size E hook and light brown, work a ch of 10 sts. Skip 2 ch, work 1 sc into each of the foll 8 ch. Work 8 rows.
Next row: 4 ch, skip 2 ch, work 1 sc into each of the next 2 ch, work to end. Rep this row 6 times in all (20 sc across row). Work 16 rows on these 20 sc. Dec 1 sc at beg and end of the next row and each alt row until 12 sc are across row. Fasten off. Work 2 pieces like this.

Hands
Using size E hook and light brown, work a ch of 7 sts. Skip 2 ch, work 1 sc into each of the next 5 ch. Inc 1 sc at beg and end of next row and each alt row until 9 sc are across row. Work 6 rows on these 9 sc. Dec 1 sc at beg and end of next row and each alt row until 5 sc rem. Fasten off.
Work 2 pieces like this.

Arm
Using size E hook and purple, work a ch of 24 sts. Skip 2 ch, work 1 sc into each of the foll 22 ch. Work 26 rows.
Next row: 1 ch, * 1 sc into next sc, skip 1 sc. Rep from * to end. Fasten off. Work 2 pieces like this.

Turban
Using size E hook and green, work a ch of 19 sts. Skip 3 ch, work 1 dc into each of the foll 16 ch. Turn each row with 2 ch. Work a further 26 rows dc. Fasten off.

Waist band
Using size E hook and green, work a ch of 9 sts. Skip 3 ch, 1 dc into each of the foll 6 ch. Work 18 rows on these 6 dc. Fasten off.

Feet
Using size E hook and yellow, work a ch of 14 ch. Skip 2 ch, work 1 sc into each of the foll 12 ch. Work a further 3 rows sc.
Next row: 1 ch, 1 sc into each of the next 5 sc. Turn and work on these 5 sc only. Work to end of row (outside edge).

Next row: 1 ch, skip 1 sc, 1 sc into each of the next 4 sc. Keeping inside edge str dec 1 sc at beg of each row at outside until 1 sc rem. Fasten off.
Work 4 pieces like this.

171

Hands Fold in half leaving the center edge open; fill with stuffing and sew opening. Work both hands in the same way and sew in position. Sew arms to body.

Feet Place two pieces together and sew around edge, leaving a small opening. Insert stuffing and join opening. Make both feet the same. Sew feet to body.

Using a piece of stiff cardboard $\frac{1}{2}$in x 4in *(2cm x 10cm)* insert half this into head and pad in place to support head. Put the remaining half into neck opening, pad in position and pull neck up over neck of head part and sew edge firmly over neck.

Using gold thread, work as illustrated along the pants. Work up center front and wind thread around the neck as desired. Black yarn could be used instead of gold thread if desired.

Mohair Jacket

Sizes
Directions are to fit 34in *(86cm)* bust. Changes for 36in *(91cm)* and 38in *(96cm)* bust are in brackets [ ].
Waist : 24 [26 : 28]in *(61 [66 : 71]cm)*
Hips : 36 [38 : 40]in *(91 [96 : 102]cm)*
Length from shoulder : $26\frac{5}{8}$ [$26\frac{5}{8}$: $27\frac{1}{4}$]in *(68 [68 : 69]cm)*
Sleeve Seam : $16\frac{3}{8}$ [17 : $17\frac{5}{8}$]in *(42 [42 : 45]cm)*

Gauge
With size I hook, 3 dc = 1in *(2.5cm)* and 3 rows dc = 2in *(5cm)*.

Materials shown here:
Bernat Mohair Plus ($1\frac{1}{2}$oz balls)
A–4 [5 : 5]; B–2 [2 : 2];
C–3 [3 : 4]; D–1 [1 : 1].
Crochet hooks size H and I
4 buttons
Note: Turning chain counts as one stitch.

To make the Jacket
Upper part. Color sequence: * 2 rows A; 1 row B; 1 row C; 1 row A; 1 row D; 2 rows A; 1 row C; 1 row A; 2 rows C; rep from *. With size I hook and A make 107 [113 : 119] ch.
Row 1: (RS) 1 dc in 3rd ch from hook, 1 dc in next and each ch to end, turn—106 [112 : 118] sts. *Row 2:* 3 ch as first dc, 1 dc in next and each st to end, turn. Row 2 forms str patt. *Rows 3–7:* Work 5 rows patt str.
Shape neck. *Row 8:* 3 ch, 2 dc tog, patt to last 2 sts, 2 dc tog, turn—104 [110 : 116] sts. *Rows 9–12:* Rep last 2 rows twice—100 [106 : 112] sts.
Divide for right front, back and left front. Mark with contrasting thread the 23rd [24th : 25th] sts in from each edge and the 2nd [3rd : 4th] st beyond each of those.

Finishing
Press each piece under a damp cloth with a warm iron.
Head Embroider the face as follows: eyes; outline each eye in black in stem stitch. Fill each eye half white, half blue in satin stitch.
Embroider the nose black in straight stitches.

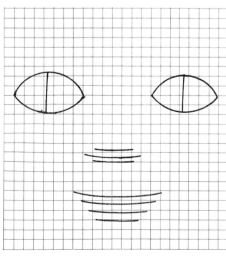

Work the mouth red in stem stitch. Place the two head pieces tog with the face towards WS and sew around the edge leaving the neck and top of head open. Turn to RS. Stuff the head and arrange turban. Shape with stuffing and sew in position. Sew curtain rings at each side for earrings.
Body Fold lining in half and cut as shape of the pants; allow $\frac{1}{2}$in *(1cm)* for seam and mark position of zip cut on one side at back of the pants. Sew around the edge of the lining, leaving the top edge open.
Place the back and front together and sew around the edge leaving the neck open. Turn to RS. Sew along the waist edge to hold the waist in position.
Insert zipper into opening. Place lining inside pants and turn back opening at the zipper and sew into place. If desired a little stuffing could be inserted in between lining and pants. Slip lining into place. Sew along top edge. Fill top of body with stuffing to form round shape. Sew each arm, leaving the top and lower edge open. Stuff and join cuff and top edge. Sew waistband in place.

172

Right front (worked from edge to first marker)

Shape armholes. Row 1: 3 ch, patt to lasts 3 sts before marker, 3 dc tog, turn—21 [22:23] sts. **Row 2:** 3 ch, 3 dc tog, patt to last 2 sts, 2 dc tog, turn—18 [19:20] sts. **Row 3:** 3 ch, patt to last 2 sts, 2 dc tog, turn—17 [18:19] sts. **Row 4:** 3 ch, 2 dc tog, patt to last 2 sts, 2 dc tog, turn—15 [16:17] sts. **Row 5:** Patt str. **Row 6:** As row 3—14 [15:16] sts. **Rows 7–12:** Rep last 2 rows 3 more times—11[12:13] sts.

3rd size only
Work 1 more row patt str.

Shape shoulder. *1st and 2nd sizes:* 3 ch (1 dc in next st) twice, (1 hdc in next st) 3 times, (1 sc in next st) 3 times, ss into next st. Fasten off.

3rd size only: (ss into next st) 4 times, 1 ch, (sc in next st) twice, 1 hdc in next st) 3 times, 1 dc in each st to end. Fasten off.

Back

Attach yarn at 2nd marker and work to 3rd marker.

Shape armholes. Row 1: 3 ch, 3 dc tog, patt to last 3 sts, (before marker), 3 dc tog, turn—48 [50:52] sts. **Row 2:** As row 1—44 [46:48] sts. **Row 3:** 3 ch, 2 dc tog, patt to last 2 sts, 2 dc tog, turn—42 [44:46] sts. **Row 4:** As row 1—40 [42:44] sts. Work 8 [8:9] rows patt str.

Shape shoulders. (Ss into next st) 2 [3:4] times, 1 ch, (1 sc in next st) twice, (1 hdc in next st) 3 times, 1 dc in each to last 8 [9:10] sts, (1 hdc in next st) 3 times, (1 sc in next st) twice, ss into next st. Fasten off.

Left front

Attach yarn in 4th marker and work to end. Work as for right front reversing all shaping.

Lower part color sequence:
* 2 rows C; 1 row A; ** 1 row C; 2 rows A; 1 row D; 1 row A; 1 row C; 1 row B; 2 rows A. Rep from * to **.

Along lower edge of upper part mark with contrasting thread the 27th [28th: 29th] st in from each edge and 1 st in center back.

Starting with RS facing, work 15 rows in patt across lower edge inc 3 sts on first and then every 6th row twice by working 2 dc into the sts corresponding to marked sts—115 [121:127] sts. Fasten off.

Sleeves color sequence: (make 2 alike) 1 row each with A, C, B, A, D, B, A, C, B etc. With size I hook and A make 41 [44:47] ch. **Row 1:** 1 dc in 2nd [4th: 6th] ch from hook, (1 dc in next ch) twice, * 3 ch, skip 3 ch, (1 dc in next ch) 3 times, rep from * ending *2nd and 3rd sizes:* 1 [2] ch, skip 1 [2] ch. *All sizes:* ss into last ch, turn—7 x 3 dc gps. **Row 2:** 6 [3:3] ch, *2nd and 3rd sizes:* Working over next ch loop work (1 dc in next ch of original ch row) 1 [2] times, 3 ch, *All sizes:* skip 3 dc, * working over ch loop of last row work (1 dc in next ch of original ch row) 3 times, 3 ch, skip 3 dc, rep from * ending (1 dc in next ch of original ch row) 1 [2:3] times, turn—41 [43:45] sts. In patt sts are always worked over ch loops of last row into top of row below, so "1 dc over ch loop into top of next dc in row below" is written, "1 dc in next dc."

Row 3: 1 [2:3] ch, skip 1 [2:3] sts, * (1 dc in next dc) 3 times, 3 ch, skip 3 dc, rep from * ending (1 dc in next dc) 3 times; *2nd and 3rd sizes:* 1 [2] ch, skip 1 [2] sts. *All sizes:* ss into 3rd ch of turning ch, turn. **Row 4:** 6 [3:3] ch, *2nd and 3rd sizes:* (1 dc in next dc) 1 [2] times, *All sizes:* skip 3 dc, * (1 dc in next dc) 3 times, 3 ch, skip 3 dc, rep from * ending (1 dc in next dc) 1 [2:3] times, turn.

Rep rows 3 and 4 until work measures 15⅜ [16:16⅝in (39 [41:43] cm) ending with a patt row 3. **Shape top Row 1:** 3 ch, *2nd and 3rd sizes:* (1 dc in next dc) 1 [2] times, *All sizes:* (ss into next dc) 1 [2: 3] times, patt to last 3 dc gp, (ss in next dc) 3 times, (1 dc in next dc) 1 [2:3] times. Fasten off and turn.

Row 2: Skip 1 [2:3] dc of last row and next 2 dc in row below and attach yarn in next dc: ** 4 ch, skip 3 dc, * (1 dc in next dc) 3 times, 3 ch, skip 3 dc, rep from * 4 times, ss in next dc, turn—5 x 3 dc gps.

Row 3: 1 ch, 1 sc in next dc, 1 hdc in next dc, 1 dc in next dc, patt to last 3 dc gp, ending 1 dc in next dc, 1 hdc in next dc, 1 sc in next dc, ss into next sc, turn—4 x 3 dc gps.

Row 4: (Ss into next st) 3 times, patt across ending ss in top of last dc, turn, leaving hdc and sc unworked—5 x 3 dc gps.

Row 5: 6 ch, skip 3 dc, patt across ending 3 ch, skip 3 dc, 1 dc in next dc, turn—4 x 3 dc gps.

Row 6: (1 dc in next dc) 3 times, patt ending ss into 3rd ch of turning ch, turn —5 x 3 dc gps.

Row 7: As row 2 from ** and working one less repeat—4 x 3 dc gps.

Rows 8–11: Rep rows 3–6—4 x 3 dc gps. **Rows 12–20:** Rep rows 2–4 three times —1 x 3 dc gps. Fasten off.

Finishing

Do not press.

With RS together join shoulder seams, set in sleeves and join sleeve seams.

Cuffs With size H hook and starting RS facing work 2 rows each with C and A evenly in sc around each cuff, joining each row with ss and turning with 1 ch between rows.

Neck-front With size H hook, starting at bottom of right front and working up right front, around neck, down left front to bottom and back again, work 2 rows each with C and A evenly in sc, turning with 1 ch. On 2nd row make 4 button-holes evenly spaced down right front between end of neck shaping and lower edge by working 2 ch, skip 2 sc.

On 3rd row work 1 sc in each ch of each buttonhole loop.

Sew buttons to left front to correspond with buttonholes.

Mohair Shawl

Size

Approx. 70in x 35in (178cm x 89cm) excluding fringe.

Gauge

With size I hook 1 Patt Rep (9 sts) = 3in wide and 3¼in deep (8cm x 9cm) (4 rows patt).

Materials shown here

Reynolds Mohair No. 1 Bayadere, 5 (40g) balls
Crochet hooks size H and I.
Note: Shawl starts at top edge with 22 flowers and by following pattern decreases to one at lower end.

Shawl

With size H hook make 206 ch.

Row 1 (RS): 1 sc in 2nd ch from hook, 1 sc in each ch to end, turn. 205 sts.

Row 2: 1 ch, 1 sc in each st to end, turn. Change to size I hook.

Row 3: 3ch, skip 3 sts, dc in next st, * 3ch, holding back on hook the last loop of each dc work 2dc at base of 3ch just made, yo and draw through all 3 loops on hook (2dc cluster made, called 2dcCL), skip 2 sts, holding back on hook the last loop of each dc work 3dc in next st, yo and draw through all 4 loops on hook (3dc cluster made, called 3dcCL), skip 2 sts, 3dcCL in next st, 3ch, 2dcCL at base of 3ch, skip 2 sts, dc in next st; rep from * to last 3 sts, skip 2 sts, dc in turning ch. Turn—22 flowers started.

Row 4: 3ch, * in center of next flower work 3dcCL, 2ch and 3dcCL, 2ch, dc in next dc, 2ch; rep from * across ending 3dcCL, 2ch and 3dcCL in center of last flower, dc in turning ch. Turn—22 flowers.

Row 5: 3ch, dc in next 2ch sp, * 3ch, 2dcCL at base of 3ch, 3dcCL in next 2ch sp, skip next dc, 3dcCL in next 2ch sp, 3ch, 2dcCL at base of 3ch, dc in next 2ch sp (between clusters); rep from * across ending dc in turning ch. Turn.

Rep rows 4 and 5, 20 times and row 4 again. Fasten off. 1 flower.

Fringe

Wind yarn around 6in (15cm) wide cardboard and cut through one edge to make strands. Take 3 strands together folded double and knot through each row end along both sides of shawl. Trim fringe.

Knitting

For some people, knitting is a relaxing and soothing occupation; for others, it is an art form through which they can find expression. For some, knitting is a form of economy, a way of providing clothes for a growing family. For many people, however, knitting is a means of acquiring smart fashion clothes at a fraction of the price they would cost to buy ready-made. The clothes in this chapter are designed using the basic stitches–plain, purl and garter stitch–and use only the simplest shaping techniques.

COMPARATIVE KNITTING NEEDLE SIZES

English	000	00	0	1	2	3	4	5
American	15	13	12	11	10½	10	9	8

English	6	7	8	9	10	11	12	13	14
American	7	6	5	4	3	2	1	0	00

Knitting needle sizes are not yet uniform in all countries. This chart tells you how English and American sizes compare. Abbreviations are given on page 169.

YARNS AND YARDAGE

The patterns in this chapter specify certain brands of yarns and for the best results, the yarn recommended should be used. Sometimes however, it is difficult to obtain a specific yarn in the color you want. If it is necessary to use a different yarn, it is most important that a gauge check be made before starting the garment.

The amount of yarn contained in a ball varies between different brands. You would be wise to check the yardage of the recommended yarn against the one you have decided to use. Always buy sufficient yarn at one time so that all the balls are from the same dye lot. Even the slightest variation in color will show up on your work and spoil the effect.

GAUGE

Whether the specified yarn is being used or not, a knitter should always knit a gauge square before starting the pattern. Even quite experienced knitters sometimes knit too tightly or loosely to achieve the correct gauge stated in the pattern. This can be corrected by changing needles to a larger or smaller size.

To make a gauge square, knit a 4in x 4in (10cm x 10cm) square of the pattern. Place the swatch on a flat surface and pin it down. Lay a ruler on the knitting and mark off 1in (2.5cm) with pins. Count the number of stitches between the pins very carefully. Now measure the number of rows and check the number against the gauge given in the pattern. If the swatch has too many stitches or rows to the inch, try a smaller size needle. If the swatch is smaller than the tension given, experiment with a size larger needle.

Girl's Tunic Dress

Sizes
Directions are to fit 22in (56)cm chest. Changes for 24, 26 and 28in (61:66: 71)cm chest are given in brackets [ ]
Length: 16 [18:21:24]in
        (41:46:51:61)cm

Gauge
7½ sts and 9½ rows = 1in (2.5cm) over st st on No. 2 needles.

Materials required:
Brunswick Fore-'n-Aft Sport Yarn
2 [3:3:4] 2oz skeins white as main color (MC) and 1 skein each navy (A), turquoise (B) and red (C)
A pair each knitting needles–Nos. 1, 2, 3 and 4.
Note: When working design carry color not being used loosely across wrong side of work.

Front
Using MC and No. 2 needles cast on 89 [97:105:113] sts and, starting with a K row, work 7 rows in st st. K 1 row on WS for hemline. Change to No. 4 needles and K 1 row, P 1 row. Cont in st st and follow chart for design. Rep from X to Y across, end as at Z. Work until row 44 is completed. Turn chart upside down and starting with row 45 follow chart until it is completed.
Change to No. 2 needles. Cont in MC st st until piece measures 11½ [13:15½:18] in (29:33:39:46)cm or desired length from hemline, ending with a P row.

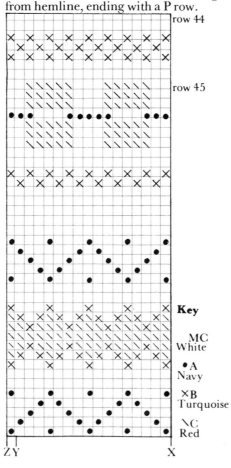

row 44

row 45

Key

MC
White
•A
Navy
×B
Turquoise
\C
Red

Z Y   X

Shape armholes:
Cont in MC st st, bind of 4 sts at beg of next 2 rows; dec 1 st at both ends of next 6 [7:8:9] rows and of foll alt row. (67 [73:79:85] sts).
Start yoke design:
Row 1: K1MC, (K1A, K1MC) to end.
Row 2: P1A, (P1MC, P1A) to end.
Using MC K1 row, P1 row, K1 row.
Row 6: P3, [2:5:4] MC, (P5B, P3MC) until 8 [7:10:9] sts rem, P5B, P3 [2:5:4] MC. Row 7: As 6th, knitwise. Row 8: As 6th. Row 9: K3 [2:5:4] C, (K1C, K3MC, K4C) until 8 [7:10:9] sts rem, K1C, K3MC, K4 [3:6:5] C.
Starting with row 8, work these design rows in reverse order, back to and inc first row. Cont in MC work 1 [3:7:9] rows in st st.
Shape front neck Next row: K20 [22:24:26], K2 tog, turn. Starting with a P row, work 7 rows in st st for left shoulder, dec 1 st at neck edge on next row and on foll alt rows 4 times—17 [19:21:23] sts.
Shape shoulders: Bind off 5 [6:7:7] sts at beg of next and foll alt row and 7 [7:7: 9] sts at beg of next alt row. Returning to sts still on needle, slip first 23 [25:27:29] sts onto a holder and complete second front shoulder to match first, reversing shapings.

Back
As front, omitting front neck opening, to beg shoulders—67 [73:79:85] sts.
Shape shoulders: Bind off 5 [6:7:7] sts at beg of next 4 rows and 7 [7:7:9] sts at beg of foll 2 rows. Leave rem 33 [35: 37:39] sts on holder.

Crew neck
Sew right shoulder seam. With RS facing and using No.1 needles, start at left front shoulder and pick up and K in MC 12 sts from each side of neck, and sts from holders at front and back. Work 5 rows in K1, P1 rib. P1 row (ridge-row on right side). Work 4 rows in K1, P1 rib. Bind off loosely using a No. 4 needle.

Edgings for side openings–work 4.
Using MC and No. 3 needles cast on 5 sts and work 4in in st st. Bind off.

Finishing
Press st st sections, using cool iron and dry cloth. Sew left shoulder seam, joining sides of neck ribbing; turn in neck ribbing on the ridge row and hem loosely on inside.
Armbands: With RS facing and using No. 2 needles, pick up and K in MC 74 [82:90:98] sts around each armhole. Work 2 rows in K1, P1 rib. Bind off in rib.
Turn up hem of front and back and catch lightly in position. Sew side opening edgings in place, from hemline for 4in up each side of front and back; and then sew remainder of side seams, joining sides of armbands. Press seams.

Sweater and Jumper

Sizes
Directions are to fit 22in (56cm) chest. Changes for 24in (61cm) and 26in (66cm) chest are in brackets [ ]
Length of Dress: 16 [18:21]in
(41:46:53)cm
Length of Sweater: 13 [14½:16]in
(33:37:41)cm
Sleeve seam: 8½ [10:11½]in
(22:25:28)cm

Gauge
6 sts and 8 rows = 1in (2.5cm) over st st on No. 5 needles

Materials required:
Brunswick Fore-'n-Aft Sport Yarn
4 [5:5] 2oz skeins white (A) and 3 [4:4] skeins blue (B)
A pair each knitting needles Nos. 3, 4 and 5

Jumper
Front
Using B and No. 3 needles, cast on 104 [110:116] sts and, starting with a K row, work 6 rows in st st.
Using A K 1 row, K1 row on WS for hemline. Change to No. 5 needles. K1 row. Fasten off A. Attach B and, starting with a P row, cont in B st st until piece measures 9 [9½:11]in (23:24:28)cm or desired length from hemline, ending with a K row.
Next row: P2, (P2 tog, P1) to end. (70 [74:78] sts). Change to No. 3 needles.
Bodice: Using B. *Row 1:* K. *Row 2:* K2, (P2, K2) to end. *Row 3:* P2, (K2, P2) to end. *Row 4:* As 2nd. Rep these last 4 rows once in A. Change to No. 4 needles and cont in this 8 row rib-and-stripe patt to complete 18 [26: 34] rows from beg of bodice.
Shape armholes: Cont in patt, bind off 12 sts at beg of next 2 rows. (46 [50: 54] sts). Working the 2 sts at each end of needle in g st, work another 7 rows in rib-and-stripe patt. Bind off in patt.

Back – work same as front.
Straps – (work 2) Using B and No. 4 needles cast on 14 sts. *Row 1:* K3, sl 1 purlwise, K6, sl 1 purlwise, K3. *Row 2:* P. Rep these 2 rows until piece measures 8 [9:10]in (20:23:25)cm or desired length from cast-on edge. Bind off.

Sweater
Front
Using A and No. 3 needles cast on 71 [77: 83] sts. *Row 1:* P1, (K1, P1) to end. *Row 2:* K1, (P1, K1) to end. Rep these last 2 rows 4 times more. Change to No. 5 needles and cont in rib as set until work measures 8½ [9½:10½]in (21:24:26)cm or desired length from cast-on edge, ending with a WS row.
Shape armholes: Cont in rib, bind off 4 sts at beg of next 2 rows; dec 1 st at both ends of next 4 [5:6] rows and of foll alt row. Work even on rem 53 [57: 61] sts until piece measures 3 [3½:4]in (8:9:10)cm from beg of armholes, ending with a WS row.
Shape front neck: *Next row:* Patt 18 [19:20] sts, turn. Patt 7 rows for left shoulder, dec 1 st at neck edge on next row and on foll alt rows 3 times—14 [15: 16] sts.
Shape shoulder: Bind off 5 sts at beg of next and foll alt row and 4 [5:6] sts at beg of next alt row. Returning to sts still on needle, slip first 17 [19: 21] sts onto a holder and complete 2nd front shoulder to match with first, reversing shapings.
Back
As front, omitting front neck opening, to beg shoulders—53 [57:61] sts.
Shape shoulders: Bind off 5 sts at beg of next 4 rows and 4 [5:6] sts at beg of foll 2 rows. Leave rem 25 [27:29] sts on holder.

Turtleneck
Sew right shoulder seam. With RS facing and using No. 3 needles, start at left front shoulder and pick up 11 sts from each side of neck, and sts from holders at front and back. Working in A in K1, P1 rib, work 8 rows on No. 3 needles and 16 rows on No. 5 needles. Using B, K1 row; bind off loosely in rib.

Sleeves
Using A and No. 3 needles, cast on 34 [36:40] sts and work 4 rows in K1, P1 rib. Using B, K1 row, work 3 rows in K1, P1 rib. Rep these last 4 rows once in A, then once in B. Using A, K1 row, rib 2 rows.
Next row: Rib 1 [3:1]; (work twice in next st, rib 2) to end. (45 [47:53] sts). Change to No. 5 needles and cont in A in K1, P1 rib, inc 1 st at both ends of every 5th row until you have 57 [63:69] sts. Work even until sleeve measures 8½ [10:11½]in (21:25:29)cm or desired length from cast-on edge, ending with a WS row.
Shape top: Bind off 4 sts at beg of next 2 rows, 2 sts at beg of next 12 [14:16] rows and 4 sts at beg of next 2 rows. Bind off rem 17 [19:21] sts.

Finishing
Press st st sections. Sew side seams of dress; turn up hem and catch lightly in place. Fold each strap on the sl sts and then join sides. Sew straps in position. Sew left shoulder seam of sweater, joining sides of turtleneck; sew side seams and sleeve seams and set in sleeves. Press st st seams.

Ribbed Sweater

Directions are to fit 34in *(86cm)* bust/chest. Changes for 36, 38, 40, 42 and 44in *(91, 96, 102, 107 and 118cm)* bust/chest are in brackets [ ].

Sizes
Length from shoulder 25½ [26:26½: 27½: 28: 28½]in *(65: 66: 67: 70: 71: 72)cm*
Sleeve seam including turn-back cuff 20½ [20½:21:21½:22]in *(52:52:53:55: 56:56)cm*

Note: The first three sizes are intended for a woman and the last three for a man. Either turtleneck or crew neck can be made for any size.

Gauge
6 sts and 8 rows 1in *(2.5cm)* over st st on No. 5 needles.

Materials required:
Reynolds Firefly, 8 [9:10:11:11:12] 50 gr balls
1 pair each knitting needles, Nos. 3, 4 and 5.

Note: It is important to note that the occasional diamond and chevron pattern effects obtained with Firefly yarn are entirely random and the position of these cannot be determined in advance.

Back
With No. 3 needles, cast on 111 [117: 123:119:125:131] sts. Work in single rib as follows:
Row 1: RS K2, *P1, K1; rep from * to last st, K1.
Row 2: K1, * P1, K1; rep from * to end.
Rep these 2 rows 7 times more. Change to No. 5 needles and patt.
Row 1: RS K0 [0:2:0:3:6], P13 [16: 17:17:17:17], * K17, P17; rep from * once, K17, P13 [16:17:17:17:17], K0 [0:2:0:3:6].
Row 2: P0 [0:2:0:3:6], K13 [16:17: 17:17:17], * P17, K17; rep from * once, P17, K13 [16:17:17:17:17], P0 [0:2:0:3:6].
Cont in patt as now set and shape as follows:
Women's sizes only Dec 1 st at both ends of row every 1in *(2.5cm)* 5 times—when work measures 3 [4:5:6:7]in *(8:10:13:15:18)cm.* Cont without shaping until work measures 11in *(28cm)* from beg. Inc 1 st at both ends of next row and again when work measures 13in *(33cm)* and 15in *(38cm)* from beg.
Men's sizes only Cont in patt without any shaping until work measures 5in *(13cm)* from beg. Inc 1 st at both ends of next row and every 3in *(7.5cm)* 3 times.
For all sizes When shapings are completed, cont on these 107 [113:119:127: 133:139] sts until work measures 18 [18:18:18½:18½:18½]in *(46:46:46:47: 47:47)cm* from beg ending with a WS row.

Armhole shaping Bind off 5 sts at beg of next 2 rows and 4 [5:6:4:5:6] sts at beg of next 4 rows—81 [83:85:101:103:105] sts. RS rows will now beg and end K15 [K16:K17:P8:P9:P10]. Cont in patt until work measures $24\frac{1}{4}$ [$24\frac{3}{4}$:$25\frac{1}{4}$:$26\frac{1}{4}$:$26\frac{3}{4}$:$27\frac{1}{4}$]in *(62:63:64:67:68:69)cm* from beg ending with a WS row.

Shoulder and neck shaping *Row 1:* Bind off 7 sts, patt until there are 23 [24:25:31:32:33] sts on right-hand needle, leave these sts on a spare needle for right back, cont along row, bind off 21 [21:21:25:25:25] sts, then patt to end. Cont on the 30 [31:32:38:39:40] sts now rem on needle for left back.

Row 2: Bind off 7 sts, patt back to neck edge.

Row 3: Bind off 4 [4:4:3:3:3] sts, patt to end. Rep last 2 rows once (once: once: twice: twice: twice). Bind off rem 8 [9:10:8:9:10] sts. With WS facing, attach yarn to inner edge of right back sts and work this side to correspond.

Front

Work as for back until armhole shaping is completed, then cont without shaping until work measures 23 [$23\frac{1}{2}$:24:25:$25\frac{1}{2}$:26]in *(58:60:61:63:65:66)cm* from beg, ending with a WS row.

Neck and shoulder shaping *Row 1:* Patt 34 [35:36:42:43:44] and leave these sts on a spare needle for left front, cont along row, bind off 13 [13:13:17:17:17] sts, patt to end. Cont on the 34 [35:36:42:43:44] sts now rem on needle for right front and work 1 row even.

Bind off 3 sts at beg of next row, dec 1 st at same edge of next 6 rows, then dec 1 st at same edge on next alt row. Now bind off 7 sts for shoulder shaping at beg of next row, then dec 1 st at neck edge on foll row. Rep last 2 rows once (once: once: twice: twice: twice). Bind off rem 8 [9:10:8:9:10] sts **.

With WS facing, attach yarn to inner edge of left front sts and work this side to correspond.

Sleeves

With No. 3 needles cast on 53 [55:57:65:67:69] sts and beg with a first row work 43 rows in rib as on waist. You have ended with a RS row to reverse rib on cuff. Change to No. 5 needles and patt.

Row 1: RS K1 [2:3:7:8:9], P17, K17, P17, K1 [2:3:7:8:9].

Row 2: P1 [2:3:7:8:9], K17, P17, K17, P1 [2:3:7:8:9].

Cont in patt as now set and inc 1 st at both ends of next row and every foll 8th [6th: 6th: 6th: 6th: 5th] row until there are 81 [87:93:101:107:113] sts working extra sts into patt. When all incs are completed, the RS rows will beg and end K15 [P1:P4:P8:P11:P14]. Cont without shaping until work measures $20\frac{1}{2}$ [$20\frac{1}{2}$:21:$21\frac{1}{2}$:22:22] *(52:52:53:55:56:56)cm* from beg ending with a WS row. Place marker loops of contrast yarn at each end of last row to indicate end of sleeve seam. Work 18 [20:22:18:20:22] rows even.

Shape top: Bind off 4 sts at beg of next 10 [10:10:12:12:12] rows and 4 [5:6:6:7:8] sts at beg of next 6 rows = 17 sts rem for all sizes. Cont on these sts working in st st for shoulder yoke, until this strip is long enough to fit across one front shoulder edge. Bind off.

Turtleneck

With No. 3 needles cast on 139 [139:139:147:147:147] sts. Work in rib as on waist for $2\frac{1}{2}$in *(6cm)* then change to No. 4 needles and work a further 2in *(5cm)* in rib. Bind off in ribbing.

Neckband—**for crew neck**

With No. 4 needles, cast on 135 [135:135:143:143:143] sts. Work in rib as on waist for 8 rows, change to No. 3 needles and work 8 rows, then change back to No. 4 needles and work 8 rows. Bind off in ribbing.

Finishing

Press patt sections lightly on WS with warm iron and damp cloth. First pin sleeves into armholes, matching markers to beg of armhole bound-off sts so that these bound-off edges are pinned to straight row of sleeves above markers, then pin bound-off edges of sleeves to sides of armholes and sides of sleeve extension strips to shoulder edges of front and back. The bound-off edge of shoulder yokes forms part of neckline. Sew sleeves in place as pinned, backstitching these and all seams. Press seams. Remove markers. Join side seams. Join sleeve seams to within 4in *(10cm)* of lower edge, then join rem on reverse side. For turtleneck hold edges tog with RS inside and join for 3in *(8cm)* from bound-off edge, then join rem of seam on reverse side. Placing seam level with left back shoulder seam and having right side of main part facing RS of the reversed part of collar seam, sew cast-on edge of collar to neck edges. Turn collar out and turn down 2in *(5cm)* at bound-off edge onto RS. For crew neck, join ends with RS inside. With RS tog and seam level with left back shoulder seam, backstitch cast-on edge to neck edges. Fold band in half to WS and sl-st bound-off edge to previous seam.

Pants Suit

Sizes

Directions are to fit 22in *(56cm)* chest. Changes for 24in *(61cm)* and 26in *(66cm)* chest are given in brackets [ ]

Length of Sweater: 12 [13:14]in *(30:36:41)cm*

Length of Vest: 13 [14:15]in *(33:36:38)cm*

Length of Pants: 23 [$24\frac{1}{2}$:$25\frac{1}{2}$]in *(58:63:65)cm*

Gauge

7 sts and 9 rows = 1in *(2.5cm)* on No. 3 needle

Materials required:

Brunswick Fore-n-Aft Sport Yarn

Sweater: 4 [5:6] 2oz *(56g)* skeins red (A)

Vest and Pants: 1 [1:1] skein red (A); 8 [9:10] skeins navy (B) and 3 [4:4] skeins white (C)

1 pair each knitting needles Nos. 2, 3 and 4

1 set (4) double-pointed needles No. 2

4 (4:5) buttons

$\frac{3}{4}$yd *(18.5cm)* $\frac{1}{2}$in *(1.25cm)* elastic.

Sweater back

With No. 2 needles and A, cast on 82 [90:98] sts. Work 1in *(2.5cm)* K1, P1 rib. Change to No. 3 needles and st st. Work even until back measures 8 [$8\frac{1}{2}$:9] in *(20:21:23)cm* from beg.

Shape armholes: Bind off 5 sts at beg of next 2 rows, then dec 1 st at each end of every alt row until 68 [72:78] sts rem. Work even until armholes measure 4 [$4\frac{1}{2}$:5]in *(10:11:13)cm.*

Shape shoulders Bind off 7 [7:7] sts at beg of next 4 rows. Bind off 6 [8:9] sts at beg of next 2 rows. Leave rem 28 [28:32] sts on holder.

Front

Work same as back until armholes measure $2\frac{3}{4}$ [3:$3\frac{1}{2}$]in *(7:8:9)cm* ending with a P row.

Shape neck K across 28 [30:32] sts, leaving 12 [12:14] sts on holder, K rem 28 [30:32] sts.

Working one side at a time dec 1 st every alt row at neck edge until 20 [22:23] sts rem. Work even until piece measures same as back.

Shape shoulders: From arm edge bind off 7 [7:7] sts twice then 6 [8:9] sts once.

Attach yarn to other side of neck and work to correspond.

Sleeves

With No. 2 needles and A, cast on 42 [48:54] sts. Work in K1, P1 rib for 1in *(2.5cm)*. Change to No. 3 needles, work in st st and inc 1 st at each end of every 8th row until there are 60 [66:74] sts. Work even until sleeve measures $9\frac{1}{2}$ [$10\frac{1}{2}$:$11\frac{1}{2}$]in.

Shape top: Bind off 5 sts at beg of next 2 rows, then dec 1 st at each end of every alt row until 26 [30:34] rem. Bind off 4 sts at beg of next 4 rows, bind off rem 10 [14:18] sts. Sew shoulder seams.

Collar

With set of 4 double pointed needles No. 2, pick up and K100 [106:114] sts around neck inc sts from holders. Work in K1, P1 rib for 3 [$3\frac{1}{2}$:4]in *(8:9:10)cm.* Bind off in rib.

Finishing
Press pieces with cool iron. Join side and sleeve seams and set in sleeves.

Vest back
With No. 3 needles and B, cast on 64 [70:76] sts and work in g st (every row k) for 12 rows. Change to No. 4 needles and st st. At 7]7½:8]in *(18:19:20)cm* from beg work first and last 10 [12:12] sts in g st for 1in *(2.5cm)*.

Shape armholes: Bind off 5 [6:6] sts at beg of next 2 rows. Then dec 1 st at each end of every alt row 4 [5:6] times working dec inside g st border—46 [48: 52] sts. When armhole measures 3 [3½: 4]in *(8:9:10)cm*, work center 18 [20:20] sts in g st for 12 rows.

Shape neck: Work 19 [19:21] sts, bind off center 8 [10:10] sts, work rem 19 [19: 21] sts. Working one side at a time, dec 1 st at neck edge every row 3 [2:1] times.

Shape shoulders: Bind off 8 [8:10] sts once, 8 [9:10] sts on second row, still

181

keeping a g st border of 5 [6:6] sts. Attach yarn at neck edge and work other side to correspond.

Left front

With No. 3 needles and B, cast on 28 [32:36] sts and work 12 rows in g st. Change to No. 4 needles and st st keeping 5 sts at front edge in g st. Inc 1 st at end of each K row inside front g st border 11 [12:14] times—39 [44:50] sts. When side measures 7 [7½:8]in (18:19:20)cm from beg work 10 [12:12] sts in g st at side edge for 1 in (2.5cm).

Shape armholes: Bind off 5 [6:6] sts at armhole edge, then dec 1 st every alt row at side edge 4 [5:5] times, at the same time shaping front by dec 1 st every 3rd row twice, then 1 st every alt row at neck edge inside border 16 [17:20] sts rem. When armhole measures 4½ [5: 5½]in (11:13:14)cm in depth shape shoulders as given for back.

Right front

Work as given for left front, but reverse shapings and make 4 [4:5] buttonholes in g st border by K2, yo, K2 tog, K1.

Finishing

Press pieces with a damp cloth. Join side and shoulder seams. Sew on buttons.

Pants

Make two sections, reversing pattern for second piece. With No. 3 needles and B, cast on 100 [108:116] sts. Work in K1, P1 rib for 1in (2.5cm). K1 row on WS for hemline. Starting with a K row work in st st and dec 6 sts evenly across every 12th row 4 times—76 [84:92] sts. At same time, work 36 [38: 42] rows colour B, 4 rows C, 2 rows B, 4 rows C, 2 rows B, 10 rows A and 2 rows B. Then start pattern.

Pattern stitch With C work 1 row K, 1 row P. *Row 3:* with B, *K1, sl 1 purlwise, rep from * across. *Row 4:* With B, *K1, sl 1 purlwise, rep from * across. Rep these 4 rows for pattern.

Continue in patt and inc 1 st at each end of every 8th row until there are 92 [100: 108] sts. When leg measures 14 [15:16] in (36: 48: 51)cm from hemline bind off 6 sts at each end of row. Then dec 1 st at each end of row every 1in (2.5cm) there are 76 [84:92] sts. When work measures 8 [9:10]in (20:23:25)cm from 6 bound off sts change to colour A and shape top working in st st. Knit 19 [21:23], purl back; k38 [42:46] purl back. Continue knitting 19 [21:23] more sts until all sts are worked off. K1 row on WS to form hemline. Work 1in (2.5cm) st st. Bind off.

Finishing

Press pieces with cool iron. Join leg seams and front and back seams. Insert elastic in top hem, turn down and sl stitch to inside. Sew hems at lower edge.

182

Man's Sweater

Sizes

Directions are to fit 38in (96cm) chest Changes for 40in (102cm) and 42in (106cm) chest are in brackets [ ] Length: 23¾ [24:24½]in (60 [61:62]cm) Sleeve seam: 18½in (47cm)

Gauge

6 sts and 8 rows = 1in (2.5cm) on No. 5 needles.

Materials required:

Brunswick Fore-n-Aft Sport Yarn, 4 [5:5] 2oz skeins Camel (A), 4 [5:5] skeins Tangerine (B), 2 [2:2] skeins Dark Lime (C) and 1 [1:1] skein Wood Brown (D)
1 pair each knitting needles, Nos. 2, 3, 4 and 5
Note: The sweater is in st st throughout.

Sweater back

With No. 3 needles and B, cast on 114 [118:126] sts. Work 5 rows st st. K1 row on WS for hemline. Change to No. 5 needles and start check patt: Attach A. *Row 1:* *K2 B, 2 A, rep from * to last 2 sts, K2 B. *Row 2:* *P2 B, 2 A, rep from * to last 2 sts, P2 B. *Row 3:* * K2 A, 2 B, rep from * to last 2 sts, K2 A. *Row 4:* * P2 A, 2 B, rep from * to last 2 sts, P2 A. Rep rows 1 to 4 for check pattern. Work 16 more rows in patt. Change to No. 4 needles. Work in st st and work 4 rows D, 16 rows C and 4 rows D. Cont in st st and work stripe patt: *Rows 1 and 2:* In B, *Rows 3 and 4:* In A, for 52 rows. Then work 4 rows D, 16 rows C, 4 rows D.

Shape armholes: Change to stripe patt. Bind off 4 [5:6] sts at beg of next 2 rows. Dec 1 st at beg and end of next and every alt row until 90 [94:96] sts rem. Cont straight until armholes measure 8½

$[8\frac{3}{4}:9\frac{1}{4}]$in *(21.5[22:23]cm)*, ending with a P row.

Shape shoulder: Bind off 10 [9:9] sts at beg of next 2 rows and 9 [10:10] sts at beg of next 4 rows. Leave rem 34 [36:38] sts on holder for neck.

Front

Work same as back until armholes measure $7\frac{1}{4}$ $[7\frac{1}{2}:8]$in *(18 [19:20]cm)*, ending with a P row.
Shape neck: K35 [36:37] sts, turn, dec 1 st at neck edge on next 5 rows, then on every alt row until 28 [29:29] sts rem, ending with a P row.
Shape shoulders: Bind off 10 [9:9] sts on next row and 9 [10:10] sts on next 2 alt rows. Place center 20 [22:22] sts on holder for neck. Work other side to correspond.

Upper sleeve

Cuff: With No. 3 needles and D, cast on 78 [82:86] sts. Work 3 rows st. st. K1 row on WS for hemline. Change to No. 4 needles and st st beg K work 2 rows D, 8 rows C, 2 rows D, P 1 row D on right side. Change to stripe patt and inc 1 st at beg and end of 5th and every foll 6th row until 84 [88:92] sts. Cont straight until piece measures 6in *(15cm)* from hemline, ending on P row.
Shape top: Bind off 3 [3:4] sts at beg of next 2 rows. Dec 1 st at beg and end of next and every alt row until 66 sts rem. Bind off 6 sts at beg of next 6 rows until 30 sts rem. Bind off.

Lower sleeve

With No. 3 needles and B, cast on 54 [54:58] sts. Work hem as for upper sleeve. Change to No. 5 needles and check patt, inc at beg and end of 7th and every foll 6th row until 78 [82:86] sts when piece measures 13in *(33cm)*. Bind off fairly loosely.

Turtleneck

Press pieces carefully with cool iron. Join right shoulder seam.
With No. 2 needles and A, K 24 [25:25] sts from left shoulder to front holder, K 20 [22:22] sts from holder, K 24 [25:25] sts to shoulder, K 34 [36:38] sts from back holder (102 [108:110] sts). Work in K1, P1 rib for $5\frac{3}{4}$in *(15cm)*. Change to B and work 2 rows rib. Bind off fairly loosely in rib.

Finishing

Join left shoulder seam (join turtleneck with flat seam). Join side and upper sleeve seams. Set in upper sleeves. Turn in and sl st cuff hem. Turn up cuff. Join lower sleeve seam. Attach lower sleeve to upper under cuff, so that seam will not show. Sew down P row of upper sleeve over joining with a running st. Sew cuff to upper sleeve with several back sts. Turn in and sl st lower sleeve and bottom hems.

Dress and Jacket

Sizes

Directions are to fit 32in *(81cm)* bust. Changes for 34, 36 and 38in *(86:91:96cm)* bust are in brackets [ ]
Dress: Length from top of shoulders
$37\frac{1}{2}$ $[38\frac{1}{2}:39\frac{1}{2}:40\frac{1}{2}]$in
95 (98:100:103)cm
Jacket: Length from top of shoulders
$23\frac{1}{2}$ $[24:24\frac{1}{2}:25]$in
60 (61:62:63)cm
Sleeve seam: 16in *(41cm)* all sizes.

Gauge

11 sts and 15 rows = 2in *(5cm)* over st st on No. 5 needles.

Materials required:

Coats & Clark's Red Heart Wintuk Sport Yarn
Dress: 6 [6:7:7] 2oz skeins in main color—MC
1 [1: 2: 2] skeins each in first and second contrast colors, A and B
Jacket: 5 [5:6:6] 2oz skeins in main color—MC
1 [1:1:1] skein each in first and second contrast colors, A and B
1 pair each knitting needles Nos. 3, 4, 5
6 buttons for dress.

Dress back

** With No. 3 needles and MC, cast on 140 [146:152:158] sts and work 9 rows st st, starting with a K row.
K1 row on WS for hemline. Change to No. 5 needles. Cont in st st, starting with a K row, and work even until back measures 4 $[4\frac{1}{2}:5:5\frac{1}{2}]$in *(10:11:13:14)cm* from hemline, ending with a P row.
Shape as follows:
1st dec row: K8, K2 tog tbl, K16 [17:18:19], K2 tog tbl twice K48 [50:52:54], K2 tog, (K16 [17:18:19], K2 tog) twice, K8. 134 [140:146:152] sts. Work 15 rows even.
2nd dec row: K8, K2 tog tbl (K15 [16:17:18], K2 tog tbl) twice, K46 [48:50:52], K2 tog, (K15 [16:17:18], K2 tog) twice, K8. 128 [134:140:146] sts. Work 15 rows even.
3rd dec row: K8, K2 tog tbl, (K14 [15:16:17], K2 tog tbl) twice, K44 [46, 48, 50], K2 tog, (14 [15: 16: 17], K2 tog) twice, K8. 122 [128:134:140] sts. Work 15 rows even.
4th dec row: K8, K2 tog tbl, (K13 [14:15:16], K2 tog tbl) twice, K42 [44:46:48], K2 tog, (K13 [14:15:16], K2 tog) twice, K8. 116 [122:128:134] sts. Work 15 rows even.
5th dec row: K8, K2 tog tbl, (K12 [13:14:15], K2 tog tbl) twice, K40 [42:44:46] K2 tog, (K12 [13:14:15], K2 tog) twice, K8. 110 [116:122:128] sts. Work 15 rows even.
6th dec row: K8, K2 tog tbl (K11 [12:13:14], K2 tog tbl) twice, K38 [40:42:44], K2 tog, (K11 [12:13:14], K2 tog twice, K8.—104 [110:116:122] sts. ** Work 15 rows even.

7th dec row: K8, K2 tog tbl, (K10 [11:12:13] K2 tog tbl) twice, K36 [38:40:42], K2 tog, (K10 [11:12:13], K2 tog) twice, K8.—98 [104:110:116] sts. Work 15 rows even.
8th dec row: K8, K2 tog tbl, (K9 [10:11:12], K2 tog tbl) twice, K34 [36:38:40], K2 tog, (K9 [10:11:12], K2 tog) twice, K8.—92 [98:104:110] sts. Fasten off MC.
Attach A.
Change to No. 4 needles and P1 row. Work 12 rows K1, P1 rib. Fasten off A.
Attach B.
Change to No. 3 needles and cont as follows:
Next row: K8, sl 1, K2 tog, psso, K16 [18:20:22], sl 1, K2 tog, psso, K32 [34:36:38], K3 tog, K16 [18:20:22], K3 tog, K8. 84 [90:96:102] sts. Work 13 rows K1, P1 rib. Fasten off B.
Attach MC.
Change to No. 4 needles and cont as follows:
Next row: K8, sl 1, K2 tog, psso, K14 [16:18:20], sl 1, K2 tog, psso, K28 [30:32:34], K3 tog, K14 [16:18:20], K3 tog, K8. 76 [82:88:94] sts. Cont in st st in MC and work 7 rows even, starting with a P row.
Shape sides: Inc 1 st at each end of next and foll 5th row. 80 [86:92:98] sts. Change to No. 5 needles and cont inc 1 st at each end of every foll 5th row until there are 94 [100:106:112] sts.
Work even until bodice measures 8in *(20cm)* from end of col band, ending with a P row.
Shape armholes: Bind off 4 [5:6:7] sts at beg of next 2 rows. Dec 1 st at each end of every row until 68 [72:76:80] sts remain, then on foll 2 alt rows. 64 [68:72:76] sts.
Work even until bodice measures 15 $[15\frac{1}{2}:16:16\frac{1}{2}]$in *(37 [37.5:40:40.5]cm)* from end of col band, ending with a K row.
Shape shoulders and neck: *Next row:* P19 [20:21:22], bind off 26 [28:30:32], P to end. Cont on these 19 [20:21:22] sts for first side as follows:
Row 1: Bind off 5 [6:6:6], K to last 2 sts. K2 tog. *Row 2:* P2 tog, P to end. *Row 3:* As first.
Work 1 row straight. Bind off rem sts. With RS facing, attach yarn to rem sts and K to end. Finish to correspond with first side.

Front

Work as for Back from ** to **. 104 [110:116:122] sts.
Work 10 rows straight.
Divide for front opening as follows:
Next row: P46 [49:52:55] and slip these sts on a spare needle, bind off 12, P to end. Cont on 46 [49:52:55] sts for first side as follows: Work 4 rows even.
Next row: K8, K2 tog tbl, (K10 [11:12:13], K2 tog tbl) twice, K12 [13:14:15]. 43 [46:49:52] sts. Work 15 rows straight.

Next row: K8, K2 tog tbl, (K9 [10:11: 12], K2 tog tbl) twice, K11 [12:13:14]. 40 [43:46:49] sts. Fasten off MC.
Attach A.
Change to No. 4 needles and P1 row. Work 12 rows K1, P1 rib. Fasten off A. Attach B.
Change to No. 3 needles and cont as follows:
Next row: K8, sl 1, K2 tog, psso, K16 [18: 20:22], sl 1, K2 tog, psso, K10 [11:12: 13]. 36 [39:42:45] sts. Work 13 rows K1, P1 rib. Fasten off B. Attach MC.
Change to No. 4 needles, and cont as follows:
Next row: K8, sl 1, K2 tog, psso, K14 [16: 18:20], sl 1, K2 tog, psso, K8 [9:10:11]. 32 [35:38:41] sts.
Cont in st st in MC and work 7 rows even, starting with a P row.
Inc 1 st at side edge of next and foll 5th row. 34 [37:40:43] sts.
Change to No. 5 needles and cont inc 1 st at side edge on every foll 5th row until there are 41 [44:47:50] sts. Work even until front matches back at side edge, ending with a P row.
Shape armholes: Bind off 4 [5:6:7] sts at beg of next row. Work 1 row even. Dec 1 st at each end of next row.
Dec 1 st at armhole edge on every row, and *at the same time* dec 1 st at front edge on every foll 4th row until 25 [27:29:31] sts rem. Dec 1 st at armhole edge on foll 2 alt rows and 1 st at front edge on foll 4th row. 22 [24:26:28] sts.
Now keep armhole edge straight and cont dec 1 st at front edge on every 4th row, 2 [3:4:5] times more, then on every foll 6th row until 16 [17:18:19] sts rem. Work even until front matches back at armhole edge, ending with a P row.
Shape shoulders: Bind off 5 [6:6:6] sts at beg of next and foll alt row. Work 1 row even. Bind off rem sts.
With RS facing, attach MC to 46 [49: 52: 55] sts on spare needle. Work 4 rows even.
Next row: K12 [13:14:15], K2 tog, (K10 [11:12:13], K2 tog) twice, K8 43 [46:49:52] sts. Work 15 rows even.
Next row: K11 [12:13:14], K2 tog, (K9 [10:11:12], K2 tog) twice, K8. 40 [43: 46:49] sts. Fasten off MC.
Attach A.
Change to No. 4 needles and P1 row. Work 12 rows K1, P1 rib. Fasten off A. Attach B.
Change to No. 3 needles and cont as follows:
Next row: K10 [11:12:13], K3 tog, K16 [18:20:22], K3 tog, K8. 36 [39:42:45] sts. Work 13 rows K1, P1 rib. Fasten off B.
Attach MC.
Change to No. 4 needles and cont as follows:
Next row: K8 [9:10:11], K3 tog, K14 [16:18:20], K3 tog, K8. 32 [35:38:41] sts. Finish to correspond with first side, reversing shaping.

184

Finishing
Using a warm iron and damp cloth, press parts lightly on WS, omitting ribbing.
Join shoulder seams.
Armhole borders: With RS facing, No. 3 needles and MC, starting at underarm, pick up and K108 [114:120: 126] sts all around armhole edge. Work 6 rows K1, P1 rib. Bind off in rib.
Front borders: *Right:* With No. 3 needles and A, cast on 166 [170:174: 178] sts and work 2 rows K1, P1 rib. Fasten off A.
Attach B and shape point as follows:
Row 1: K to last 8 sts, turn. *Row 2:* Sl 1, rib to end. *Row 3:* Rib to last 6 sts (thus working 2 sts more than on first row), turn. *Row 4:* As row 2. *Row 5:* Rib to last 4 sts, turn. *Row 6:* As row 2.
Make buttonholes as follows:
Row 7: Rib 67 [71:75:79], bind off 3, (rib 14, bind off 3) 5 times, rib 9, turn (thus leaving 2 sts unworked). *Row 8:* (do not slip first st), rib to end, casting on 3 over those bound-off. *Row 9:* As row 5. *Row 10:* As row 2. *Row 11:* As row 3. *Row 12:* As row 2. *Row 13:* In rib as first. *Row 14:* As row 2. Fasten off B. Attach A and K1 row, then rib 2 rows. Bind off in rib.
Left: With No. 3 needles and A, cast on 158 [162:166:170] sts and rib 2 rows. Fasten off A. Attach B and K1 row, then rib 13 rows.
Fasten off B. Attach A and K1 row, then rib 2 rows. Bind off in rib.
Starting at end of point, i.e. 8 sts up from tip, pin edge of right border to front edge from base of opening and around to center back of neck, last buttonhole to come ½in (1cm) below start of front shaping.
Pin left border in position from base of opening to center back of neck.
Join borders neatly at back, then sew in position all around using a flat seam, stitch left border neatly to bound-off sts at center front. Sew point in position on right side.
Join side seams and armhole borders. Fold hem at ridge to wrong side and sl st loosely in position. Press seams. Sew on buttons.

Jacket
Back
With No. 3 needles and MC, cast on 96 [102:108:114] sts and work 14 rows K1, P1 rib.
Change to No. 5 needles and st st, starting with a K row, and work even until back measures 14½in (37cm), ending with RS facing. Place a marker at each end of last row, then work 12 more rows.
Shape armholes: Bind off 2 [3:4:5] sts at beg of next 2 rows, then dec 1 st at each end of next and every alt row until 72 [76:80:84] sts rem. Work even until back measures 23½ [24:24½:25]in (60:61:62:63)cm ending with a P row.

Shape shoulders: Bind off 7 [7:8:8] sts at beg of next 4 rows, then 7 [8:7:8] sts at beg of next 2 rows. 30 [32:34:36] sts.
Change to No. 3 needles and K1 row, then rib 3 rows; fasten off MC. Attach B and K1 row, then rib 2 rows. Fasten off B. Attach A and P1 row, then rib 2 rows. Bind off loosely in rib.
Left front
With No. 3 needles and MC cast on 50 [52:56:58] sts and work 14 rows K1, P1 rib inc 1 st at center of last row on *2nd and 4th* sizes only. 50 [53: 56: 59] sts.
Change to No. 5 needles and work even in st st until front matches back to markers, ending with a P row.
Shape front: Dec 1 st at end of next and every foll 4th row until 47 [50:53: 56] sts. Work 3 rows even, thus ending with a P row.

Cont shaping front edge.

Shape armholes: *Next row:* Bind off 2 [3:4:5], K to last 2 sts, K2 tog.

Dec 1 st at armhole edge on every alt row, and *at the same time* dec 1 st at front edge on every foll 4th row as before until 29 [31:33:35] sts rem.

Now keep armhole edge straight and cont dec at front edge on every foll 4th row until 21 [22:23:24] sts rem. Work a few rows even until front matches back at armhole edge, ending with a P row.

Shape shoulders: Bind off 7 [7:8:8] sts at beg of next and foll alt row. Work 1 row. Bind off rem sts.

Right front

Work to correspond with left front, reversing shaping.

Sleeves

With No. 3 needles and A, cast on 44 [46: 48:50] sts and work K1, P1 rib for 2 rows; fasten off A. Attach B and K1 row, then rib 2 rows. Fasten off B. Attach MC and P1 row, then work in rib until cuff measures 3in *(8cm)* ending with WS facing.

Next row: Rib 2 [3:4:5] MIL, [rib 8, MIL] 5 times, rib 2 [3:4:5]. 50 [52:54: 56] sts.

Change to No. 5 needles and st st, starting with a K row, shaping sides by inc 1 st at each end of 3rd and every foll 10th [9th: 8th: 7th] row until there are 68 [72:76:80] sts. Work even until sleeve seam measures 16in *(41cm)* ending with a P row.

Shape top: Bind off 2 [3:4:5] sts at beg of next 2 rows. Dec 1 st at each end of next and every alt row until 46 [42: 38:34] sts rem. Work 1 row even, then dec 1 st at each end of every row until 30 sts rem. Bind off 3 sts at beg of next 2 rows. Bind off rem sts.

Finishing

Press as for dress.

Left border: With RS facing, No. 3 needles and MC, pick up and K62 [66: 70:74] sts from shoulder edge to start of front shaping and 98 to cast-on edge. 160 [164:168:172] sts.

Rib 3 rows. Fasten off MC. Attach B and K1 row, then rib 2 rows. Fasten off B. Attach A and P1 row, then rib 2 rows. Bind off in rib.

Right border: Starting at lower edge, work as for left border. Join shoulder seams, then join borders using a flat seam. Join side and sleeve seams; insert sleeves. Press seams.

Stitch cast-on edge to neck edges. Fold band in half to WS and sl-st bound-off edge to previous seam.

Useful Addresses of Stockists and Suppliers for Needlecraft and Crafts Materials

Batik
Screen Process Supplies
1199 East 12th Street
Oakland, California 94606

Stephen Blumnich
Apt 1, Box 25a
Halseys, Oregon 97348

Helio Dyes
2140 West 4th Avenue
Vancouver 9 BC
Canada

Quilting
Needleart Guild
2729 Oakwood, N.E.
Grand Rapids, Mich. 49505

Gibbs Manufacturing Company
Canton, Ohio

Lee Wards
Elgin, Illinois 60120

Basketwork
H. H. Perkins Company
228 Shelton Avenue
New Haven, Conn 06506

Lampshade Frames
Oriental Lamp and Shade Company
810 Lexington Avenue
New York, NY 10021

Candlemaking
American Handicrafts Company
5655 Main Street
Buffalo, NY

Pourette Manufacturing Company
6818 Roosevelt Way
N.E. Seattle, Washington 98115

J&E Polish Company
2724 NE 82nd Street
Seattle, Washington 98105

Celebration Candle Supplies
PO Box 28, Dentwater
Mich. 49448

Macramé
The Mannings
RD 2
East Berling, Pa. 17316

House of Harvey
2724 NE 82nd Street
Seattle, Washington 98105

Macramé and Weaving Supply Company
63 East Adams
Chicago, Illinois 60603

Beadwork
Allcraft Tool and Supply Company
150 Frank Road
Hicksville, NY 11901

Index

Acknowledgments

The publishers would like to thank the following designers and contributors :

Feltcraft *page 8* Audrey Hersch: *pages 10–12* Valerie Janitch; **Papercraft** *pages 15–17* Bruce Angrave; *pages 18–23* Valerie Janitch; **Corn Weaving** *pages 24–29* Irena Clanfield; **Rugmaking** *pages 30–35* Patons & Baldwins Limited, designs courtesy of 'Stitchcraft'; **Jewelry** *pages 36–43* Alison Richards; **Toymaking** *page 44* Lister Yarns Limited: *page 46* Diana Biggs: *page 47–48* Anne Hulbert: *page 49* Katie Dyson; **Appliqué** *page 57* Patricia Philpott; **Beadwork** *page 58* Pam Hartland: *page 60* Anne Hulbert: *page 61* Joyce Thyer: *page 63* Audrey Hersch; **Patchwork** *pages 64, 68–70* Lynette Syme; **Smocking** *page 72* Lynette Syme; **Quilting** *page 78* Shirley Lane: *page 80* Jill Newton: *page 81* Shirley Lane; **Candlemaking** *pages 88–91* David Constable; **Macramé** *page 92* Anne Croot: *pages 94–95* Maxine Fitter: *page 96* Anne Croot: *pages 97, 99* Hobby Horse Limited, London; **Tie Dyeing** *pages 100–105* Frances Diplock, Ruth Francis; **Pebble Polishing** *pages 106–109* Len Cacutt; **Tatting** *pages 110, 114, 115* Mary Konior: *page 114* below: Hobby Horse Limited, London; **Basketwork** *pages 116–121* Anne Hulbert; **Fabric Craft** *page 123* Shirley Lane: *page 122* Audrey Hersch: *pages 124–125* Valerie Janitch; **Collage** *page 134* Valerie Janitch: *page 137* Frances Rhodes: *pages 138* and *139* Valerie Janitch; **Batik** *pages 140–143* Frances Diplock, Ruth Francis; **Embroidery** *page 146* Jane Simpson: *page 147* Valerie Janitch: *page 148* Jane Simpson; **Crewel** *pages 154–159* Lydia Cole-Powney; **Needlepoint** *pages 162–165* Mary Rhodes: *page 163* Jane Simpson: *page 166* J&P Coates Limited: *page 167* Margaret Beautement; **Knitting** *page 168* Wendy Wools Limited: *page 170* Wendy Wools Limited: *page 171* Lister Yarns Limited: *page 173* Wendy Wools Limited: *page 174* Wendy Yarns Limited: *page 177* Patons.

The publishers would like to thank the following companies for their help in the preparation of material for this book:

Candlemakers Suppliers Limited (candlemaking materials); Carter & Parker Limited (Wendy and Peter Pan Yarns); J. & P. Coates Limited (embroidery and tapisserie threads); Dylon International Limited; George Lee & Sons Limited (Lee Target Yarns); Lister & Co (Lister Lavenda Yarns); Patons & Baldwins Limited (Patons Turkey rug wool and Patons brown check canvas, knitting and crochet yarns).

The publishers would like to thank the following individuals and organizations for their kind permission to reproduce the photographs in this book:

Bruce Angrave: *16, 17*; Nilson Anthony: *52*; Camera Press: *14, 130, 144, 150* below; J. P. Coates Ltd: *166*; Dylon International Ltd: *100–105, 140–143*; William Howes: *106–109*; PAF International Ltd: *54–55, 84–87, 131* above; Syndication International: *150* above.

All other photographs are the copyright of Octopus Books Ltd.

Book design and artwork: Chuck Goodwin

Special photography for this book: John Ledger